+Huckaby

The Federal Vision

Edited by
Steve Wilkins
&
Duane Garner

Athanasius Press

Monroe, Louisiana

Steve Wilkins & Duane Garner, *The Federal Vision*
Copyright 2004

Published by Athanasius Press,
205 Roselawn Ave., Monroe, LA 71201
318-323-3061

Cover design by Hannah Grieser

Contents

Introduction 11
Steve Wilkins

Covenant and Election 15
John Barach

Covenant, Baptism, and Salvation 47
Steve Wilkins

Paedobaptism and Baptismal Efficacy: Historic Trends
and Current Controversies 71
Rich Lusk

What's for Dinner? Calvin's Continuity with the Bible's
and the Ancient Church's Eucharistic Faith 127
Mark Horne

Merit Versus Maturity: What Did Jesus Do for Us? 151
James B. Jordan

"Judge Me, O God": Biblical Perspectives on Justification 203
Peter J. Leithart

Justification and the Gentiles 237
Steve Schlissel

The Church: Visible or Invisible 263
Douglas Wilson

New Life and Apostasy: Hebrews 6:4–8 as Test Case 271
Rich Lusk

Acknowledgements

Special thanks are in order to Holly McCabe and Sarah Garner for their fastidious transcription and proofreading and to Hannah Grieser for amazing us with her wonderful artwork. We are deeply grateful for all of the support we have received from the great many who have contributed to the establishment of Athanasius Press, without whose help this book would not have been possible.

Duane Garner
Managing Editor
Athanasius Press

Contributors

Steve Wilkins has been pastor of Auburn Avenue Presbyterian Church in Monroe, Louisiana since 1989. He and his wife Wendy have six children and one grandchild.

John Barach was ordained in August 1999 and pastored Trinity Reformed Church (URCNA) in Lethbridge, Alberta until November 2002. In January 2003 he became the pastor of Covenant Reformed Church (URCNA) in Grande Prairie, Alberta.

Rich Lusk is assistant pastor of Auburn Avenue Presbyterian Church in Monroe, Louisiana. He has written a number of papers and articles. Previously he served for seven years at Redeemer Presbyterian Church in Austin, Texas. He and his wife Jenny have four children.

Mark Horne is a pastor in the Presbyterian Church in America and author of *The Victory According to Mark: an Exposition of the Second Gospel.* He is prime contributor to Theologia, a collection of theological papers online at http://www.hornes.org/theologia. He is married to Jennifer and has four children.

James B. Jordan graduated from the University of Georgia with a degree in Comparative Literature. After a tour in the US Air Force, Mr. Jordan attended Reformed Theological Seminary (Jackson, Mississippi) and Westminster Theological Seminary (Philadelphia, Pennsylvania), graduating with a Th.M. in Systematic Theology. Since the late 1980s Mr. Jordan has been director of Biblical Horizons, now located in Niceville, Florida. Mr. Jordan was awarded an honorary D.Litt. degree from the Central School of Religion (England) for his work on the Mosaic dietary laws. Mr. Jordan is author of numerous books, most prominently *Through New Eyes: Developing a Biblical View of the World,* and many scholarly monographs and short essays. He can be reached at Biblical Horizons, Box 1096, Niceville, FL 32588, or at jbjordan4@cox.net.

Peter J. Leithart is an ordained minister in the Presbyterian Church in America and currently serves as organizing pastor for Trinity Reformed Church in Moscow, Idaho, and as Senior Fellow of Theology and Literature at New St. Andrews College, also in Moscow. He has written a number of books and articles and lives in Moscow with his wife, Noel, and their ten children.

Steve Schlissel has pastored Messiah's Congregation in New York City since 1979. He and his wife, Jeanne, have six children and three grandchildren. He oversees Urban Nations—a ministry to the vast immigrant population of New York City, and Meantime—a ministry for women who were sexually abused as children.

Douglas Wilson is the minister of Christ Church in Moscow, Idaho. He is the author of various books including *Reforming Marriage* and *The Case for Classical Christian Education.*

Introduction

Steve Wilkins

The purpose of this book of essays is to introduce (or, more properly, to re-introduce) the modern Church to covenantal reading and thinking. Covenant is the central teaching of the Word of God; it describes a relationship with the Triune God through Jesus Christ, His only Begotten Son. To be in covenant is to be in real communion with God, attendant with real privileges and real blessings. It is to be brought into the circle of the eternal fellowship that has always existed between Father, Son, and Spirit (John 14:23–24; 17:20–23). It is to be made partaker of the divine nature (2 Pet. 1:2–4). It is to be beloved of the Father for the sake of His Son and is founded upon union with Christ (John 17:20–23).

Sadly, most Christians have lost sight of the glorious reality of covenant and consequently ended up (inadvertently) looking more to their own experiences for assurance of salvation than they have to Christ. The gospel has been abstracted and reduced to a collection of propositional statements about Christ which require intellectual assent. The Church has been reduced to an institution that is merely a place of potential blessing rather than the Spirit-filled, blessing-filled body of Christ. The sacraments have become nothing more than mere symbols that visibly picture the gospel but do not actually accomplish anything when they are administered according to the Scriptures. To many in the Church, the covenant is a meaningless, indefinable concept which merely allows infants to be baptized (for some unknown reason).

Even those whose knowledge is better than this have fallen into a trap. We have allowed our theological system to become a filter *through which* we read the Word of God. Consequently, it becomes almost impossible to refine or even seriously examine the system by the Word. If an interpretation of the Scriptures is suggested that contradicts a particular point of the system, it is rejected out of hand. The assumption is that since the system is biblical the Scriptures *cannot* contradict it. Rather than allowing the Scriptures to mold our system, we now force the Scriptures into the mold of the system. Strangely, in our zeal to avoid becoming like Rome, we have become as Romish as could be. We have identified the teaching of the Scriptures with our confessions and catechisms and thus have embraced the very position we profess to abhor—that of allowing man-made theological formulations to have supremacy over the Scriptures.

We have lost the perspective of our fathers in the faith and even more, we have lost the perspective which the apostles, prophets, and our Lord Himself had. We find ourselves afraid to speak as the *Bible* speaks, indeed, in some circles, even quoting certain passages from the Scriptures provokes the raised eyebrow of suspicion. For these and other reasons, it seems clear to the authors that we have strayed from the paths which our fathers walked with confidence and joy—and the time has come to examine ourselves.

The 2002 Auburn Avenue Pastors Conference ("The Federal Vision") brought together four men to speak on the covenant and its nature. There was nothing novel or particularly creative about the lectures given (most if not all of the points made by the speakers had been made by numerous theologians at one time or another in the past), but the conference became the catalyst to provoke a great deal of discussion on the covenant and its practical outworkings. The papers that follow seek to expound what was set forth only cursorily in January 2002.

It should be noted that many of the things written in the following articles have been written by others long before us. These things have been taught in every age of the Church. You find statements, allusions, and clear teaching of these matters in the early fathers (Justin Martyr, Cyril, Irenaeus, Augustine); in the Medieval fathers and the Reformers (Anselm, Aquinas, Calvin, Bucer, Luther, Cranmer, Ursinus); in many theologians of the seventeenth–nineteenth centuries (Cornelius Burges, Richard Hooker, Jonathan Edwards, M. F. Sadler, John Nevin); and we could add many contemporary theologians as well. The views expressed herein are also reflected in many of the creeds and confessions of the Church (the Nicene Creed, Calvin's Strasbourg and Geneva catechisms, the baptismal liturgy of the French Reformed Church, the Book of Common Prayer, the Second Helvetic Confession, the 1560 Scots Confession, the French Confession, the Gallican Confession, the Augsburg Confession, the Belgic Confession, and the Westminster Confession). Though no one of these witnesses held all the things set forth here, all the things set forth here have precedent in the history of the Church and we are self-consciously seeking to build upon this foundation.

By putting forth this collection (and the one that will follow, D.V.), we do not intend to make a bad situation worse. We have not (and will never) fling charges of heresy against our brothers who disagree with our position. We refuse to do this because such charges are utterly unwarranted. We have the greatest confidence in the sincerity of those who differ from us, of their love for the Savior, and their desire to preserve the purity of the faith once for all delivered to the saints. We are confident that we will spend eternity with these brothers and would welcome them at any time into our congregations to commune with us. Our own frailties and shortcomings are so great that we say all that we say with an eye to ourselves, lest while seeking to pluck splinters out of our brothers' eyes, we neglect the telephone poles in our own.

Nor do we have any delusions of our own importance. We haven't the slightest notion that our views will "straighten out everything that's wrong with the Church." Our desire is far less ambitious: we simply hope to further more reasonable and charitable discussion of these issues among our fathers and brethren to the end that we all come to understand the Word of God more clearly so as to proclaim it more faithfully.

We intend no disrespect toward any who take a different position; indeed, we welcome their comments and critique. We are all firmly convinced that our formulations need refinement and clarification at numerous points. It is our prayer, however, that these essays will be of service in assisting the Church to consider the teaching of God's Word afresh from the perspective of covenant, all to the glory of God. If this is the outcome, nothing will please us more.

Chapter One

Covenant and Election

John Barach

The relationship between covenant and election is a controversial topic today. But it also has been controversial in the past. One of my great theological heroes, Klaas Schilder, discovered it to be somewhat controversial in his own ministry.[1]

We have to recognize that when we start talking about election we are dealing with a subject that many people would rather not discuss. It is tempting not to talk about election. There are many evangelical churches where preachers don't talk about election at all because they know that many people in their congregations have questions about it and throughout history people have held diverse views on it. So they shy away from getting into something so controversial.

Even in Reformed churches there are people who see election as a problem: "Am I elect? How do I know? Can I really be confident of these things?" Unfortunately, there are also others in Reformed churches who treat election as an academic subject, a theological datum with little relevance for us today, something that can easily be set to the side. It is tempting to avoid the subject of election and many churches do, but we must not give in to that temptation. Scripture speaks and so we must speak.

The Canons of Dort were one of the Reformed Church's first great formulations of the doctrine of election. They were written largely in response to the Arminian Remonstrants and they talk about how to teach election properly. The First Head of Doctrine, Article 14, says:

> Just as, by God's wise plan, this teaching concerning divine election has been proclaimed through the prophets, Christ Himself, and the apostles,

in Old and New Testament times, and has subsequently been committed to writing in the Holy Scriptures, so also today in God's Church, for
which it was specifically intended, this teaching must be set forth—with
a spirit of discretion, in a godly and holy manner, at the appropriate time
and place, without inquisitive searching into the ways of the Most High.
This must be done for the glory of God's most holy name, and for the
lively comfort of His people.

In the very conclusion to the Canons of Dort something more is
said about the way we teach election:

> This Synod urges all fellow ministers in the gospel of Christ to deal with
> this teaching in a godly and reverent manner, in the academic institu-
> tions as well as in the churches; to do so, both in their speaking and
> writing, with a view to the glory of God's name, holiness of life, and the
> comfort of anxious souls; to think and also speak with Scripture accord-
> ing to the analogy of faith; and, finally, to refrain from all those ways of
> speaking which go beyond the bounds set for us by the genuine sense of
> the Holy Scriptures and which could give impertinent sophists a just
> occasion to scoff at the teaching of the Reformed churches or even to
> bring false accusations against it.

Notice that, in that last sentence about giving "impertinent sophists a just occasion to scoff" at the Reformed churches, the "sophists"
referred to there are the Arminians. The Synod of Dort was afraid that
the Arminians would be given opportunity and occasion to scoff at the
Reformed teachings if Reformed pastors spoke in the way that would
make God look stingy ("unjust, a tyrant"), that would make people
"carnally self-assured," teaching them to ignore the warnings of Scripture, or that would suggest that God has predestined "the greater part
of the world to sin and to eternal condemnation" or that "reprobation
is the cause of unbelief and ungodliness" or "that many infant children
of believers are snatched in their innocence from their mothers' breasts
and cruelly cast into hell so that neither the blood of Christ nor their
baptism nor the prayers of the Church at their baptism can be of any
use to them." The Canons of Dort identify these as "slanderous accusations . . . which the Reformed churches not only disavow but even
denounce with their whole heart."

We have to take this caution to heart as we begin to think about election. How are we to speak about God's election? The Canons of Dort, these wise pastors, tell us that we are to speak *reverently* (to the glory of God), *pastorally* (focusing on holiness of life and on the comfort of God's people), and *scripturally* ("without inquisitive searching into the ways of the Most High," but rather speaking "with Scripture according to the analogy of faith").

Think of Deuteronomy 29:29: "The secret things belong to the LORD our God, but the things revealed belong to us and to our sons forever, that we may observe all the words of this law." We need to think about election and talk about it and preach it on the basis of what Scripture says. We also have to speak and talk and teach and preach about election on the basis of the *way* Scripture says it.

Before we get into the relationship between election and covenant proper, let me first say something about God's predestination. The Bible tells us that God predestines all things that happen; we already know that from Genesis 1:1. The first verse of the Bible tells us that all things happen by God's will. God is the initiator. We read in Ephesians 1:11 that God is the one "who works all things after the counsel of His will." Everything that happens is the outworking of God's will. Everything—your salvation, but also your birth and your baptism. All the events of your life, including your perseverance in faith and your final glorification with Christ.

The Bible teaches that all things happen according to God's will, so that if anyone enters into final glory with Christ Jesus, that is the outworking of God's eternal plan. God has predestined some people who deserve eternal damnation to eternal glory with Christ instead, while not so predestining others. This is the Bible's teaching from Genesis 1:1 on through the whole of Scripture. God didn't predestine anyone to glory because of something in that person, but simply out of His sheer love and grace in Christ. God initiates, not because He sees anything in us, but out of sheer grace.

That predestining choice is unchangeable. The number of people who will enter into final glory is the number of people God always *intended* to enter into final glory with Christ. That predestining choice is also unthwartable. Apostasy, we are told in Romans 9, doesn't thwart God's plan. Yes, some people fall away. Yes, Israel has fallen away. Yes,

Israel has been cut off, but that has not thwarted God's plan. God preserves a remnant, and even that apostasy happens in accord with God's will, we are told, to show His wrath, to make His power and His justice known.

It is *scriptural* to emphasize God's predestination as Scripture does. It is also *pastoral* to underscore God's eternal predestination. It teaches us humility and gratitude. It teaches us to praise God for His sheer grace, the grace, which Paul says in 2 Timothy 1:9, "was granted us in Christ Jesus from all eternity." It also teaches us confidence. As we look at all the different events that happen in life, as we see that some people do fall away and apostatize, we can know that no matter what happens, God's purposes cannot be frustrated. What our confessions say about God's election and predestination is true. We need to glory in that truth and we need to teach it.

However, if all that is revealed in Scripture is the *fact* of predesti-nation, the fact that God has predestined some people to eternal glory, then we wouldn't get the *fruit* of God's election. If God chose some people, but I don't know if He chose *me*, and I certainly don't know if He chose *you*, then I am left with a kind of agnosticism. I don't know if God really predestined me to share in Christ's glory forever. I don't know if He predestined you. I don't know if He predestined anyone.

So we take God's election, which was revealed for our comfort, and we move it up into some kind of noumenal realm, out of our reach, so that we don't know about it. At best we can guess; at best we can make charitable judgments about other people in the Church, but we don't know. That is the case if all Scripture tells us is the *fact* of predes-tination. But thank God He has told us more than simply *that* He predestined some people.

We are bound to what Scripture says about election, but we are also bound to the *way* Scripture speaks about election. We are bound, that is, to the *tone* of Scripture, to the manner in which Scripture pre-sents all of its talk about God's predestination and election.

When Scripture speaks about election, it speaks about it as good and joyful news. Election is never to be presented, and it is never pre-sented in Scripture, as some kind of terrible, frightening mystery, something that should cause us qualms when we think about ourselves and our relationship to God. Scripture does not present God as a stingy miser who is parsimonious with His grace. The Canons of Dort, responding to all the charges and attacks on election being made by the Arminians, warned specifically against teaching things that justified those charges. They warned against teaching that God is "unjust, a tyrant." Scripture doesn't present election with that tone.

You may say, "Aren't you presenting a caricature here? Who preaches that way?" I wish it were a caricature. If you have never encountered the kind of teaching about election that makes God look stingy, you should be thankful, but there are ministers and churches that bear the name Reformed that do present God's election in this way. There are churches where perhaps twenty people out of seven hundred partake of the Lord's Supper because they are taught that they need to wait to find out if they are *really* elect. They aren't sure that they are in the covenant. All God's promises are only for the covenant and the covenant, they say, is made with the elect only and they don't know if they are elect. They are given the impression that they need to wait for some kind of experience of God's grace and love to know that they are elect before they can even be confident that they were really baptized, that they are really God's covenant people, that Jesus really died for them. They need to wait for some kind of experience apart from Scripture. That is not a caricature. I wish to God that it were.

But the Bible doesn't present election as something to cause fear and trembling and worry. It presents election as something to be certain of and to rejoice in and to glory in. Election is good news. It's encouragement. It's comfort. It's a declaration that God has given you a great privilege. God chose you out of the whole human race to belong to Him. He set His love on you. He wanted you. He made you special.

Now here is the big question. Who is that "you" who is elect? Who is that "you" who receives that comfort? Scripture's tone in talking about election drives us to realize that Scripture's talk about election is not just general. It has an address on it. It is addressed to certain particular people. God, in Scripture, identifies people as His elect. He calls them His "chosen." Who are those people whom God addresses in this way?

That question gets us into the relationship between election and covenant. That relationship has been viewed in several different ways. There are some who say that God simply chooses a general category of people, a class of people (Israel, the Church), but that God has not predestined any individual to eternal glory with Christ. That is the Arminian position. We need to reject that position because the Bible tells us that God works out all things according to His will. And "all things" includes not only our entrance into God's covenant people in history but also who will persevere to the end. It includes who is going to enter into eternal glory with Christ. Those things also, we know from Ephesians 1, God is working out according to His will.

There is another view more popular in our circles which says that only the elect, that is, only those whom God has predestined to eternal glory with Christ, are really in the covenant. Others may be in the *sphere* of the covenant. They may be *externally* in the covenant, but only those predestined to eternal glory with Christ are *really* in the covenant or *internally* in the covenant. God makes no promises, then, to those who are not predestined to eternal salvation.

That is one Reformed view, but it is only *one* Reformed view. There have been many Reformed views in history. This particular view is held by people in the Protestant Reformed Churches and the Netherlands Reformed Churches. It is held by Reformed Baptists, and it is held by many Presbyterians.

This view even appears to have some support from the Westminster Larger Catechism, Q & A 31: "With whom was the covenant of grace made? The covenant of grace was made with Christ as the second Adam, and in Him with all the elect as His seed." Some people see that answer as giving support to the view that only the elect, only those predestined to glory with Christ eternally, are really in the covenant. Others are only externally in the covenant or in the sphere of the covenant.[2]

This view presents a number of pastoral problems. If we don't know who is predestined to eternal glory with Christ and if we believe that these are the only ones who are really in the covenant, then it follows that we don't know who is really in the covenant. So you find sometimes that ministers who hold this view will not address their congregation as the congregation of Jesus Christ because they don't know whether they belong to Christ.

On this view, if a child is baptized, the question remains whether that child has really been *baptized*. Or was that baptism just a sprinkling with water? Baptism is tied to God's covenant but if we don't know if this person is elect then we cannot be sure that this person is in the covenant.

Writers such as Abraham Kuyper have taught that just as there is sometimes a false labor that doesn't result in birth, so sometimes there is what he calls *schijndoop*, an apparent baptism. It looks like baptism. The minister is there. He pours the water over the head of that child. He says the words. But it was only apparent baptism. It was not a real baptism because that child turns out later on not to have been elect. If the child is elect it was a real baptism. If the child was not elect then it wasn't a real baptism.[3]

On this view, then, we don't know if our children are in the covenant. Can we teach our children to pray to God as their *Father* if we don't know if they have been predestined to eternal glory with Christ? Can we teach our children to sing "Jesus loves me, this I know; for the Bible tells me so" if we don't know if they are predestined to eternal glory with Christ? Can we teach our children any of the Psalms if we don't know that they have the right as God's people to sing those Psalms? So it follows that we no longer treat our children as God's covenant people and we no longer treat the whole congregation as God's covenant people.

As pastors become consistent with this view they are inclined to preach in the third person, and stay away from the words *I* and *we* and *you* when it comes to election. Of course they can talk about *sin* in the first and second person: "I have sinned; we have sinned; you have sinned." They can talk about our duty in the first and second person: "We must obey God's commandments. You must love the Lord." Yet when it comes to talking about salvation they suddenly switch to the third person: "Jesus died for *the elect*." They cannot say *we* or *you* to the congregation because pastors don't know if what they're saying is really for everyone in their congregation. They don't know if the people are in the covenant and if God's covenant promises are for them.

If we hold this view consistently, then, the covenant no longer functions in our thinking and our practice because we have made the covenant as invisible and as unknowable for us as God's eternal predestination. We end up trying to do theology and our pastoral work in terms of the secret things which belong to the Lord instead of the things which He has revealed to us and to our sons for our comfort. In fact, on this view we also end up with a problem that is even worse. We lose the ability to use the language of Scripture and to apply it directly to the flesh-and-blood people who are sitting in the pews.

In the Bible God makes His covenant with believers and their children. We see that in Genesis 17. God establishes His covenant with Abraham and what does He tell him? He tells him to include his children and to have his sons circumcised. The covenant is with believers and their children, even though those children may later break covenant with God. That was true in the Old Covenant, and that is true in the New Covenant.

The Bible tells us that people can and do break the New Covenant. Hebrews 10:29: "How much severer punishment do you think he will deserve who has trampled under foot the Son of God, and has regarded as unclean the blood of the covenant by which he was sanctified, and has insulted the Spirit of grace?"

Notice what Hebrews says. It says that this person has "regarded as unclean the blood of the covenant by which he was"—brought into the sphere of the covenant? No—"by which he was sanctified," really and truly, and he "has insulted the Spirit of grace."

The New Covenant can be broken. Jesus taught us that. He says in John 15, "I am the true vine, and my father is the vinedresser. Every branch *in me* that does not bear fruit, He takes away." He doesn't say, "Every bit of tumbleweed that is stuck in my branches." He says, "Every branch *in me*."

These branches were not stuck to the tree with Scotch Tape. These branches were genuinely in Christ. That's good Pauline language and it's the language of Jesus. "Every branch in me that does not bear fruit He takes away." That is not a reference to mere chastening. Jesus says, "If anyone does not abide in me" that is, if anyone does not *stay* in me, where he really is, then "he is thrown away as a branch and dries up; and they gather them, and cast them into the fire, and they are burned."

Jesus teaches us that some who are in Him get cut off and burned. They apostatize and they go to hell. Scripture tells us that not all who are in the covenant have been predestined to eternal glory with Christ. They don't end up in eternal glory, and they don't end up there because they have not been predestined to end up there.

What, then, is the relationship between covenant and election? As we read Scripture we discover that the covenant includes believers and their children. Abraham and his seed are included, even the hypocrites.

There are people in the covenant and in the Church who will not be in the Church on the last day but will have been cut off and burned. There are people in the covenant and in the Church whom God has not predestined to persevere to the end and to inherit eternal glory with Christ forever.

Previously, I mentioned a view that was only one of the Reformed views. This view I have just presented is another strand of Reformed thought, and it has very good credentials. This happens to have been Calvin's view.[4] Many of the other early reformers held a similar view. It is the view, I believe, which is taught in the Three Forms of Unity: the Heidelberg Catechism, the Belgic Confession, and the Canons of Dort.[5] It has been the view of many Reformed and Presbyterian theologians as well, but you will find all kinds of variations of thinking about the relationship between covenant and election all through history. We need to give each other some breathing room, as the Church historically has, on the issue of covenant and election.

Reformed theologians haven't always agreed on the relationship between covenant and election. We sometimes think that our view alone is the Reformed view: "Anybody who disagrees with me has disagreed with *the* Reformed view." Greg Bahnsen once said that we tend to calculate the mainstream by gerrymandering a canal right where we are standing so that we can say, "I am the mainstream. Everybody who diverts from this is not."[6]

It seems clear to me, however, that the view I have just presented is biblical. I believe that the Bible teaches that God makes His covenant with believers and their children, but some in the covenant have not been predestined to eternal glory with Christ.

But is that all we can say about the relationship between covenant and election? There are people who take that approach. They have a radical form of this view which sharply distinguishes covenant from election. Election is over here and covenant is over there, and never the two shall meet. God predestined some people to glory with Christ but that has nothing to do with who is in the covenant.

That isn't the way Scripture speaks, however, and so we are back to the question that we asked earlier: To whom does God address the statements in Scripture about His election? Whom does God call "elect"?

We discover in Scripture that God addresses His faithful covenant people as His "chosen ones" and as His "elect ones." Sometimes God applies that language to the whole of the covenant people: "You are my chosen nation." Sometimes He applies it, in particular, to a remnant which is faithful while the rest are apostate. We find that language in particular in the Old Testament. Too many of our Reformed treatments of election deal almost strictly with the New Testament, but the Old Testament isn't silent on election, and we need to hear what it says.

In the Psalms, Israel is often referred to as God's chosen ones. We see the same thing many times in Deuteronomy. We find it in Deuteronomy 4:37, and notice the connection here between choosing and exodus: "Because He loved their fathers, therefore He chose their descendants after them. And He personally brought you from Egypt by His great power."

We hear something similar in Deuteronomy 10:14–15: "Behold, to the LORD your God belong heaven and the highest heavens, the earth and all that is in it. Yet on your fathers did the LORD set His affection to love them, and He chose their descendants after them, even you above all peoples, as it is this day."

The classic passage in this connection is Deuteronomy 7:6ff.:

> You are a holy people to the LORD your God; the LORD your God has chosen you to be a people for His own possession out of all the peoples who are on the face of the earth. The LORD did not set His love on you nor choose because you were more in number than any of the peoples, for you were the fewest of all peoples, but because the LORD loved you and kept the oath which He swore to your forefathers, the LORD brought you out with a mighty hand, and redeemed you from the house of slavery, from the hand of Pharaoh king of Egypt.

Again, notice the connection here between election and exodus. The Lord didn't *choose you* because you were great in number, Moses says. But He *brought you out of Egypt* because He set His love on you and kept the oath He had made some time in the past to your forefathers.

This close tie between election and exodus may appear to present a bit of a problem. It seems as if God's choice or election of Israel was made *in history*. God chose you, Moses says, because He was keeping an oath He made some time ago to the forefathers. This election happens in history and appears to be identical, in Deuteronomy 7, with the Exodus.

However, the *historical* character of this choice shouldn't trouble us. We find the same thing often in Scripture.[7] Think of the choice of a king for Israel. We read in Deuteronomy 17 that the Israelites are to choose for themselves a king whom the Lord chooses, or, as some translations put it, whom the Lord *will* choose. When did God choose David? When each of Jesse's other sons passed Samuel, he said, "The LORD has not chosen these." But when David was brought in, the LORD said, "This is he" (1 Sam. 16:6–13). That is when God chose David to be Israel's king.

Now this choice, which happens in history and which is visible and obvious to everyone present, reflects—and is the outworking and historical manifestation of—God's eternal predestinating choice as we said at the very beginning. All things, including what happened here with Samuel and David, and what happened earlier with Israel at the Exodus, happen according to God's will.

From eternity God chose David to be king of Israel. From eternity He chose Israel to be His people, but He enacted that choice of David in history when Samuel poured oil over his head, and He enacted His choice of Israel out of all the nations in history at the Exodus. That is when God, in history, but according to His eternal plan, took Israel out of the nations for Himself. God chose Israel to be in the covenant, and that is good news. That is unconditional election. Deuteronomy 7 is one of the passages that teach us unconditional election: "Not because you were great in number, but because God loved you and He is faithful to His oath."

In Deuteronomy 9:4–6 God goes further and says that He isn't blessing Israel because of her righteousness, either. Her blessings weren't due to anything in Israel herself. It was entirely God's grace. This election is a privilege. Israel, out of all the nations on the earth, is God's special people, a holy people. That is the whole point of Deuteronomy 7: You are a holy people because God chose you for Himself.

This choice of Israel involves not just a group or a class, as many Arminians would like it to, but it involves the members as well. No Israelite had the right to say, "God chose the nation, the class as a whole, but He didn't choose me," because God chose each Israelite to belong to that nation. They couldn't take what God said to Israel here and say, "Well, this refers to the class, but *I* don't need to keep these laws because nothing God says here applies to me as an individual. It just applies to the whole class." No, of course they took what Moses said here to refer them personally, as members of God's covenant people.

Each Israelite was grafted into God's people as an act of God's electing love. That election, that choice to belong to the people of God, that choice of Israel as a nation, involves a special calling and a special responsibility. God chose His people unconditionally, not because of anything that was true of them. He chose them to belong to Him, but their life in covenant with God was *conditional*. It involved faith and obedience and perseverance.

All through history we see that individual Israelites apostatize. Israel as a whole apostatizes, though God preserves a remnant. It is out of the whole of Israel that God selects some whom He preserves according to His eternal plan and predestination. That is how God works out His eternal plan in the course of history. Though God declares Israel "my people" early in her history, we discover in Hosea that God later calls Israel "not my people" (Hos. 1:9). He made them His special people, and then He reprobated them in history: "Not my people." Later in Hosea He promises to call Israel "my people" again. He promises to preserve a remnant and to bring in the Gentiles as well. He promises to choose, to elect, Israel one more time.

That sounds strange to us, but it is scriptural language. We hear in Isaiah 14:1: "When the LORD will have compassion on Jacob, and *again choose Israel,* and settle them in their own land . . ." God chooses Israel *again.* He *continues* to choose Israel as His people even though many of them apostatize.[8] He preserves a remnant and He adds the Gentiles, so that He can have a people as He always eternally intended.

We might say, "Well, that's why many Reformed theologies don't deal with the Old Testament. The Old Testament election involved the whole body and it involved history. But that was the Old Testament. Election revealed in the New Testament is a different kind of election."

But that isn't what 1 Peter teaches us. In 1 Peter 2:9ff., Peter says to the church, "You are a chosen race, a royal priesthood, a holy nation, a people for God's own possession, that you may proclaim the excellencies of Him who has called you out of darkness into His marvelous light." There is the exodus motif again, "for you once were not a people but now you are the people of God; you had not received mercy, but now you have received mercy."

Peter teaches us to view the Church and to view ourselves the way that Moses describes Israel. Our being God's covenant people isn't our doing. Paul says in 1 Corinthians 1:26ff. that in the Church there are

> not many wise according to the flesh, not many mighty, not many noble;
> but God has chosen the foolish things of the world to shame the wise,
> and God has chosen the weak things of the world to shame the things
> which are strong, and the base things of the world and the despised,
> God has chosen, the things that are not, that He might nullify the things
> that are, that no man should boast before God.

We are God's chosen people, not because of anything in ourselves, not because of anything we have done, but because of His sheer grace. Others stumble over Christ, Peter says, to which he adds, "they were also appointed." They were destined to stumble over Christ, Peter tells us, but we are God's chosen people, sheerly by God's grace. We are the people who have gone through the Exodus from darkness to light. We are the fulfillment of Hosea's prophecy: "You once were not a people, but now you are the people of God." Peter doesn't let us apply this statement simply to the Church as a *class*. This statement applies to individuals in the Church as well. It applies to all of us as members of the Church.

Everything Peter says in this letter applies to his hearers personally. Peter teaches us at the very beginning of this letter to regard each of ourselves and every member of the Church as God's chosen: "Peter, an apostle of Jesus Christ, to those who reside as aliens, scattered throughout Pontus, Galatia, Cappadocia, Asia, and Bithynia, who are chosen according to the foreknowledge of God the Father . . ." (1 Pet. 1:1–2a). Peter writes to this group of people throughout Asia Minor and calls them God's chosen and elect nation. He's teaching them to see themselves not just as a class but as individuals too, as chosen pilgrims, elect according to the foreknowledge of God.

That is a privilege we need to embrace. We belong to God. God has claimed us for Himself in history. He exodused us out of darkness into His marvelous light to belong to Him, and this great privilege is also our calling. Every gift in Scripture is a mandate. If that is who we are, Peter says, if we really are God's chosen people, then we need to live as God's chosen people, that is, as "aliens and strangers" in the world (1 Pet. 2:11).

Paul teaches us something similar. In Ephesians 1, he writes:

> Paul, an apostle of Christ Jesus, by the will of God, to the saints who are at Ephesus and who are faithful in Christ Jesus: Grace to you and peace from God our Father and the Lord Jesus Christ. Blessed be the God and Father of our Lord Jesus Christ, who has blessed us with every spiritual blessing in the heavenly places in Christ, just as He chose us in Him before the foundation of the world, that we should be holy and blameless before Him. In love He predestined us to adoption as sons through Jesus Christ to Himself, according to the kind intention of His will, to the praise and glory of His grace, which He freely bestowed on us in the Beloved (1:1–6).

Paul goes on: "In Him we have redemption . . . in Him . . . in Him . . . in Him." All of these blessings that Paul names here have been lavished on us *in Christ*. That includes our election to be holy and blameless. It includes God's predestination of us to be adopted as sons through Jesus Christ and to enjoy an inheritance. All of that is *in Christ*.

Christ is the Elect One. That's how the LORD describes Him in Isaiah 42:1: "My chosen one in whom my soul delights." Peter says in 1 Peter 2:6 that He is the "chosen cornerstone."[9] Christ is the Elect One, and in Him we have been chosen. But to whom does Paul say all of this? He says this to the "saints who are at Ephesus, and who are faithful in Christ Jesus."

Is Paul addressing only the elect ones in the congregation, only the ones who were predestined to eternal glory with Christ, whoever they may be? Does Paul have some special apostolic insight to know with absolute certainty that every last person in that congregation in Ephesus was predestined to eternal glory with Christ? No, he is writing to the whole church.

He distinguishes between "we" and "you" in this chapter, and the "we" may be Jewish Christians. It may be the apostles. Yet it doesn't make any difference for our application because what he says about "we" and "us" here, he goes on to apply to "you" later (1:13). Everything that "we" have "you" have, he is saying in this chapter. Paul is writing here to the whole church. He is writing to husbands and wives, parents and children, slaves and masters, as he goes on to say (5:22–6:9). Everything he says in this letter presupposes that he is not speaking to a few of the Ephesians but to all of them, head for head.

The whole church is in Christ. They have been baptized into Christ. They have clothed themselves with Christ (Gal. 3:27). Paul wants them to know that all of these blessings he is praising God for are theirs in Christ. There is nothing missing in Christ Jesus. Everything you need is found in Him and *you* are in Him. That's the good news Paul wants the Ephesians to know. Everything is in Christ and you're in Christ, and all of these blessings, then, are for you. Then, having just referred to them as elect, Paul goes to warn them in chapter five about sin that would bring down God's eternal wrath on them. He says: Don't do these things because nobody who does them "has an inheritance in the kingdom of Christ and God" (Eph. 5:3–5).

Paul doesn't appear to see a conflict, a tension, or an apparent contradiction between what he says at the beginning of the letter and the warning he gives in chapter five. Having called them "chosen in Christ before the foundation of the world," he goes on to say to the same people, "Don't do these things because nobody who does them has an inheritance in the kingdom of Christ and of God." There is no conflict in Paul's letters between comfort and warning.

Think of Romans 8. Paul says there that nobody can bring a charge against God's elect (8:33). The Romans were not supposed to say, "Well, wouldn't it be great to be one of those elect people, then. I just don't know if I am." No, they were to take this statement as applying to themselves. Paul is writing to comfort and encourage *them*: "Who can bring a charge against God's elect? And you Romans are God's elect," he is saying. They are supposed to see and know and be assured of their privileged status in Christ. Paul isn't getting confused in his letter when later on he writes to them in chapter 11 and says, "If the natural branches were chopped off, don't boast, because you could be chopped off too" (cf. 11:20–21). Paul doesn't see a contradiction or some kind of neo-orthodox tension between the assurance of chapter 8 and the warning of chapter 11. Paul warns the very same people he comforts.

Paul talks about God's election in 2 Thessalonians 2:13 also. He says to the church, "But we should always give thanks to God for you, brothers beloved by the Lord, because God has chosen you from the beginning for salvation through sanctification by the Spirit and faith in the truth." How can Paul speak that way? Does Paul have apostolic insight to know that every last person in the church there at Thessalonica is predestined to glory with Christ? If that were the case, if Paul can address them the way he does because he has a special insight that we don't have and he knows that everybody there in Thessalonica is pre-destined to glory in Christ, then that means that we can't learn from Paul how to talk to the Church. We can't learn from the apostle Paul, who told us to imitate him, how congregations ought to be addressed.

This *reductio ad absurdum* demonstrates that there is a problem with our argument. If we come to the conclusion that we can't learn from Paul how to address the Church, then we must admit that our premise is wrong, namely, the premise that Paul can address the Church as God's chosen because he has an apostolic insight we don't have. If Paul isn't speaking to the whole church this way because he knows that they are all going to end up in eternal glory with Christ, then is it possible that Paul is speaking to some only: "Brothers, beloved by the Lord, you subset of the Church, we give thanks for you"?

No! If Paul were speaking only to some of the people in the church, to some of the people who heard this letter read to the church, but not to others, then that would rob the whole church of the very comfort Paul wants to give them. They'd all be asking, "Is Paul talking to *me*?" If Paul isn't writing to the whole church, then no one in the church would know if Paul is writing to him.

Is Paul making a good guess here, then: "It sure looks like they are all elect"? Is this wishful thinking? Is Paul just making a charitable judgment: "I will treat them as if they are elect even though they may not be"? No. To whom is Paul speaking here in this verse? That is a burning question for every preacher who preaches 2 Thessalonians 2:13. Pastors must deal with this question. This isn't an academic question that can be left in the study or to the scholars and theologians. It isn't a question with implications for this text only. This question comes up, in one way or another, in every sermon. To whom is Paul speaking here? Did he know to whom he was speaking? Did Paul have names and faces in mind? Yes, he did.

Did the Thessalonians have to wonder whether Paul was speaking about them or about the guy sitting on the other side of the room? Did they have to say to themselves, "I bet Paul means Bill and Bob, probably not Jack, *maybe* Steve. I hope he means *me*." Did they have to guess? No, they *knew* to whom Paul was speaking because Paul is writing to the church. That is how he begins 1 Thessalonians: "Paul and Silvanus and Timothy to the *church* of the Thessalonians" (1:1). No guesswork was necessary on Paul's part or on their part. Paul isn't making a charitable judgment here. He is writing to the whole church, the church that had received the word in faith, the church which was living in terms of that faith. And if they were members of that church, they could be confident in faith that Paul was addressing them and that he was addressing their fellow members, too.

It wasn't as if they were living perfectly as God's people either. Paul goes on in this letter and says, "Some among you are busybodies and aren't doing any work" (cf. 3:6–12). Not everyone in Thessalonica was living a great Christian life, yet Paul addresses the church as "brethren beloved by the Lord" and tells them, "God has chosen you for salvation." He says that this choice, with its goal of salvation, is why God called them through the gospel into the Church (2:13–14). Through the call of the gospel God's choice became a reality in history.

What does Paul say next? "Stand firm and hold to the traditions which you were taught" (2:15). "Don't apostatize," Paul says. The declaration that God chose you isn't an invitation to sit back and put your feet up. It's a calling to stand firm and not to apostatize.

We need to hold three things together as we think about the relationship between covenant and election.

First, God has eternally predestined an unchanging number of people out of the whole world to eternal glory with Christ. We read that from Genesis 1:1 on. We know that from Ephesians 1:11: God "works all things after the counsel of His will."

Second, God's covenant includes some who have been so predestined to eternal glory with Christ, but it also includes others who have not been predestined to eternal glory with Christ but who will apostatize.

Third, God addresses His people as a whole, and that includes each one in the covenant, head for head, as His elect. That is the big issue we need to think through. God, in the Bible, through His prophets and apostles, addresses His people publicly as elect, as chosen.

Now the big question is this: May we speak the language of Scripture? May pastors address their congregations the way Moses and the Psalms and Peter and Paul do, the way that God does? Or maybe the bigger question is this: May we do anything but? Shall we not learn from Scripture how congregations are to be addressed?

If we try to do our theologizing and our pastoring and our speaking to God's people from the perspective of God's eternal predestination we run into all kinds of difficulties with the way God speaks in Scripture. We start to think that God shouldn't talk the way He does, and we don't want to talk that way either.

We are uncomfortable sometimes saying to our churches or to members of our churches or to our children, "God chose *you*." But *God* speaks that way. We are uncomfortable sometimes saying to them, "Jesus died for your sins." We start to reason that Jesus died for the full and final salvation of those and those only whom God has predestined to eternal glory in Christ and we don't know with infallible certainty that this child, this church member, this congregation has been so predestined.

If we try to work from the perspective of God's eternal predestination, we have trouble saying things to the flesh-and-blood people in our churches that Peter and Paul and the other writers of Scripture had no trouble saying to the churches they addressed.

If we try to do our theologizing, our pastoring, our preaching from the perspective of what God has hidden, on the basis of the secret things of His predestination, we discover that we have a hard time applying not only the *promises* but also the *warnings* of Scripture to the real flesh-and-blood people in the pews.

Who is being addressed by those warnings? The ones infallibly predestined to eternal glory with Christ? If that's the case, then what function does that warning play? If we're thinking in terms of God's predestination, we're inclined to say, "Well, those people who are being warned can't fall away. They won't fall away. And therefore these warnings and threats doesn't really apply to them."

So people have sometimes said that the warnings in Scripture are only *hypothetical* for the elect. They're warning against something that can't happen and won't happen anyway. What is a hypothetical warning? Whatever it is, it's not found in Scripture. The Westminster Confession 14.2 isn't speaking of merely hypothetical warnings when it says that faith trembles. Does faith tremble at things that are only hypothetical? No. Faith trembles at the warnings. Why? Because those warnings are real. That's why those warnings are frightening. *Unbelief* thinks the warnings are hypothetical and brushes them off, but *faith* knows better. Faith trembles.

The Canons of Dort aren't speaking of merely hypothetical warnings when they say that "God . . . preserves, continues, and completes His work by the hearing and reading of the gospel, by meditation on it, by its exhortations, *threats*, and promises, and also by the use of the sacraments." God causes people to persevere through the threats of the gospel. Those are real threats, real warnings, but if we try to do all our thinking from the perspective of eternal predestination to glory with Christ, we have a hard time with those warnings. We have a hard time applying them to the elect, but we also have a hard time applying them to the reprobate. What good does the warning do him? He won't respond to it anyway!

When a pastor preaches from this perspective, he can't apply the promises effectively and he can't apply the warnings effectively. When you proclaim the promises, people aren't sure if those promises are really for them. When you proclaim the warnings, people brush them off because they figure that if they're elect they can't incur God's wrath and if they aren't there's nothing they can do about it anyway.

God calls us to think and to theologize and to pastor, not in terms of the secret things which belong to Him, but in terms of the things He has revealed for us and for our sons, that they may observe the way of the Lord and keep His law. God calls us to think covenantally, and in doing so, let me affirm again, we are not denying that God predestines some to eternal glory with Christ. We are affirming that, but we want to affirm the rest of what Scripture says as well. Even if we don't understand how all these things fit together, even if we don't all agree with each other about how these things fit together, let us agree on this—we *must* speak the language of Scripture to our people. We *may not* do otherwise.

We are not wiser than God. We are not better theologians than God. We must learn from Scripture, from God Himself, from His prophets and apostles, how to address God's people. We must follow the pattern of the prophets and apostles and call our congregations "God's chosen people" and assure them, as Peter and Paul and all the rest do, that Jesus died for them, that they are God's temple, the temple of the Holy Spirit.

We don't have to understand all the connections perfectly. We don't have to have all of our theology worked out in exhaustive detail before we can do what Scripture teaches us to do, but here is a possible objection: What if I say to the church, "God chose you for salvation and Jesus died for you," and then some of those people fall away and apostatize and end up in hell? Haven't I lied to them? No, you haven't. You have spoken the truth. In Scripture, truth is more than just conformity to the facts. It is trustworthiness and faithfulness.[10] You have spoken to these people in a trustworthy manner. You have spoken to them in a faithful manner, a manner that they can bank their whole lives on, because you have spoken to them in accordance with God's revelation.

There is a tough, challenging, and surprising passage in Ezekiel 33:13ff. The LORD says there:

> When I say to the righteous, he will surely live, and he so trusts in his righteousness that he commits iniquity, none of his righteous deeds will be remembered; but in that same iniquity of his which he has committed he will die. But when I say to the wicked, "You will surely die," and he turns from his sin and practices justice and righteousness, if a wicked man restores a pledge, pays back what he has taken by robbery, walks by the statutes of life [NASB margin] without committing iniquity, he will surely live; he shall not die. None of his sins that he has committed will

be remembered against him. He has practiced justice and righteousness; he will surely live.[11]

Yet we want to say to God, "You said to the righteous man, 'You will surely live'—*living you will live*, in the Hebrew idiom—but he died. You said to the wicked man, 'You will surely die'—*dying you will die*—and he lived. You lied to them, didn't you? You didn't tell the truth to them." But who are we to teach God how to speak the truth?

This is how God speaks. He says to people, "You will surely live," and then they die because they trust in their own righteousness instead of trusting in Him. But God was telling the *truth* when He says to them, "You will surely live." He was not lying to them. He was saying something trustworthy. When He says to the wicked man, "You will surely die," He's saying something trustworthy to that man and the man takes heed to what God has said. He trusts what God has said. He believes that if he stays on the path on which he is going he will surely die. In faith he trembles at the warning and he will surely live.

God speaks this way and we must learn from Him how to speak. God speaks to His people and He calls them elect, and therefore we also need to speak to God's people this way. We must. We have no other choice but to let God teach us how to address His people, even if we don't have it all worked out in our minds. If we are not comfortable with biblical language, not only hearing it but also saying it, if biblical language sounds strange to us, and if our theology gets in the way of our speaking and receiving the language of Scripture, then what has become of us—we, who are to live by every word that proceeds from the mouth of the Lord?

God's speech to us is trustworthy because it is God who is speaking, and He speaks to us in a *promissory* way. In speech God pledges Himself to us, to be our God.[12] We tend to think of a promise as a prediction: "This is going to happen no matter what." But that is not how God's promises work in Scripture. By *promise* I mean that God is pledging and giving Himself to us in words.

We tend to think that promises relate to the future, but in our confessional and theological heritage that word *promise* can also refer to past events. Luther puts it this way: "This is my body" is a plain indicative statement which becomes promissory. It becomes a promise by the addition of the words "for you."[13]

So also, the Heidelberg Catechism, Lord's Day 7, says that Christians must believe all that is *promised* in the gospel. Those promises, it says, are summed up in the Apostles' Creed. But most of the Creed has to do with the past. How do those statements in the Creed become promises? Those events happened *for us*.

When we hear that God is the maker of heaven and earth, that isn't simply a report on past history; it's a promise. God has created heaven and earth *for* us. Jesus died; that's a past event. He died *for us*; that's a promise.

God administers His salvation by speaking to us, by proclaiming it to us, by telling us who we are in Christ and all that we have in Christ. He addresses us with the promise of salvation, including the promise of His choice, the promise of His election. He doesn't simply say, "I chose some people." He says to us, "I chose you. You're mine. You're special. You belong to me." That promise is good news. God selected you out of the whole world to belong to Him, to belong to His covenant. Covenant membership is not just a bare legal relationship. The covenant is not just a means to an end, the goal of salvation. The covenant in history is the early form of that final goal. It is the early form of that end, that salvation. The covenant is a bond with the triune God of Scripture.

God chose you to be in His covenant, to have that bond with Him in Christ. That choice, worked out in history when you were baptized, is grounded in God's eternal predestination. *He* had you baptized, according to His eternal plan. God doesn't just predestine the ends. He predestines the means as well. In eternity God chose to have you baptized, engrafted into the Church, joined to Christ, the Elect One, joined to Christ's body, the Church, made a member of His chosen nation. That's glorious good news. That is privilege.

It is a privilege for pastors to preach this good news to their congregations week after week so that the people *know* that this privilege is for them: "God has selected you out of the whole human race to belong to God and to have Him say, 'I will be *your* God and you will be my people.'" Yet in God's wisdom, He has decreed that some of those whom He has chosen to bring into a covenant relationship with Him will enjoy that relationship only for a time. God truly brings those people into His covenant, into union with Christ. They are "in Him," to use Jesus' words in John 15. They share in His blessings (think of Hebrews 6). They experience His love, but that covenant relationship is conditional. It calls for repentance and faith and new obedience. God's *choice* was not conditional, but life in the covenant is.

God chooses not to work in these people so that they persevere. When they fall into sin, in His unsearchable wisdom, He allows them to harden themselves in sin. He even hardens them Himself. They may have been believers in a sense (John 2:23–24). They had a privileged status, but they fell from privilege. They hardened their hearts. They rejected God's gifts. They grieved the Spirit (Eph. 4:30). They quenched the Spirit (1 Thess. 5:19); that is, they put out the Spirit's fire. That is Scriptural language, and there comes a point when the Spirit will no longer strive with them and they apostatize.

Using our traditional theological and confessional language, we would say that these were non-elect members of the covenant. Using Calvin's terminology, these people were "generally elect" but not "specially elect."[14] Using the language of Scripture, they were among God's chosen people. They were the people that God addresses as elect. They were joined covenantally to Christ, the Elect Cornerstone, but they have been cut off from Christ. They have stumbled and fallen, as Peter says, just as they were appointed to do (1 Pet. 2:8). Affirming the reality of apostasy is not denying God's predestination. Even their apostasy is included in God's plan. Though He predestined these people to enter His covenant, He didn't predestine their perseverance. He didn't keep working in them for whatever wise reason of His own. He didn't keep working in them to will and to do (Phil. 2:13).

On the last day, these apostates will look back and see God's grace and love which they rejected. The fault wasn't in Christ or the gospel or in God's covenant. God assured them, as He assures us, that everything we need for life and godliness is ours in Christ (2 Pet. 1:3). The fault was not in Christ or in God. The fault was in them. God in His grace causes others, whom He has chosen to belong to Him and to be His covenant people, to belong to Him forever. When they sin, He brings them back. He keeps working in them by His Spirit constantly and graciously so that they keep trusting Him, so that they get up when they fall, so that they persevere to the end.

Peter says in 2 Peter 2, "Therefore, brethren, be even more diligent to make your call and election sure, for if you do these things you will never stumble; for so an entrance will be supplied to you abundantly into the everlasting kingdom of our Lord and Savior Jesus Christ" (2:10–11, NKJV).[15] Peter doesn't say to them, "Find out if you are called and elect." He calls them "called and elect." He doesn't say, "Make yourselves sure about your call and election." He says, "Make your call and election sure." What does he mean? The context here is not dealing with personal assurance. He is also not saying that we can somehow contribute to God's election or that God's election is based on something in ourselves or something we have done. But what he is saying is that by our lives we have to ratify and confirm God's calling and election. We have to work it out. We have to live it out, and as we do that, Peter assures us, we will not fall short of God's everlasting kingdom.[16]

On the last day we will look back and we will see God's grace every inch of the way. God gave us life. God worked in all the details in our lives. God, in grace, united to us in Christ, the Elect One, and He kept us in Him. He worked in us to will and to work (Phil. 2:13). He worked in us so that we responded to Him in faith and trust and we persevered. We owe it all to Him, to His choice, to His grace. We will enter into final glory with Christ exactly according to God's eternal predestinating decree.

For those who do not persevere to the end, God's choice to have them belong to His covenant was His choice to show them grace and love for a time, and both their entrance into His covenant and their subsequent rejection of His grace and love by their apostasy is the historic outworking of His predestinating decree.

For those who do persevere to the end, God's choice to have them belong to His covenant was His choice to have them belong to Him forever. Their entrance into His covenant, their perseverance in faith, and their rich entry into the everlasting kingdom of Jesus Christ (2 Pet. 1:11) are the historic outworking of His predestinating decree.

In history, we are to view ourselves the way God teaches us to. We are God's covenant people. God has called us elect. Pastors need to address their congregations that way. He tells us that He chose us.

Pastors must tell their congregations that He chose them. We must speak the language of Scripture, calling people to respond in faith.

Yet if apostasy is a real danger, can we ever have assurance? Not in ourselves, but in God and in His promises. Left to myself, I would most assuredly fall away, but in Christ I can be confident because no one who trusts in Him is ever put to shame (Isa. 28:16; Rom. 10:11). As we look to Christ in faith, as we trust God who speaks to us these words so rich with promise, the Spirit works in us so that we do persevere.

There is no room for presumption in God's covenant. The warnings apply to every covenantal member, but there is also no room and no need for the worry: "Am I really elect?" We believe God's promise and we live in terms of it.

Appendix

One question which may arise in connection with my approach in this article is whether this approach has antecedents in the history of Reformed theology. I do not claim that anyone has expressed this view exactly as I have, though I am certainly indebted to many other Reformed writers, some of whom I have mentioned in the endnotes.

Among the early Reformers, Zwingli appears to have held a similar view. In speaking about God's relationship to the infants of believers, Zwingli says:

> For when he includes us under Abraham's covenant this word makes us no less certain of their election than of the old Hebrews'. For the statement that they are in the covenant, testament and people of God assures us of their election until the Lord announces something different of someone.

He says later, "Indeed it is my opinion that all infants who are under the testament are doubtless of the elect by the laws of the testament." It appears that Zwingli is saying that God's covenant law teaches us that these children are elect. Peter Lillback summarizes:

> Zwingli's point seems to be that men will make errors in their attempts to judge if someone is elect or not. But God's Word or Law is absolutely reliable. If the law declares that the children of God's people belong to

Him, one must receive it as the truth, until the law shows they do not belong to Him, as in the case of an adult unbeliever from a Christian family.

Zwingli then applies this view to Esau:

> What then of Esau, if he had died as an infant? Would your judgment place him among the elect? Yes. Then does election remain sure? It does. And rejection remains also. But listen. If Esau had died an infant he would doubtless have been elect. For if he had died then there would have been the seal of election, for the Lord would not have rejected him eternally. But since he lived and was of the non-elect, he so lived that we see in the fruit of his unfaithfulness that he was rejected by the Lord.[17]

Lillback discusses the difference between a man named Cellarius, who had no use for externals because only the elect were really in the covenant, and Zwingli, who emphasized the importance of baptism. Lillback summarizes it this way:

> Zwingli believed that infant baptism was a sign of the covenant which brought a promise of salvation to the children. The very covenant sign for Zwingli was critical because it was an attestation of the decree of election for the parents and their child. One might later prove that he was not truly one of Christ's by not manifesting the faith that was the fruit of election. But to assume that of any infant, or even to remain in an uncertain state as taught by Cellarius, was to deny the law of God which undergirded the covenant sign.[18]

We find a somewhat similar approach to the election of believers' infants, when those infants die in infancy, in the Canons of Dort. The First Head of Doctrine, Article 17, says:

> Since we must make judgments about God's will from His word, which testifies that the children of believers are holy, not by nature, but in virtue of the gracious covenant, in which they together with their parents are included, godly parents ought not to doubt the *election* and salvation of their children whom God calls out of this life in infancy.

"Godly parents ought not to doubt," that is, they are forbidden to doubt, may not doubt, are not permitted to doubt "the election and salvation of their children whom God calls out of this life in infancy." Why? Because, say the Canons of Dort, those children have been included in God's covenant together with their parents. They have not grown up and apostatized, and their membership in the covenant is therefore sufficient to assure us that they were elect.

The historic Reformed Baptismal Form links baptism with the promise of election. The Form talks about the promises given to us by the Triune God when we're baptized into His name. The Father promises to adopt us as His children. The Son promises to wash away our sins.[19] That Form also talks about the Holy Spirit who promises to present us "without spot among the assembly of the elect in life eternal."[20] If the Spirit promises that you will be among the elect in life eternal, you can bank on it and trust that you are among the elect *now*.

Therefore, every member of the Church can confess in faith the words the Heidelberg Catechism puts in the mouths of its students:

Q. 54 What do you believe concerning the "holy catholic church"?

A. I believe that the Son of God, through His Spirit and Word, out of the entire human race, from the beginning of the world to its end, gathers, protects, and preserves for Himself a community *chosen for eternal life* and united in true faith. And of this community *I am and always will be*, a living member (emphasis mine).

The Heidelberg Catechism links the doctrine of election here with the doctrine of the Church. In a warm and pastoral way, it teaches all the Church's children, those who have been grafted into the Church through baptism (Q & A 74) to confess together with the whole Church: "The Son of God is gathering His elect Church, and I am and always will be a living member of it." That isn't a wish or a boast; it's a confession of faith, grounded on God's grace in bringing us into His covenant.

Notes - Chapter 1

[1] For more information concerning Schilder and the debates on covenant and election in the Reformed churches in the Netherlands in the 1940s, see J. Geertsema, ed., *Always Obedient: Essays on the Teachings of Dr. Klaas Schilder* (Phillipsburg, NJ: P&R, 1995); Cornelis van Dam, ed., *The Liberation: Causes and Consequences: The Struggle in the Reformed Churches in the Netherlands in the 1940s* (Winnipeg: Premier, 1995); J. Kamphuis, *An Everlasting Covenant*, trans. G. van Rongen (Launceston, Australia: Free Reformed Churches of Australia, 1985); and Rudolf van Reest, *Schilder's Struggle for the Unity of the Church*, trans. Theodore Plantinga (Neerlandia, AB: Inheritance, 1990). See also Klaas Schilder, *Extra-Scriptural Binding—A New Danger* (Neerlandia, AB: Inheritance, 1996).

[2] Notice, though, that the Westminster Larger Catechism says that the children of believers are also in the covenant (Q & A 166). Q & A 31 is not the only statement in the Catechism about who is in covenant with God. You can make a case that the Westminster Larger Catechism has a broader view of who is in the covenant than the view I am describing here.

[3] Abraham Kuyper, *Voor een distel een mirt: Geestelijke overdenkingen bij den heiligen Doop, bij het doen van belijdenis en het toegaan tot het Heilig Avondmaal* (Amsterdam, 1891), p. 54 cited in J. Kamphuis, *An Everlasting Covenant*, pp. 24–25.

[4] Peter A. Lillback, *The Binding of God: Calvin's Role in the Development of Covenant Theology*, Texts and Studies in Reformation and Post-Reformation Thought (Grand Rapids: Baker, 2001).

[5] Cf. Heidelberg Catechism, Q & A 74 (the infants of believers are "included in the covenant" and are "by baptism . . . grafted into the Christian church"); Belgic Confession, Art. 34 ("Christ shed His blood . . . for the washing of the children of believers"); Canons of Dort I.17 (God's Word testifies that the children of believers are included in the covenant). Note also that the conclusion of the Canons of Dort rejects the view that when the infants of believers die they perish "so that neither . . . their *baptism* nor the prayers of the church at their *baptism* can be of any use to them."

[6] "I have spoken purposely of the history of respectable Reformed thought, not of a mythological 'mainstream of Reformed thought' because the latter is usually found by gerrymandering a canal under one's own feet." Greg L. Bahnsen, "God's Law and Gospel Prosperity: A Reply to the Editor of the Presbyterian Journal" (distributed by the Session of St. Paul Presbyterian Church, Jackson, MS, 1978, and available at www.cmfnow.com, #PE041), cited in Robert R. Booth, "Covenantal Antithesis," *The Standard Bearer: A Festschrift for Greg L. Bahnsen*, ed. Steven M. Schlissel (Nacogdoches, TX: Covenant Media Press, 2002), p. 29.

[7] In what follows, I am indebted to B. Holwerda's "De verkiezing in de Schrift," *Populair-wetenschappelijke bijdragen* (Goes: Oosterbaan & LeCointre, 1962), pp. 49–64. This article was written in 1942, during the controversy over the relationship between covenant and election in the Reformed churches in the Netherlands. A few

years later, Holwerda was appointed Professor of Old Testament at the Theological College of the Reformed churches (liberated).

[8] Holwerda, p. 59, points out that the phrase here in Isaiah 14:1 could be rendered "I will *still* choose Israel."

[9] My own translation. The NASB translates this phrase "a choice stone, a precious cornerstone." The NKJV is more accurate: "A chief cornerstone, elect, precious." The same word (*eklekton*) is used for the stone in 2:4, 6 as for the race in 2:9. Cf. the discussion in P. H. R. van Houwelingen, *1 Petrus: Rondzendbrief uit Babylon*, Commentaar op het Nieuwe Testament (Kampen: Kok, 1991), pp. 76–79; Wayne A. Grudem, *The First Epistle of Peter*, Tyndale New Testament Commentaries (Grand Rapids: Eerdmans, 1988), pp. 98–99.

[10] See the discussion in B. Holwerda, *Seminarie-Dictaat: Jozua en Richteren*, 4th ed. (Kampen: Van den Berg, 1978), p. 13. I am *not* saying that our speech here is out of conformity with the facts. It is in conformity to the fact that the people we are addressing are God's covenant people, in God's sight as much as in ours, and the fact that God teaches us how we are to address them in a way that is trustworthy and faithful to Him and to them.

[11] Note that this passage is not preaching works-righteousness. It is not telling us that this wicked man has earned his salvation by doing good works. But it is speaking about covenant faithfulness which flows out of faith in God's word—in this case, faith in the *warning* God has uttered, in particular.

[12] In what follows, I am building on Cornelis Trimp's discussion of *promise* in "Preaching as the Public Means of Divine Redemption," trans. Nelson D. Kloosterman, *Mid-America Journal of Theology* 10 (1999): pp. 39–75 and in "The Promise of the Covenant: Some Observations," *Unity in Diversity: Studies Presented to Prof. Dr. Jelle Faber on the Occasion of His Retirement*, ed. Riemer Faber (Hamilton: Senate of the Theological College of the Canadian Reformed Churches, 1989), pp. 71–77.

[13] Trimp sums up Luther's view: "The phrase '*for you*' grants the testament its typical characteristic of promise. Christ does not make a general declaration, but He addresses the disciples and pledges to them that by His death He gives Himself for them." ("Promise," p.73).

[14] Cf. Lillback, pp. 214ff.

[15] For the following exegesis of this passage, I am indebted to P. H. R. van Houwelingen, *2 Petrus en Judas: Testament in tweevoud*, Commentaar op het Nieuwe Testament (Kampen: Kok, 1993), pp. 39–41. Van Houwelingen is Professor of New Testament at the Theological University of the Reformed Churches in the Netherlands (liberated).

[16] I don't deny that this passage can and should be applied for our assurance, but the focus of the passage is not on personal assurance of salvation. Nothing in the passage suggests that when Peter says that we should make our election sure he means that we should assure ourselves concerning our election.

[17] All quotations are from Lillback, *The Binding of God: Calvin's Role in the Development of Covenant Theology*, pp. 104–105. I am not necessarily endorsing everything Zwingli says here, of course.

[18] Lillback, p. 108.

[19] Note that this promise is not a promise to wash away our sins in the future sometime. Rather, it is His pledge that He *does* wash away our sins, which fits with the prayer after baptism, which says, "We thank and praise Thee that Thou hast forgiven us and our children all our sins."

[20] I am quoting here from the version of the Form (Form # 1) in the Christian Reformed Church's 1976 *Psalter Hymnal*. You can find this form online at http://www.thirdmill.org/files/english/html/worship/infant.baptism.1.html.

Chapter Two
Covenant, Baptism and Salvation
Steve Wilkins

The foundation of all of God's dealings with man is covenant. It is the basis of all that God has done, is doing, and will do in time and on earth. Nothing can be understood rightly apart from an understanding of covenant.

Yet, the truth is, very few Christians have seriously considered the covenant and its implications for their lives and the lives of their children. Even those churches that profess to believe in "covenant theology" seem to have little understanding of covenant as it is revealed to us in the Scriptures. This has greatly contributed to the weakness and ineffectiveness of the Church in this century. If we are to be what God commands us to be, we must understand and rejoice in the covenant God has established with His people. Covenant as it relates to man, simply and perhaps too simplistically stated, is the relationship of love and communion with the living, Triune God. But to understand this, we need to look at God Himself.[1]

The Covenant and God

All things find their origin in the Triune God, covenant included. There is no explicit reference in the Scriptures to any covenant existing between the three persons of the Godhead. Usually, Reformed theologians, if they speak of any covenant within the Godhead, are referring to the idea of a pretemporal "covenant of redemption"—the agreement in which the Son voluntarily placed Himself under obligation to the Father to carry out the work of redemption.

In fact, the reality that God is not only one but eternally three persons implies the very thing that covenant is about. Indeed, for God to have personality at all implies that He experiences relationships within Himself. It is this that distinguishes the Triune God from the Unitarian divinity of the Jews or the Muslims. Ralph Smith observes, "The most exalted non-Christian idea of deity involves a being who is eternally alone—with no other to love, no other with whom to communicate, and no other with whom to fellowship." The implications of this are momentous. This means that love, fellowship, and communication are not essential to his being. That is, the Unitarian monad is and must be reduced to an impersonal force. As Smith observes, "A god for whom a relationship with another is eternally irrelevant is an abstraction, an idea or a thing more than a person."[2] Sadly, because of a lack of understanding of the Trinity, this is precisely the view of most Christians.

Unitarianism cannot posit love in God, because there is nothing in Him to be the object of that love. If they say, "God demonstrates His love to the world after He creates it," then they are forced to admit that God changes in time. If they say, "No, He loved the world from eternity," then they are forced to maintain that His personhood (at least His attribute of love) was dependent upon something outside of Himself—in this case the world that He planned to create. In either case (whether God changes or is dependent upon something outside of Himself to mold His character), you end up with something less than the Triune God of Scripture who is infinitely, eternally, and unchangeably, perfect love. The Unitarian god ends up inevitably becoming nothing more than "the Force"—a god who manifests himself primarily through raw, arbitrary power.

Ralph Smith raises a further problem here:

> If Muslims and Jews applied their notion of god consistently to their worldview, man's personality, too, would be found to lack ultimate meaning. That man speaks, laughs, and loves can only be accidental truths at best. There would be nothing in the deity to correspond to such things. And what could it mean for man to be created in the image of such a god? If man is to be like such a god, would that mean that the ideal life in this world is one that lacks these personal qualities? Should man look forward to an eternity of silent self-contemplation?[3]

Unitarianism leads to a dreadful and nightmarish dead end.

Polytheism is, of course, no better. By definition no god can be omnipotent and perfect, completely and absolutely sovereign—i.e., none can be ultimate. Inevitably, polytheism results in rivalries among the gods. In the end, all of them must be subject to some ultimate defining principle. This means that the impersonal is ultimate and we end with the same problem as before.

It is only in the biblical doctrine of the Trinity that these pitfalls are successfully avoided. The Bible teaches us that God is One God who exists eternally in three persons. All three persons are equally divine (they are all the same in substance, equal in power and glory) and yet all three are distinct, eternal persons. This is God's nature; He has always existed as three persons—Father, Son, and Holy Spirit—and always will. And since God is truly three persons, He is a community of holy, undivided fellowship.

We see that the Father eternally loves the Son and eternally seeks to exalt Him. John says that in the beginning the Word was with God (John 1:1–3). The covenantal fellowship of the persons of the Trinity can be seen here. Ralph Smith notes:

> Thus, John begins his Gospel with three assertions about Christ the Word: 1) that He has existed from all eternity, 2) that He was 'with God,' an assertion that employs both a preposition that implies intimacy and an expression that is commonly used for covenantal presence and blessing, and 3) that the Word was God. Part of what John intends to say may be paraphrased as, 'Jesus lived eternally in covenantal fellowship with God because He is God.'[4]

The Son eternally loves the Father and seeks to honor Him, delighting to do His will, and by the power of the Spirit carrying out His purposes to the honor and glory of the Father. This is the "oneness" that is so often mentioned by the Savior. Throughout John's gospel, this covenantal unity of the Father and the Son is emphasized. Jesus, who is in the bosom of the Father, is the only One who is able fully to reveal (or expound) Him (John 1:18). He is the only One who has "seen" the Father (John 6:46). So perfect is the covenantal unity of the Son and the Father that Jesus can say that if anyone has seen Him they have seen the Father (John 14:9–11).

He plainly asserted His oneness with the Father to the Jews: "I and the Father are one" (John 10:30). Calvin notes that in the context Jesus is not speaking of metaphysical oneness—He is not emphasizing that He and the Father are one in Being, as true as that is. Rather, Jesus is emphasizing their oneness of purpose in saving the world. Thus, Calvin says, "The ancients misused this passage to prove that Christ is *homoousion* [one substance] with the Father. Christ is not discussing the unity of substance, but the concord He has with the Father; so that whatever Christ does will be confirmed by His Father's power."[5] The context of this statement confirms Calvin's point (cf. 10:17–18, 25–29).

Because He was one with the Father, He constantly sought to do the Father's will (John 4:34; Heb. 10:4–7). What was true when He came into the world had always been the case prior to His incarnation. The Son always delighted in pleasing and honoring the Father. Thus Paul says it was *because* He was in the likeness of God that He willingly humbled Himself in obedience even to the point of death (Phil. 2:5–7). He was willing to humble Himself *because* he was "in the form of God," i.e., of the essence and being of God—and this is the way God always acts. He always humbles Himself for the good of others.

In the same way, the Spirit loves and honors both the Father and the Son and carries out the will of God to the glory of both. Being sent by the Father and the Son, it is His privilege to glorify them both. Thus, Jesus says, "When the Spirit comes, He will glorify Me." God's purpose of glorifying Himself, therefore, is not selfish or egotistical. Indeed, it is exactly the opposite. Each Person of the Godhead continually seeks the glory of the other Persons. The Father seeks to glorify the Son and the Son seeks the glory of the Father. The Spirit seeks to glorify the Father and the Son, and the Father and the Son give glory to the Spirit (John 13:31–32; 17:1, 5). Neither Person seeks His own glory, but rather the glory of the other.

Each of the Persons of the Godhead exists in sacrificial relations with the others. The glory of God then consists not in self-seeking, but in self-giving. Therefore, the fact that God is love in His relation to the creation and mankind is simply the consequence of the fact that God is love in Himself. What we see revealed in creation of the love of God is the manifestation in time of what is eternally true of God in Himself. It is the outflowing of His fullness of grace and love which the Persons of the Godhead have for each other.

The covenant into which we are brought is this very same covenant that has always existed within the Godhead from eternity. The sacrificial love that Christ displays for the Church is not simply a love for sinners, but the overflow of the love and communion that He shared with the Father and the Spirit from all eternity. Thus when John says "God is love," he is saying that the love that exists between the Father, Son, and Holy Spirit is definitive of who God is—there can be no understanding of God apart from understanding that He is a Triune Being who exists in a unity of love. If we are beloved of God, that means we are swept up into the holy, covenantal fellowship of love that has always existed in the Godhead.

Our Savior tells the disciples that they have been made partakers of the same love that exists between Himself and the Father (John 15:9–10): "*As* the Father loved Me, *I also have loved you*; abide in My love. If you keep My commandments, you will abide in My love, just as I have kept My Father's commandments and abide in His love." This is what God has done through the redemptive work of Christ: "He has delivered us from the power of darkness and conveyed us into the kingdom of the Son of His love" (Col. 1:13).

The glorious love that exists within the Godhead is freely and graciously extended and exercised toward us in and through Christ Jesus. God did not create the world and man in order to have something over which He might rule or dominate, but to have a world and a people with whom He might share His own life and bring into the joys of His fellowship. Jonathan Edwards remarks, "There was, as it were, an eternal society or family in the Godhead, in the Trinity of Persons. It seems to be God's design to admit the Church into the divine family as His Son's wife."[6] We are by His grace brought into the divine communion of love (John 14:21, 23): "'He who has My commandments and keeps them, it is he who loves Me. And he who loves Me will be loved by My Father, and I will love him and manifest Myself to him' . . . Jesus answered and said to him, 'If anyone loves Me, he will keep My word; and My Father will love him, and We will come to him and make Our home with him.'"

Further, we are brought into the family not only as the Bride of the Son but as children of the Father (1 John 3:1–3). As His children, we become the recipients of the same love that exists between the Father and the Son (John 17:23–24).

This is what it means to be in covenant. Covenant is a gracious relationship with the Triune God, in which we are made partakers of His love and participants in the communion and fellowship that has existed from all eternity in the Godhead. Consequently, all who are brought into this covenant are called upon to live as God lives—in loving, sacrificial, self-denying service to others.

The Covenant and Image-bearing

Adam was created after God's image (Gen. 1:26) which means, in part, that he was to reflect the fellowship of the Trinity. Adam initially reflects this reality by the fact that he is created not in isolation but in covenant with the Triune God. But this status was not fully sufficient to manifest the image of God in the way God desired. Thus, God declares that it is "not good" that man be alone.

Image-bearing demands that man (like God) live in community. Man's identity (like God's) is essentially tied to his relationships with others. This is implied in the language of creation (Gen. 1:26–27). God made man after His image and commanded *them* to take dominion. It is not only that each individual bears the image of God but particularly, *male and female in a communal relationship with each other* show forth that image. Since man is created after the image of the Triune God, it is not good that man be alone. It is impossible for man, in isolation from his fellows, to show forth the image of God in the fullest sense. He must have communion with other men, in the family, in the society, and ultimately in the Church, if he is to glorify the Triune God Who is in Himself a holy community of love and fellowship.

The image of God is not displayed merely by the human individual possessing certain characteristics (as it has been defined in our confessions and catechisms, i.e., "knowledge, righteousness, and holiness") but by humanity as a whole as it reflects God's uncreated and eternal community. Each individual can fully show forth the image of God only within the context of life in community with others. Only in fellowship with others can we display to the world what God is like. This is so because the true God is *the* community of love and fellowship. Therefore, covenant is essential to image-bearing.

For this reason, when man fell, it wasn't just the individual souls of Adam and Eve that were affected but their entire existence. Their relationships with the Lord, with one another, and with the creation itself were destroyed by sin. Sin is a negation of the image of God in that it is a failure to maintain covenant—faithful communion with God and others. Thus, when Adam sinned, he lost everything that defined life for him.

The covenant structured his life around three central institutions:

1. *Worship.* Adam was first and foremost to be a *worshiper.* His first purpose was to glorify the One who created Him by returning to Him suitable thanksgiving and praise.
2. *Wedlock.* The covenant defined him as a *covenant head or husband.* As God's representative in creation, man is to exercise headship under God. In this role, Adam was given a wife to love, protect, and lead, and with whom he could be fruitful by the blessing of God.
3. *Work.* The covenant defines man as *worker;* one who has been given the job of taking dominion over the creation as God's vice-regent. As God's representative, Adam was entrusted with the entire creation to subdue and take dominion over it in God's name and according to His Word.

These three institutions define the covenant structure of life. This is how man is to glorify God and enjoy Him—by worship, marriage, and work. This is life. The one who rebels against this covenantal structure is, by definition, dead. This is exactly what happened at the Fall. God had said that in the very day Adam rebelled he would die. As we look at the Fall from the perspective of covenant, we understand these words. Adam in his rebellion was rebelling against life at every point and embracing death.

By his sin, Adam also forfeited a holy and happy posterity. All mankind descending from Adam by "ordinary generation" would come into the world not upright but covenantally dead in sin, cut off from covenant, strangers to "life," and in need of reconciliation and rebirth.

Sin fragments the covenantal unity of life. It destroys meaning and purpose and man himself is destroyed. Cut off from the covenant, man loses himself in a universe which has become incomprehensible. He is alienated from God, from the creation, and from others. Since the "fear of the Lord" is the beginning of wisdom, a man without that fear understands nothing rightly. Man (and now, the entire creation) is in need of a thorough restoration which is the foundational meaning of "salvation" (to be made whole). This requires a second Adam.

Covenant and Redemption

In the first Adam we lost everything. Man now stands in need of a "Second Adam" in whom all things can be restored. Of course, the Fall cannot be reversed by simply pretending it didn't happen and starting over. The "Second Adam" inherits the circumstances of the Fall and must remedy them if mankind is to be restored to communion with God as His image-bearers. This demands that man first be freed from the dominion of sin and reconciled to God.

In order to restore man, sin must first be dealt with. The curse of the covenant that hangs over mankind and all creation must be removed if man is to be reconciled to God and restored to His favor. Thus, the job of the second Adam is to undertake redemption by making atonement for sin and, through death and resurrection, to restore all things. This task was undertaken by the Second Person of the Godhead.

All the blessings and benefits of salvation therefore are found "in Christ." In the first Adam there is only death. In the second Adam there is life and peace. By virtue of union with the Second Adam we have wholeness and restoration—new birth, regeneration, new life. And by virtue of our union with Him who is the true image of God (Col. 1:15), we are restored to full image-bearing (Rom. 8:29). A new humanity is re-created in the Second Adam.

To be reconciled to God is to be restored back into covenant communion with Him. Christ is the only Mediator of the covenant—the one Mediator between God and man (1 Tim. 2:4). Our covenant relationship with God is in and through Him. In Him we are granted all the promises of God and everything necessary for life and godliness (2 Cor. 1:19–20).

The Bible teaches us that baptism unites us to Christ and His body by the power of the Holy Spirit (1 Cor. 12:13). Baptism is an act of God (through His ministers) which signifies and seals our initiation into the Triune communion (we are "baptized *into the name* of the Father, Son, and Holy Spirit").[7] At baptism we are clothed with Christ, united to Him and to His Church which is His body (Gal. 3:26–28). The Church, therefore, is not to be divorced from Christ and the blessings of covenant. "We are members of His body, of His flesh and of His bones," Paul says (Eph. 5:30). It is for this reason that the Westminster Confession states that outside the Church there is no ordinary possibility of salvation (WCF 25.2). This is true simply because there is no salvation outside of Christ.

All that man must have is found in Him. He is the Elect One of God, the chosen servant to accomplish for His people what they could not accomplish on their own. He is the well-beloved of the Father in whom we find acceptance in God's sight. He is the faithful and righteous One, in whose righteousness we are able to stand in God's presence. He was baptized and lived–His life faithfully according to that baptism, keeping covenant as the second Adam, doing all that the first Adam failed to do, walking by faith in obedience in the power of the Spirit. Moreover, He did what the first Adam could not have done, taking our curse upon Himself, dying in our place, paying the penalty for our sins.

He is the Justified One. At His resurrection He was vindicated by the Father, publicly declared to be the Righteous One. We might say that by His resurrection He was the first One to be born again, born from above by the power of the Spirit as He died to sin and was raised in newness of life. In being delivered from death, He not only purchased salvation and secured it for His people, but we may also say that in one sense, He as our substitute, was the first to receive salvation in all its fullness. He received it in the middle of history and thus became the surety that we too shall be made recipients of this salvation at the end of history.

By virtue of our union with Him, we are made recipients of all that is His. This is how we receive the grace of God. We often think of grace exclusively as the "unmerited favor" of God toward sinners, but the term refers to "favor, pleasure, or goodwill." Grace is not a thing or a substance, but the favor of God. Christ, in this sense, was the object of God's grace—not that He had any sin which had to be forgiven, but in that He was the peculiar object of God's favor and good pleasure. He is the One who is "well-pleasing" to God and, thus, all God's favor or grace is found only in Him. We receive the grace of God "in Him." We are accepted in the Beloved (Eph. 1:5–6). To be saved by grace then requires that we be united to Christ (Eph. 2:5–6). Thus, Christians are called to persevere in the grace of God (Acts 13:43)—i.e., never forsake the Lord Jesus in Whom alone we may find grace and favor.

Salvation is relational. It is found only in covenant union with Christ. As we abide in Him, all that is true of Him is true of us. It has been the common practice in Reformed circles to use the term "elect" to refer only to those who are predestined to eternal salvation. Since God has ordained all things "whatsoever comes to pass" (Eph. 1:11), He has certainly predestined the number of all who will be saved at the last day. This number is fixed and settled, not one of these will be lost. The Lord will accomplish all His holy will. But the term "elect" (or "chosen") as it is used in the Scriptures most often refers to those in covenant union with Christ who is *the* Elect One.

In the Old Testament, Israel is called God's elect or chosen people (Deut. 7:6; Ps. 135:4; Isa. 45:4). Consequently, Paul and the other apostles refer to the members of the Church, the "new Israel," as the "elect" as well (Col. 3:12; 1 Pet. 1:1–2; 2:9; 5:13; 2 John 1, 13).

Election was not something hidden or unknown to the apostles or the prophets but something that could be rightly attributed to all who were in covenant. Paul even addresses the Ephesians in startling language (Eph. 1:3–5), saying that they were chosen in Christ "before the foundation of the world." We have to remind ourselves that he was not giving a theological lecture but stating what was objectively true of all those in the church in Ephesus. Being united to the Elect One, all who are baptized may be truthfully addressed as the "elect of God." Thus, if you were to ask Paul, "Do you know who the elect are?" he might have replied, "Of course! The elect are all who are in Christ!"

This is not to say that election is only "general" or "corporate" and not individual. God's promise to Israel was both to the nation as a whole and to the particular individuals who made up the nation. Each Israelite was grafted by God into the body of His people as an act of His sovereign, electing love. Though the promises were given to the nation of Israel, every individual Israelite could say, "This belongs to me."[8]

Think of the promise Paul relates to the members of the church at Rome (Rom. 8:28–34). Throughout this passage, Paul refers to the "elect," those whom God "foreknew" and "predestined," and then asks these questions: "What shall *we* say to these things? If God is for *us*, who can be against *us*? Christ died, rose again and makes intercession for *us*, who can separate *us* from the love of God?" Clearly, Paul is not stating promises that are true only for some unknown group called the "elect." Nor is he speaking only to a portion of the congregation whom he judges to be "regenerate." Rather, he is applying these promises to all the members of the Church who have been baptized and united to Christ in His death, burial, and resurrection (Rom. 6). Yet, in spite of these clear affirmations of their elect status, Paul does not hesitate to warn them against the possibility of apostasy (Rom. 11:9–22).

We see similar language in 2 Thessalonians 2:13–14:

> But we are bound to give thanks to God always for you, brethren beloved by the Lord, because God from the beginning chose you for salvation through sanctification by the Spirit and belief in the truth, to which He called you by our gospel, for the obtaining of the glory of our Lord Jesus Christ.

How could Paul say this? If someone insists that Paul was given special insight into whom God had chosen, then we must respond with John Barach, "we suddenly discover that we cannot learn from the apostle Paul, who told us to imitate him, how to talk to our churches." Pastor Barach continues:

> Or is Paul speaking to some only? Brothers, beloved by the Lord, you subset of the church, we give thanks for you? . . . If he were speaking to some only then that would rob the church of the very comfort that Paul wants to give the church. Is Paul making a good guess here? . . . Is it wishful thinking? Is he just making a charitable judgment? . . . To whom is Paul speaking? . . . [The Thessalonians] knew to whom Paul was speaking because Paul tells them that he is writing to the church. That is how

he begins 1 Thessalonians 1:1, 'Paul and Silvanus and Timothy to the church of the Thessalonians.' He is writing to the whole church. The church that had received the word in faith. The church which was living in terms of that faith. There is no guess work necessary. He didn't need to make a charitable judgement.[9]

The elect are those who are faithful in Christ Jesus. If they later reject the Savior, they are no longer elect—they are cut off from the Elect One and thus, lose their elect standing. But their falling away doesn't negate the reality of their standing prior to their apostasy. They were really and truly the elect of God because of their relationship with Christ.

Being "in Christ" is the key to understanding covenant. Many Reformed folk speak of the covenant as if it is a *thing*—a special room with enriched, purified air, good food, and friendly people. The covenant is viewed as a wonderful environment; a place that is far, far better and safer than walking the streets of the world; a place that offers many benefits and gives many opportunities to those who are privileged to be in it (whether they are "elect" or not). You get to worship God, study His Word, fellowship with other saints—but it is only a place of greater opportunity. There is no *real* grace or salvation necessarily there for men.

In fact, covenant is *a real relationship, consisting of real communion with the Triune God through union with Christ.* The covenant is not some *thing* that exists apart from Christ or in addition to Him (another *means* of grace)—rather, the covenant *is* union with Christ. Thus, being in covenant gives all the blessings of being united to Christ. There is no salvation apart from covenant simply because there is no salvation apart from union with Christ, and without union with Christ there is no covenant at all.

Because being in covenant with God means being in Christ, those who are in covenant have all spiritual blessings in the heavenly places. Union with Christ means that all that is true of Christ is true of us. This seems clear by how the apostles address the churches. Note, for example, how Paul addresses the historic church in Corinth in his first epistle:

- They are sanctified in Christ Jesus (1:2).
- They are called to be saints (1:2) with everyone who calls on the name of Jesus Christ.
- They have been given the grace of God (1:4) by Christ.
- Because of this, they have been enriched in everything by Him in all utterance and knowledge (1:5).
- He assures them that they will be confirmed to the end blameless in the day of Christ (1:7–8).
- He says that they have been called into the fellowship of Jesus Christ by God (1:9).
- Being "in Christ" they share in his wisdom, righteousness, sanctification, and redemption (1:30–31).
- They have received "the Spirit who is from God" so that they might know the things that have been freely given them by God. The "natural" man cannot receive these things but they can since they have been given the mind of Christ (2:14–16).
- They are the temple of God because the Spirit of God dwells in the Church (3:16–17).
- All things belong to them, because they are Christ's and Christ is God's (3:21–23).
- Through Paul's ministry, they have been "born" through the gospel (4:15 "in Christ Jesus I have begotten you [gennao] through the gospel.").[10]
- Christ has been sacrificed for them (5:7).
- They have been washed (or baptized) which has brought about sanctification and justification in the name of Christ, by the Spirit of God (6:9–11).[11]
- They will, therefore, be raised up just as God raised up the Lord Jesus (6:14).
- The Holy Spirit is in the body and, therefore, they must remember that they are not their own; they have been bought with a price (6:19–20).
- The Corinthians are the "children" of the Fathers of Israel who were also "redeemed" out of Egypt, baptized in the Red Sea, and granted fellowship with God and communion with Christ—yet, God was not well-pleased with them; thus, they must not imitate them (10:1–5). These things were written to teach us not to do what Israel did in breaking covenant: lusting after evil things, becoming idolaters, com-

mitting sexual immorality, tempting Christ, murmuring against God (10:6–11).
- They have communion with the body and blood of Christ and are thus one body with Him (10:15–17).
- They have all been baptized into one body by the Spirit (whether Jews or Greeks) (12:13).
- He emphasizes that they are the body of Christ and individually members of it (12:27).
- Paul emphasizes that Christ died for "our" sins (including those of his hearers; 15:3).

Paul declares these things to be true of the members of the church in Corinth in spite of the fact that he knew of their sins. He was not able to speak like this because he had some special insight into the secret decrees of God. He was speaking about what was true of these people objectively by virtue of their union with Christ in covenant. All this was true of each of the members, but, like Israel, they were required to persevere in faith. If they departed from Christ, they would perish like Israel of old. All their privileges and blessings would become like so many anchors to sink them into the lake of fire. This is his point in chapter 10. Note, however, Paul's method: he declares what is objectively true of them by virtue of their covenant union with Christ and then calls upon them to be faithful because of this union. "How can you who are members of Christ do these things?" (1 Cor. 6:15–17)

You see the same sort of language throughout the epistles. Paul and the other apostles addressed the Church in this way and did not feel compelled in the least to qualify or hedge their statements—even when they knew about serious sins within the particular churches.

The apostles did not view the covenant as a place of potential blessing or a place of fantastic opportunity—they viewed it as salvation, because it meant fellowship and communion with the Triune God. It is union with Christ in His obedient life, His sacrificial, substitutionary death, triumphant resurrection, and glorious ascension and session at the right hand of the Father.

All in covenant are given all that is true of Christ. If they persevere in faith to the end, they enjoy these mercies eternally. If they fall away in unbelief, they lose these blessings and receive a greater condemnation than Sodom and Gomorrah. Covenant can be broken by unbelief and rebellion, but until it is, those in covenant with God belong to Him and are His. If they do not persevere, they lose the blessings that were given to them (and all of this works out according to God's eternal decree which He ordained before the foundation of the world).

Thus, when one breaks covenant, it can be truly said that he has turned away from grace and forfeited life, forgiveness, and salvation. For this reason the Scriptures describe apostates as those who:

- "possessed the Kingdom" (Matt. 21:42–45);
- received God's gifts (Matt. 25:14ff., the parable of the talents);
- received the word with joy (Matt. 13:20) and believed for a while (Luke 8:13);
- bore fruit (though not to maturity, Luke 8:14);
- had union with Christ as branches in a vine (John 15);
- had real communion with Christ (1 Cor. 10:4–5);
- had the Spirit's work within them (being "enlightened, tasted of the heavenly gift, made partakers of the Holy Spirit, tasted the Word and the powers of the world to come," Heb. 6:4ff.);
- received the knowledge of the truth (Heb. 10:26);
- had been sanctified by the blood of Christ (Heb. 10:29);
- had been made members of the heavenly city, sprinkled by the blood of Jesus (Heb. 12:22ff.);
- had been cleansed from former sins (2 Pet. 1:9);
- were bought by the Lord (2 Pet. 2:1);
- escaped the pollutions of the world (2 Pet. 2:20);
- knew the way of righteousness (2 Pet. 2:21); and
- had "the adoption, the glory, the covenants, the giving of the law, the service of God, and the promises" (Rom. 9:4).

The apostate fails to persevere in the grace of God and, thus, has his name removed from the book of life (Rev. 3:5: "He who overcomes shall be clothed in white garments, and I will not blot out his name from the Book of Life; but I will confess his name before My Father and before His angels"). The Book of Life is the book of the covenant (see also Ex. 32:31–33; Rev. 13:8; 17:8; 20:12, 15; 21:27). Those who "take away from the words of the book" will in turn be "taken away" from the Book of Life (Rev. 22:19).

This is not a hypothetical impossibility but a very real possibility for those who are in covenant with Christ and members of His Church. We must not view these and similar warnings as mere devices which are placed in the Scriptures in order to frighten the elect into heaven. The clear implication of these passages is that those who ultimately prove to be reprobate may be in covenant with God. They may enjoy for a season the blessings of the covenant, including the forgiveness of sins, adoption, possession of the kingdom, sanctification, etc., and yet apostatize and fall short of the grace of God.

The apostate forsakes the grace of God that was given to him by virtue of his union with Christ. It is not accurate to say that they only "appeared" to have these things but did not actually have them—if that were so, there would be nothing to "forsake" and apostasy is bled of its horror and severity. That which makes apostasy so horrendous is that these blessings actually belonged to the apostates—though they only had them temporarily, they had them no less truly. *The apostate doesn't forfeit "apparent blessings" that were never his in reality, but real blessings that were his in covenant with God.*

This seems to be the point of John 15:1–8. Jesus here declares that He is the vine and His hearers are branches united to Him. He then exhorts them to continue abiding in Him so that they might bear fruit. If they refuse to abide in Him, they will be fruitless and incur the wrath of the Divine husbandman and, finally, will be cast into the fire. Here, then, we have those who are joined to Christ in a vital union (i.e., a union that could and should be fruitful) and yet who end up cursed and condemned.

Often this passage is interpreted along these lines: There are two kinds of branches. Some branches are not really in Christ "in a saving way," but only in an *external* sense—whatever fruit they bear is not genuine and they will eventually be destroyed. Other branches are truly joined to Christ *inwardly* and savingly, and they bear more and more fruit as they are pruned and cultivated by the Father. As Norman Shepherd has noted,

If this distinction is in the text, it is difficult to see what the point of the warning is. The outward ("external") branches cannot profit from it, because they cannot in any case bear genuine fruit. They are not related to Christ inwardly and draw no life from him. The inward branches do not need the warning, because they are vitalized by Christ and therefore cannot help but bear good fruit. Cultivation by the Father, with its attendant blessing, is guaranteed.[12]

The Calvinist embraces this implausible interpretation because he (understandably) does not want to deny election, effectual calling, or the perseverance of the saints. The exegetical problems one must embrace with this position, however, are nearly insurmountable. If the branches are not truly joined to the vine, how can they be held accountable for their lack of fruit? The distinction of "external" and "internal" union seems to be invented and is not in the text. All the branches are truly and vitally joined to the vine. All can and should be fruitful. The pressure to preserve the Scriptural teaching of God's sovereignty in salvation ought not be allowed to push us to deny these obvious points. But in order to resist this pressure the text must be interpreted as it is intended to be interpreted—i.e., covenantally.

The picture of the vine and branches was a common way in which God referred to His covenant people Israel in the Old Testament (Ps. 80:8–16; Isa. 5:1–7; Jer. 2:21). The Jews were used to thinking of themselves as the vineyard of Jehovah. "The vine" was a figure of God's chosen people. Here in John 15 Jesus says that "He is the real vine." He identifies Himself with His people. He is their covenant head. He is their life. He is not only their Creator but their Redeemer. They are His body, united to Him by God's gracious inclusion of them in covenant.

Jesus is merely reiterating what the prophets had proclaimed. If they do not abide faithful to God, they are going to bring down judgment upon themselves. They will be cut off from covenant with God. They will lose the blessings of His grace and mercy and will be destroyed like the ungodly (only their condemnation will be greater since they despised the grace of God and have done despite to the Spirit of grace—which was really and truly given to them in Christ).

Thus, in the Scriptures, those in covenant with God are warned against breaking the covenant that has been established by God. The reality of covenant is gloriously held forth and men are exhorted to beware of breaking this covenant by impenitence and unbelief. God doesn't deny the objective, real nature of union with Christ, rather, He upholds the reality which covenant has given to His people and on that basis, calls them to repent and believe and warns them of judgment if they don't. Paul therefore pleads with the Corinthians "not to receive the grace of God in vain" (2 Cor. 6:1). They have a real, objective, blessed relationship with God which must be preserved.

Covenant, therefore, is a gracious relationship, not a *potentially* gracious relationship. To be in covenant is to have the treasures of God's mercy and grace and the love which He has for His own Son given to you. But the covenant is not *unconditional.* It requires persevering faithfulness.

The Necessity of Faith

Since man is the image of God and since faith is central to man's life, we would expect to find some sort of analogy to faith within the Trinity.[13] If we understand faith as an entrusting of oneself to another, then we can see that there is "faith" within the Godhead. Each person of the Godhead entrusts Himself to the others. The Spirit refuses to glorify Himself but entrusts His glory to the Son and the Father. The same is true of the other Persons of the Godhead. Jesus does not seek His own glory but the glory of His Father. He describes Himself as the One "who seeks the glory of the One who sent Him" (John 7:18). He in turn depends upon the Father and the Spirit to glorify Him (John 17:1, 5; 16:13–15).

Similarly, the Father refuses to glorify Himself but receives glory through His work of glorifying the Son (Phil. 2:9–11). The Father vindicates His Son (by raising Him from the dead and exalting Him, giving Him a name above every name), and when every tongue confesses that Jesus is Lord, it brings glory to the Father. Each Person of the Godhead denies Himself, entrusting His glory to the other two Persons. By analogy, every image-bearer is to do the same. This was Adam's calling.

Adam was to believe God, trusting himself to his Creator and obeying His Word. His glory would come in refusing to seek his own glory and in seeking the glory of the Triune God. This was the point of

Satan's temptation. The serpent challenged Adam to doubt God's trust-worthiness (Gen. 3:4–5). If Adam had continued in faith, refusing to glorify himself, he would have been glorified by God. But because he sought his own glory (by setting himself in judgment of God) he was put to shame. The covenant is dependent upon persevering faith. This is illustrated most clearly by Jesus acting as the Second Adam.

Jesus came into the world with the same responsibility as Adam (He was to live as a man as He had always lived as the Second Person of the Trinity—i.e., denying Himself and seeking to glorify His Father). He was to walk by faith, entrusting Himself to the Father, believing His Word, and obeying. As with the first Adam, Satan tempted Jesus to doubt God's trustworthiness, seeking to get Jesus to satisfy His own desires and grasp at glory apart from the will of His Father. But Jesus continued to trust and remained faithful throughout His life, learning "obedience by the things which He suffered" (Heb. 5:7–9).

Even in death, He continued to entrust Himself to His Father (Luke 23:46). Through His sufferings He became mature, growing in wisdom, showing forth the image of the Godhead. And because He was faithful, He became the author of eternal salvation. Philip Hughes in his commentary on Hebrews 12:2 ("looking unto Jesus, the author and finisher of *our* faith, who for the joy that was set before Him endured the cross, despising the shame, and has sat down at the right hand of the throne of God.") calls Jesus the "man of faith par excellence":

> [T]he incarnate Son is himself the man of faith par excellence, and this seems to be the primary sense intended by the Greek original of the expression, which reads literally, "the pioneer and perfecter of faith," . . . His whole earthly life is the very embodiment of trust in God (Heb. 2:13—"And again: 'I will put My trust in Him.' And again: 'Here am I and the children whom God has given Me.'"). It is marked from start to finish by total dependence on the Father and complete attunement to his will (10:7–10). His faith expresses itself, necessarily, in prayer (5:7; John 17; Mark 1:35, etc.), and is completely victorious as, surmounting all temptations and afflictions, he is made perfect through suffering (Heb. 2:10; 4:15), thus becoming "the source of eternal salvation to all who obey him" (5:8f.). In looking to Jesus, then, we are looking to him who is the supreme exponent of faith, the one who, beyond all others, not only set out on the course of faith but also pursued it without

wavering to the end. He, accordingly, is uniquely qualified to be the supplier and sustainer of the faith of his followers.[14]

Covenant life is always founded upon persevering faith in the faithful One. If we are to abide in union with Him, we, by the grace and power of the Spirit, must be faithful. Thus the elect are marked by *abiding* in the Word of Christ (John 8:31–32). Those who turn away and refuse to "hold fast to the word" break covenant with Christ and are referred to by Paul as having "believed in vain" (1 Cor. 15:1–2). The blessings purchased by Christ are enjoyed only by those who "continue in the faith" (Col. 1:21–23). The gospel is only saving to those who "hold fast to the word" (1 Cor.15:1–2). Paul knew of some who had "fallen away" from the faith and warns Timothy about them (1 Tim. 1:18–20). Unbelief is a denial of God's image and breaks covenant, cutting us off from the blessings of salvation (communion with the Triune God).

The covenant then is participation in the life (or fellowship) of God:

> As His divine power has given to us all things that *pertain* to life and godliness, through the knowledge of Him who called us by glory and virtue, by which have been given to us exceedingly great and precious promises, that through these you may be *partakers* of [Gr. *koinonos*, become fellowshippers with] the divine nature, having escaped the corruption *that is* in the world through lust. (2 Pet. 1:3–4)

We must embrace this straightforward covenantal framework and allow it to direct our understanding of God's work of salvation as it unfolds in time. We cannot judge men based upon the secret decrees of God or the hidden operations of the Spirit. The secret things belong to God (Deut. 29:29). We are to be concerned with those things that are revealed. The questions of *when* a man is "regenerated," or given "saving faith," or "truly converted," are ultimately questions we cannot answer and, therefore, they cannot be the basis upon which we define the Church or identify God's people.

What we do know is whether or not a man is in covenant with God. If he is not in covenant, he must repent of his sins and believe in Christ Jesus, be joined to the people of God by baptism, and persevere in faithfulness all his days (by the power of the Holy Spirit who works in him "to will and do" for God's good pleasure). If he has been baptized, he is in covenant with God and is obligated to walk in faithfulness, loving the Lord with all his heart, soul, mind, and strength. If he is unfaithful, he is to be called to repentance. If he refuses to repent, he is to be cut off from the body of Christ and delivered over to Satan with the prayer that he be taught not to blaspheme.

Viewing salvation from the perspective of the covenant does indeed force us to rethink some of our categories and terminology. But the payback will far outweigh the costs incurred. The covenant perspective enables us to assure the people of God of their blessedness without tolerating or condoning ungodly presumption upon the grace of God. It enables us to assure Christians of their acceptance with God without needlessly undermining their confidence in God's promises (by forcing them to ask questions of themselves they cannot answer with certainty).[15] We can preserve the sovereignty of God's grace in salvation without promoting pietism or legalism. We can declare the powerful significance and blessings of the sacraments without becoming sacerdotalists. We can boldly declare the centrality of the Church in salvation without falling into the errors of Roman Catholicism.

These and many other benefits await a careful rethinking of covenant and its implications. All that we as Calvinists have been concerned to preserve (the absolute sovereignty of God in salvation, the absolutely gracious nature of salvation, the supremacy of Christ over all, etc.) can be preserved without falling prey to the error of forcing the Scriptures to submit to a preconceived logical or theological construct and, thus, subtly departing from Scripture as the supreme rule of faith and life. The benefits are well worth the time and effort needed to hammer out a clear exposition of the nature and blessedness of being in covenant with the living God.

Notes - Chapter 2

[1] Throughout this paper I am leaning heavily upon a number of contemporary essays as well as older works. In addition to the writings of Calvin, Nevin, Old, and others, I am indebted to the more recent work of Ralph Smith, *Eternal Covenant* (Moscow, ID: Canon Press, 2003); Jim Jordan's unpublished paper *Thoughts on Sovereign Grace and Regeneration*; numerous papers by Dr. Peter Leithart, Dr. Joel Garver, Rich Lusk, and other more recent studies.

[2] Smith, *Eternal Covenant*.

[3] Ibid.

[4] Ibid.

[5] Calvin, *The Gospel According to St. John*, vol. 1, (Grand Rapids, MI: Eerdmans Publishing Co., 1959), p. 273.

[6] Quoted in Amy Plantinga Pauw, *The Supreme Harmony of All: The Trinitarian Theology of Jonathan Edwards*, (Grand Rapids, MI: Eerdmans Publishing Co.), 2002, pp. 42–43.

[7] Through baptism one is given a new name. He is brought out of his old Adamic family and into the fellowship of the new family of the Father, Son, and Spirit.

[8] Here and in the argument that follows, I am indebted to John Barach's treatment of this subject in his 2003 lecture, "Covenant and Election" given at the 2003 Auburn Avenue Presbyterian Church Pastors Conference.

[9] Ibid.

[10] Peter also speaks this way in his first epistle (1:22–23, 25). He uses the word *anagennao* which means "give new birth or life to." Peter speaks in the second person plural throughout without any qualifiers. All of the members of the Church have been "born again" by means of the word preached to them. Again, what is striking is that both Paul and Peter say this to the *visible* Church (even though they could not see the hearts of their hearers).

[11] Some commentators read 1 Corinthians 6:11 in this way: "But you received a justifying and sanctifying washing in the name of the Lord Jesus Christ and by the Spirit of our God." The grammar of the text may suggest the Spirit instrumentally confers justification and sanctification through the washing. Thomas Edwards, in *A Commentary on the First Epistle to the Corinthians* (Minneapolis, MN: Klock and Klock, 1979), sees *apelousasthe* as a reference to baptism with "sanctified" and "justified" explaining the term. Thus, to be washed is to be justified and sanctified (p. 144) R. C. H. Lenski in his *Interpretation of First Corinthians* notes, "Paul is, of course, speaking about baptism, but when he uses *apolouein* he at once names the effect of baptism, the spiritual washing away of all sin and guilt, the cleansing by pardon and justification." (Minneapolis, MN: Augsburg Press, 1961), p. 250.

[12] Norman Shepherd, *The Call of Grace*, Phillipsburg, NJ: P & R Publishing, 2000, pp. 89–90.
[13] I am indebted here to Tim Gallant's essay "Paradoxology: Thoughts on the Trinitarian Grounding of Human Faith." (http://www.timgallant.org/paradoxology.htm)
[14] Philip Hughes, *A Commentary on the Epistle to the Hebrews*, Grand Rapids, MI: Eerdmans Publishing Co., 1977, p. 522–523.
[15] Questions like, "Have you truly believed?"; "Have you sincerely repented?"; "Do you have a new heart?"; "Have you been truly converted?"; etc.

Chapter Three
Paedobaptism and Baptismal Efficacy:

Historic Trends and Current Controversies

Rich Lusk

In 1857, Charles Hodge wrote an essay in the *Princeton Review* lamenting the decline of the practice of infant baptism in America.[1] Using statistics provided by the General Assembly of the Presbyterian Church, Hodge pointed out that from 1812 onward, the number of children being brought for baptism was radically declining in relation to the overall number of communicants. In 1811, there had been 20 paedobaptisms per hundred communicants; by 1856, the ratio was just over 5 per hundred. Hodge sounded the alarm: "[M]ore than two-thirds of the children of the Church have been 'cut off' from the people of God by their parents' sinful neglect, and by the Church's silent acquiescence therein."

Hodge reported a similar downgrade was occurring in other ostensibly Reformed denominations. The Dutch Reformed ratio was only slightly better than the Presbyterian in 1856, at around 7 paedobaptisms per hundred communicants. Things were even worse in other bodies. The New School Presbyterians were leaving six out of seven children unbaptized. Paedobaptism was so rare among Congregationalists by the mid-1850s that Hodge could truthfully claim, "in the Congregational churches in New England, infant baptism is, beyond doubt, dying out." Only the high church Episcopalians seemed relatively unaffected by the trend.

What caused this sharp decline in the maintenance of covenant baptism? Why did the Church's historic practice lose so much ground in America so quickly? It is far beyond the scope of this essay to enter into all the theological and social forces that factored into the decline of paedobaptism in our culture. One thing is certain: America became progressively "baptist" on a massive scale in the early-to-mid-nineteenth century.[2] Without going into detail, a few obvious connections can be made between two powerful cultural-theological movements and the loss of paedobaptism: namely, experiential Revivalism and Enlightenment rationalism. Let us look at each of these in turn.

The Effects of Revivalism

Note that the 50 year period of decline Hodge traced out coincides, more or less, with the institutionalization of Revivalism in American Christianity. While the First Great Awakening of the eighteenth century had been a mixed blessing, it remained basically Calvinistic in doctrinal orientation. Preachers such as Jonathan Edwards, George Whitefield, and Gilbert Tennant injected new life into decaying, dying churches. The Awakening did not always foster a high view of the Church, particularly because of itinerancy, but it did cultivate a warm and deep love for classic Reformational orthodoxy.[3]

The Second Great Awakening of the early nineteenth century brought with it a significant shift away from the earlier pattern of Protestantism. This rapidly expanding movement was full of anti-doctrinal, anti-ecclesiastical tendencies, all of which fanned the flames of the anti-paedobaptist fire. Leaders such as Charles Finney, Lorenzo Dow, Francis Asbury, and Alexander Campbell all wielded enormous influence in remaking American Christianity. Low church Revivalism trumped high-church Puritanism, pushing to the periphery of American society traditional Calvinistic and paedobaptistic bodies.

The revivals of the Second Great Awakening totally restructured American religious life in radical fashion. While there is some danger in characterizing broad historical movements, we can safely identify several features commonly attributed to the second wave of revivals.

First, these revivals undermined a traditional high view of ecclesiastical office and authority. The Protestant Reformation had insisted on an educated clergy, in contrast to the late medieval period, when priests were often ignorant and even illiterate. Because pastors were scholarly and articulate, they had become powerful leaders in society, influencing politics, economics, literature, art, and so forth. Church discipline was respected as the most powerful deterrent placed in the hands of mortal men. Pastors often wore special vestments to indicate their status as leaders of the community and representatives of Christ. Ministers were expected to be cultured, literate, and above the common man in intelligence and ability.

By contrast, in the Second Great Awakening, it was not uncommon for ministers to go on preaching tours with little or no formal training. As the need for churches on the ever expanding American frontier accelerated, older, more traditional church bodies could not supply enough ministers to keep pace. In the oft-quoted words of Peter Cartwright, "illiterate Methodist preachers set the world on fire while they [that is, preachers from 'high church' bodies] were lighting their matches."[4] Young Princeton seminarians were busy learning Latin and the latest German theology; meanwhile, the revivalistic preachers were overrunning America. Cartwright estimated that "of the thousands of preachers that the Methodists recruited in the early republic, not more than fifty had more than a common English education, and scores of preachers did not even have that much."[5]

Formal schooling was actually perceived as a distinct disadvantage for circuit riders. Preachers would strive to use informal, vulgar speech, suiting their style, message, and dress to their audiences. Francis Asbury insisted that scholarship not interfere with the more pressing task of saving souls: "I would throw by all the Libraries in the World rather than be guilty of the Loss of one Soul."[6] Charles Finney charged young seminary graduates with having "hearts as heard as the college walls."[7] In Ann Douglas' trenchant survey of nineteenth American religion, she concludes "over the course of the nineteenth century, the Protestant minister became the only professional other than the housewife who ceased to command, much less monopolize, any special body of knowledge."[8] In this context, it is easy to see why Hodge attributed the decline of paedobaptism, at least in part, to the inability of ministers to explain its biblical grounding.[9] The clergy became a new class of "Know Nothings."

Second, the revivals spawned a highly individualistic piety. Nathan Hatch has rightly referred to the period as the "democratization of American Christianity." Theologically, this meant the right of private judgment trumped traditional creeds and confessions. Popular revivalist Alexander Campbell disdained any ecclesiastical heritage as a guide or norm in biblical studies:

> I have endeavored to read the scriptures as though no one had read them
> before me, and I am as much on my guard against reading them to-day
> through the medium of my own views yesterday, or a week ago, as I am
> against being influenced by any foreign name, authority, or system what-
> ever.[10]

Robert Marshall and J. Thompson wrote, "We are not personally
acquainted with the writings of John Calvin, nor are we certain how
nearly we agree with his views of divine truth; nor do we care."[11] Free
thinking, stripped of the confining straightjacket of tradition, became
the order of the day. The doctrines of God's sovereignty and predestination, perceived as threats to personal autonomy, were jettisoned in
favor of semi-Pelagian views. Paedobaptism also fell into disfavor since
it (very undemocratically) imposed a religious identity on an unwilling
subject. Personal choice was exalted. The traditional padeobaptist praxis
of Christendom was diminished.

Third, the revivals focused on the immediacy of religious experience, to the exclusion of traditional means of grace.[12] Preaching, of
course, was still emphasized as before, but now it aimed at stirring
religious sentiment rather than communicating biblical truth. Emotional appeal in preaching, without doubt, is healthy since the whole
person—head and heart—should be touched with God's Word. But
the revivalists' methods sometimes bordered on emotional manipula-
tion. Newly created "sacraments" such as the altar call and anxious
bench replaced baptism and the Lord's Supper as God's primary locus
of activity. Sappy, sentimental hymns replaced the robust, masculine
psalter used previously. Experientialism undermined the objectivity of
the covenant. Again, it is easy to see that paedobaptism would fit very
awkwardly into such a religious matrix. In such a context, if baptism is
of any value at all, it is to stimulate religious feelings and emotions,
which of course an infant cannot experience. Hodge noted that many
who entered the Church via a revivalistic conversion experience at a
camp meeting failed to bring their children with them.[13] Instead of
"growing up Christian" under continual covenant nurture, children

were expected to undergo their own "conversion experience" at the appropriate age.[14]

Lewis Schenck explains:

> It was unfortunate that the Great Awakening made an emotional experience, involving terror, misery, and depression, the only approach to God. A conscious conversion experience from enmity to friendship with God was looked upon as the only way of entrance into the kingdom. Sometimes it came suddenly, sometimes it was a prolonged and painful process. But it was believed to be a clearly discernible and emotional upheaval, necessarily "distinct to the consciousness of its subject and apparent to those around." Preceding the experience of God's love and peace, it was believed necessary to have an awful sense of one's lost and terrifying position. Since these were not the experiences of infancy and early childhood, it was taken for granted children must, or in all ordinary cases would, grow up unconverted. Infants, it was thought, needed new birth, as well as adults. They could not be saved without it. But the only channel of the new birth which was recognized was a conscious experience of conviction and conversion. Anything else, according to Gilbert Tennent, was a fiction of the brain, a delusion of the Devil. In fact, he ridiculed the idea that one could be a Christian without knowing the time when he was otherwise.[15]

Obviously, revivalism was no friend of covenant children. The revivals only intensified the worst features of the earlier Puritanism. In New England theology, children had never been regarded as more than merely formal members of the Church:

> New England never held out a large measure of hope for the little ones on the basis of God's covenant promises. These were constantly overshadowed by an emphasis on inherent sinfulness as the result of their relationship to Adam . . . Without the presence of something akin to adult experience and insight the child was hardly ever regarded as being in a hopeful way.[16]

> The experiential rigor of Puritanism and revivalism may have seemed like a safeguard against merely "nominal" membership in the churches; in reality, skepticism of covenant children became a self-fulfilling prophecy. One generation after another grew up outside the Church, for all practical purposes, never to return. As adult-like credentials for conver-

sion and full membership were pressed more and more, infant baptism became an increasingly tenuous practice, until it finally gave out altogether.[17]

Surprisingly, the revivalists were actually aided in some ways by the theologians in driving children out of the Church. Revivalism and scholasticism conspired together against paedobaptism. Revivalism demanded a narratable conversion experience, pushing baptized children to the margins of the covenant community; scholasticism in turn created new categories of membership to account for the oddity of these church children. Distinctions were made between internal and external covenant membership, federal and experiential membership, legal and vital membership, and so forth. While the simple biblical promises to and for children were obscured, it became increasingly clear theologians and revivalists would go to great lengths to preserve their preconceived notions about the status of "covenant" children.

The Effects of Enlightenment Rationalism

Revivalism was not the only factor in the growing nineteenth-century neglect of paedobaptism. The era of decline Hodge identified also corresponds with the period during which the Enlightenment made deep inroads into American society. If Revivalism represents a drift into chaotic irrationalism, the Enlightenment, of course, meant a move towards unbridled rationalism. While the Enlightenment had already engulfed the continent of Europe in the previous century, by the nineteenth century, its effects were becoming increasingly noticeable on American soil.

The results of the Enlightenment were disastrous for traditional orthodoxy. The Enlightenment forced theology into one of two molds: either biblical truth had to be conformed to the dictates of a secular, supposedly neutral reason, resulting in rationalistic, secularized dogmatics; or religion was taken out of the realm of scientific, public fact altogether and placed in the sphere of subjective, private experience, resulting in introspective pietism. Among conservatives, the Enlightenment ethos permeated in fairly subtle ways, and there was usually a blending of both molds together. Several complex developments should be noted here.

First, in the wake of the Enlightenment, the Reformed scholastics developed an overly cognitive view of the faith. Christianity came to be defined as a rigidly dogmatic system—a kind of ideology or philosophy. Arid intellectualism in the churches and seminaries was the inevitable result. Systematic theology became more rigorously logical, and less doxological and practical than it had been in Calvin's day. Systematic theology texts gave predestination an increasingly prominent place, all the while relegating sacramental theology to an awkward position at the tail end, since the sacraments didn't fit into a neat and tidy dogmatic structure. The developing *ordo salutis*, soon to become a touchstone of Reformed scholastic orthodoxy, omitted the sacraments altogether, giving the impression they were insignificant appendages to the gospel, rather than crucial means of saving grace.[18] This rationalistic legacy of the Enlightenment is still very much with us in Reformed churches that feature hour-long sermonic discourses on systematic theology as standard fare, but only celebrate the Eucharist once a quarter to keep it "special." It is also seen in Reformed pastors who, when performing a baptism, spend more time telling their congregations what the sacrament does *not* do than what it does. Cognition is more important than ritual on such a model.

M. F. Sadler, a nineteenth-century Reformed Anglican, was a voice crying in the wilderness against the Enlightenment's truncation of the faith. He saw a close connection between the tendency to turn the Bible into a philosophical system and the loss of the sacraments as genuine means of salvific grace.

> Nothing has done more to destroy the true life of Christianity than the attempt to make it into a sort of philosophical system.
>
> The tendency of much modern popular Theology is to exhibit Christianity as a sort of science, having its causes and effects—moral and mental, of course, but still causes and effects—connected according to certain known laws. The causes are: the exhibition of certain influential motives—such as the love of God shown in the plan of redemption; the (natural) effects of these are the drawing of the heart and affections Godward, the implantation of a new principle, etc.
>
> Now, all this is true; but being only part of the truth, when held *alone*, it is held wrongly, and therefore mischievously. For the doctrine of the Sacraments at once and for ever makes Christianity (humanly speak-

ing) unphilosophical. It introduces a disturbing element, because a supernatural one; for it teaches us that there are in Christianity two ordinances
which produce a religious effect not according to the laws of cause and
effect with which *we* are acquainted. The Sacrament of Baptism grafts a
person into Christ, not because there is anything in Baptism itself calcu-
lated to do so, but because of the will of God and the promise of Christ
to be with His Church to the end of the world.

When a man heartily accepts the doctrine of Baptism as it is laid down
in Holy Scripture, he must hold *all* Christianity to be supernatural. He
believes that he is, in some inscrutable way, partaker of the nature of One
who is now at the right hand of God; he believes also that his fellow-
Christians are not merely his fellow-Christians because they hold the
same body of truth which he holds—as the members of a political party
may be united by holding the same opinions—but he believes that both
they and he have been grafted supernaturally into the Second Adam.

The teaching of the Church on Holy Baptism is also diametrically
opposed to that spirit of rationalism which refuses to contemplate Christianity as in reality anything more than a human philosophy, or
educational system, which, if it have not the same origin, at least has now
the same mode of operation, in all respects as any other philosophical or
educational system: any supernatural character which it may once have
had having long since passed away, it must now work its work as any
other system of opinions must do, by appealing to the reason, or imagination, or affections, of those brought within its influence.

Now the doctrine of Baptismal Grace is unquestionably opposed to
any such limitation of the power of God in the matter of our salvation,
for if we accept it we must, perforce, believe that each Christian, at the
commencement of his discipleship—at his first entrance into the kingdom which Christ has established—receives some mysterious
communication from Christ Himself, or is brought into a supernatural
state of union with Him as the Second Adam.[19]

In other words, preservation of sacramental efficacy was part and
parcel of the preservation of Calvinism, over against rationalism. The
downgrading of the sacraments was part of the Enlightenment trend to
question anything supernatural or unexplainable according to the principles of the newly emerging empirical science. Disbelief in the miracles
of Jesus' earthly ministry was accompanied by disbelief in the miracles
of His heavenly ministry wrought through the Church's ordinances of
baptism and the Eucharist. Faith in the efficacy of the sacraments in

the post-Enlightenment world, so far from being a matter of sheer presumption, is only possible if one believes, against the grain of public opinion, that God is active in the world and reigns over it as sovereign King.

Due to Enlightenment rationalism, faith itself came to be conceived more as a mental act than a relational disposition. The Enlightenment revived the Hellenistic view of the "primacy of the intellect," making faith a matter of assent to propositions rather than a posture of trust towards another person. Within such a view of faith, infant faith is considered an absurd notion.[20] Infants cannot reason, nor understand preaching, so therefore they cannot trust in God. Whatever effect the sacrament has for the child will not be realized until much later in life. Infants may still be baptized out of the inertia of tradition, but now with more than a touch of embarrassment. Adult baptism is made the norm, since understanding precedes belief.[21]

Second, the Enlightenment cast a heavy shadow of suspicion on public, communal rituals, most especially the sacraments.[22] Non-cognitive forms of communication, involving the body, gestures, and physical elements, were downplayed. Liturgy, replete with ceremony and symbolism, and sacraments, involving the "stuff" of water, bread, and wine, were marginalized in favor of a one-sided emphasis on doctrinal ideas and preaching. Worship was reduced to a sermon and the various features of communal living—"body life"—were lost as religious faith came to be seen more and more as an individual matter of private opinion. "Religion is what people do with their solitude" (in the words of Alfred North Whitehead) became the typical view in the aftermath of the Enlightenment. Leading liberal Adolf von Harnack, lecturing on the "essence of Christianity," said,

> The kingdom of God comes by coming to individuals, making entrance into their souls, and being grasped by them . . . Everything externally dramatic, all public and historical meaning vanish here. . . . It is not a matter of angels and devils, nor of principalities and powers, but of God and the soul, of the soul and its God.[23]

Externals such as sacraments were deemed alien to the true "genius" of Christianity, which was all "inward" and "spiritual." Conversion was no longer publicly manifested in submission to baptism and incorporation into the Church; it became a secret transaction between God and the soul. Communal and symbolic rituals were fine for the child-ish era of Old Testament religion but were obsolete in a more mature, rational, spiritual age. Not surprisingly, Enlightenment theologians disdained the sacraments and viewed any notion of baptismal efficacy as absurd and superstitious. Kant, the Enlightenment philosopher par excellence, called for a "pure religion" of universalizable rational truths and morality, devoid of particular historical claims and ritual practices. According to Kant, the enlightened man will not be defined by membership in a community or by a ritual imposed upon him in infancy; rather, he will create his own reality and give his life the meaning he chooses.

The tide of Enlightenment thought was seen in various realms, all impinging on the Church in various ways and championing the autonomy of the individual over against the community. As Peter Leithart has pointed out, a ritualized religion can never be completely privatized.[24] But if the Enlightenment was anything, it was a full scale war on public religion. The Enlightenment's attack on the sacraments was part of its larger project of squeezing religion out of public life and exalting the autonomy of the individual.

For example, the Enlightenment popularized a social contract theory of the state. Originating primarily with Thomas Hobbes and John Locke, social contract theory paved the way for modern liberal democracies. According to the social contract view, society is the product of sovereign individuals voluntarily choosing to form a community. But social contract theory is flatly contrary to a biblical theology of the state, which grounds society in God's ordinance rather than man's invention (cf. Rom. 13:1ff.).[25]

Social contract theory impacted the Church in the rise of the Baptist movement, with its individualistic approach to the faith and its voluntaristic ecclesiology. The Church came to be conceived along the lines of a "social contract." But in such a view, baptism is no longer a work of God's sovereign grace, which forms and enlarges the Church. Rather it is a human decision to enter a voluntary organization. God does not create the Church through the means of grace. Instead individuals create the Church by their decision to contract with God and each other.

Infant baptism is preposterous on such presuppositions. Membership in the Church has to be by choice, not imposition, so infants must be allowed to grow and make their own decision to join the Church. Combined with revivalistic experientialism, the social contract model of community was highly detrimental to the ongoing practice of paedobaptism in any meaningful way, for paedobaptism can never be based on a "social contract." The social contract theory served as a tool of the Enlightenment by pushing religion into the private sphere of the individual's conscience and making voluntary consent (e.g., baptistic principles of church membership) the essence of true religion.[26]

And note it wasn't just liberals who went this rationalizing, privatizing direction. The Enlightenment's influence was pervasive. The great Princeton stalwart B. B. Warfield viewed "immediacy" as a fundamental mark of Calvinism and labeled anything else "sacerdotalism."[27] Warfield's position seems eerily close to Fredrich Schleiermacher's view. Schleiermacher was known as the father of liberalism and spoke of the soul's "feeling of absolute dependence on God" as the essence of religion. The sacraments were treated with contempt at worst and suspicion at best. One easily gets the impression they could only "get in the way" of a truly personal relationship with the Deity. Certainly, the sacraments could not be viewed as powerful, saving actions of God.

William Willimon explains the shift:

> For a long time, we Protestants have been in the grip of what James White has called an "Enlightenment view" of baptism. The eighteenth century European Enlightenment deprecated the role of mystery in life. It sought to make all religion rational, reasonable, and understandable. Human understanding was stressed over divine activity. From this point of view, the question is asked, "What does this mean to me, and what am I doing when this happens?" rather than, "What does this mean to God, and what is God doing when this happens?"[28]

Enlightenment thought put the sacraments under a rationalistic microscope and made the frame of reference the individual rather than the community. But such an approach already presupposes a worldview in which the role and function of the sacraments is greatly marginalized. The mystery of God's activity through these physical instruments could not be allowed to stand. Any view of sacramental efficacy came to be regarded as "magic." The sacraments were viewed, at best, as visual teaching aids.

Finally, the Enlightenment worldview aided and abetted the creation of a nature/grace dualism in Protestant theology. In some respects, this dualism was inherited from medieval philosophy and thus predates the Enlightenment. Calvin's attempt to integrate faith and reason in the first book of the *Institutes* almost overcame this medieval dualism, but it crept back in with Reformed scholasticism, particularly through the covenant of works doctrine.[29] The covenant of works denied the presence of grace before the fall. But if grace is not present in the original creation, the creation as such loses its character as *pure gift* and takes on a measure of autonomy. Grace has to be *added to* the creation after Genesis 3. If that is the case, there is a great deal of philosophical pressure to keep grace out of created structures altogether. As a result, God's work of salvation remains extrinsic to the created order. Once nature and grace have been pulled apart, it is very difficult to get them back together again. The sacraments, therefore, cannot be genuine means of grace because God's favor doesn't inhabit or employ ordinary, creaturely means such as water, bread, and wine. God's grace can never be "at home" in the created order because creation is something of a closed system. The nature/grace dualism has a gnosticizing tendency on theology as a whole.

Obviously, no orthodox theological system can push the nature/grace dualism very hard, or it will lose the incarnation and everything else central to the faith. So the Reformed scholastics, like their medieval forerunners, were never consistent with their philosophical principles here (thankfully). Nevertheless, the nature/grace schema, embedded in bi-covenantal federal theology after the 1590s, played a significant (and often overlooked) role in the deformation of Protestant sacramentology. As the meritorious covenant of works rose to prominence in Reformed scholasticism, the efficacy of the sacraments was inevitably diminished. Grace was to be found outside these physical means.

The early Reformers (as will be shown below) had insisted the sacraments were mighty actions of God through which He applied Christ's redemption to His people, forming them into a Spirit-filled community. They were not efficacious in themselves of course, nor did they derive efficacy from the human officiant. But they were regarded as effective because God had promised in His Word to be active in them, making them genuine means of grace. There was nothing odd or impossible in suggesting that God used creaturely means to accomplish and apply His supernatural salvation. In the sacraments, God's role was to give and man's was to receive. In fact, it was precisely because the Reformers insisted on the gracious saving activity of God in the sacraments that they rejected the various other rituals regarded by Rome as sacraments. The Reformers had high views of marriage, but marriage could not be a sacrament because it was a human pledge, not a divine means of salvation. Penance could not be a sacrament because its three component parts—contrition, confession, and satisfaction— were all human acts. Confession certainly remained a human duty, but it could not be considered a sacrament since it was man's work, not God's. And so on. But the Enlightenment eviscerated the sacraments themselves of divine activity.

In short, then, in the post-Enlightenment view, the sacraments are basically treated as human acts of piety; they cannot be understood as divine acts of redemption. Their value is completely subjective— they help us remember divine truth, profess our faith, stir up emotions, and so forth. They are ways of expressing religious feeling and devotion. But as a result of this one sided view, they cannot be regarded as genuine means of saving grace, for God's grace is not actually found in the lowly natural elements of water, bread, and wine. In such a context, the sacraments obviously cannot belong to infants in any true sense since infants cannot perform the requisite acts or experience the proper emotions.

Paedobaptism in Crisis

Given the push and pull of Revivalism and the Enlightenment, perhaps the wonder is not so much that paedobaptism declined in America (as Hodge grappled with), but that it survived at all. Both of these movements were unfriendly to sacramentally-shaped piety. Even Hodge, for all his distress over the loss of paedobaptism, proved to be part of the problem. Hodge failed to develop a robust sacramental theology. For example, when John Williamson Nevin published his path-breaking work, *The Mystical Presence*, recovering a truly Calvinian understanding of the real presence of the glorified Christ in the Eucharistic meal, Hodge was reluctant to review the work of his former student and good friend. When he finally did so, "he somewhat disingenuously confessed at the beginning of his review of *The Mystical Presence*, he had let the work lie on his desk for nearly two years because he always found it hard to apply himself to books on such themes."[30] Hodge simply did not find discussions of sacramental theology particularly important. In analyzing Hodge's view of baptismal efficacy, Nichols reaches the harsh assessment: "For Hodge, infant baptism was no sacrament."[31]

But Hodge was not alone in his lack of interest in sacramental theology. This became a distinctive feature of American religiosity. Some Southern Presbyterians had severely degraded the meaning of baptism, so that baptized infants were not even regarded as genuine church members, much less recipients of salvific blessings in union with Christ.[32] Presbyterian giant James Henley Thornwell regarded baptized covenant children as enemies of the cross of Christ and under church censure until they made a mature and experience-based profession of faith:

> But in heart and spirit they [that is, baptized covenant infants] are of the world. In this aspect, how is she to treat them? Precisely as she treats all other impenitent and unbelieving men—she is to exercise the power of the keys, and shut them out from the communion of the saints. She is to debar them from all the privileges of the inner sanctuary. She is to exclude them from their inheritance until they show themselves meet to possess it. By her standing exclusion of them from the Lord's table, and of their children from the ordinance of Baptism, she utters a solemn protest against their continued impenitence, and acquits herself of all participation in their sins. It is a standing censure. Their spiritual condition is one that is common with the world. She deals with them, therefore, in this respect, as the Lord has directed her to deal with the world. . . . Is not their whole life a continued sin? Are not their very righteousnesses abominable before God? Repentance to them is not the abandonment of this or that vice; it is the renunciation of the carnal heart, which is enmity against God: and, until they are renewed in the spirit and temper of their minds, they can do nothing which the Church is at liberty to approve as done by them. . . . As *of the world* they are included in the

universal sentence of exclusion, which bars the communion of saints against the impenitent and profane. They are sharers in its condemnation. They are put, as impenitent, upon the same footing with all others that are impenitent. As rejecters of Christ, they are kept aloof from the table of the Lord, and debarred from all the rights and privileges of the saints. Their impenitence determines the attitude of the Church towards them; for God has told her precisely what that attitude should be to all who obey not the Gospel. What more can be required? Are they not dealt with, in every respect, according to their quality? . . . Is it not equally clear that their condition, as slaves, determines their treatment in all other respects, until they are prepared to pass the test which changes their status? Is not this precisely the state of things with the Church and its baptized unbelievers? Are they not the slaves of sin and the Devil, existing in a free Commonwealth for the purpose of being educated to the liberty of the saints? . . . But, until they come to Him, it as distinctly teaches that they are to be dealt with as the Church deals with all the enemies of God.[33]

For Thornwell, "covenant" children stood condemned until they passed revivalism's test of an experiential conversion and the Enlightenment's test of an articulated, cognitive profession of faith.

Even a traditionally high sacramental body such as the Lutherans struggled throughout the nineteenth century to maintain a strong sacramental identity.[34] American Christianity as a whole has been rather unsacramental in both conservative evangelical circles, as well as in liberal secular circles. As Philip Lee says, "It is significant that in the doctrinal tests so important to American fundamentalists for distinguishing between authentic Christianity and liberal heresy, the sacraments are never mentioned . . . American Protestantism has to a great degree become de-sacramentalized."[35]

The Decline of Paedobaptism:
John Williamson Nevin's Assessment

Nevin provides an interesting counterpoint to Hodge. He was part of the Mercersburg movement, along with immigrant Phillip Schaff. These two Pennsylvanian German Reformed theologians had problems of their own, of course, and so they must be read with discernment. But in America they also stood virtually alone, and quite heroically, during the nineteenth century in seeking to maintain the traditional ecclesial and sacramental theology of classic Calvinism. Nevin, like Hodge, was deeply distressed by the decline of paedobaptism in America, but probed deeper than Hodge in looking for the real source of the problem, and pressed significantly harder than Hodge in trying to solve it:

> If the sacraments are regarded as in themselves outward rites only, that can have no value or force except as the grace they represent is made to be present by the subjective exercises of the worshipper, it is hard to see on what ground infants, who are still without knowledge or faith, should be admitted to any privilege of the sort. If there be no objective reality in the life of the Church, as something more deep and comprehensive than the life of the individual believer separately taken, infant baptism becomes an unmeaning contradiction.[36]

Nevin analyzed the situation with piercing insight, pointing out that if the Reformed church had cast off the ancient view of baptismal efficacy, what was to keep it from casting off the ancient practice of paedobaptism? The loss of efficacy entailed the loss of its application to helpless infants, if consistency prevailed. A credobaptist victory was virtually inevitable unless strong views of baptismal grace were recovered:

> Another . . . undervaluation of the outward sacrament, is exhibited in the ecclesiastical practice of the Baptists; who refuse to baptize infants, on the ground that they have no power to repent and believe in Christ, so as to be the subjects of that inward spiritual conversion of which baptism is the profession and sign, and without which it can have no meaning. What conclusion, indeed, can well be more logical, if we are to believe that there is no objective power, no supernatural grace, in the sacrament itself, and that the whole virtue of it resolves itself at last into what goes forward in the minds of its subjects themselves under a purely subjective form? With such a theory of the institution, it is perfectly certain that the practice of infant baptism could never have prevailed as it did in the ancient Church. It belongs to the old order of thinking on the subject, as we have it in St. Chrysostom and the Christian fathers generally, which made baptism to be the sacrament of a real regeneration by the power of the Holy Ghost into the family of God. Why then should it not be given up, along with this, as an obsolete superstition? It is becoming but too plain, that the Paedobaptist part of the so-called

Evangelical Christianity of the present day is not able to hold its ground steadily, at this point, against the Baptist wing of the same interest. The Baptistic sentiment grows and spreads in every direction. It infects more and more, the secret thinking even of those sects which still retain, in a traditional way, the old practice. The question of infant baptism is sunk in many quarters, as by general consent, into the category of *adiaphora*—things indifferent; as though it lay wholly on the outside of the proper sense and true actual substance of the Christian life. Some of our evangelical sects, it is easy to see, could at once part with the usage altogether, and not miss it in their scheme of practical religion. Hence, as a general thing, it appears to have fallen into very alarming neglect. Some of our more respectable denominations, or rather some thoughtful persons in these denominations, have in fact begun to take alarm from this cause, and are showing a disposition to lift the whole doctrine of Christian Baptism again, if possible, into a higher sphere, such as may correspond, in part at least, with the sacramental worth assigned to it in past ages. This, as far as it goes, is matter for congratulation. But it still remains to be seen, how far any such reactionary feeling shall be able to stay and turn the tide, which still threatens to sweep all before it in the opposite direction. And who can say, what perils, not merely for the doctrine of Christian Baptism, but for the whole idea of Christian Sacraments, for the very being of the Church, and in the end for the universal interest of Christianity itself, may not be involved in the full triumph of what claims to be the perfection of religion in such spiritualistic form.[37]

He echoed the same warning in his defense of Mercersburg's proposed baptismal liturgy:

On this subject of baptismal grace, then, we will enter into no compromise with the anti-liturgical theology we have now in hand. In seeking to make the Liturgy wrong, it has only shown itself wrong; and the more its errors are probed, the more are they found to be indeed, "wounds, and bruises, and putrefying sores." Starting with Pelagianism on one side, it lands us swiftly in downright Rationalism on the other. "It is impossible," says the distinguished French Reformed divine, Pressense, in a late article, "to establish the necessity of infant baptism, except upon the ground that baptism imparts a special grace." We are most decidedly of the same opinion; and for this reason we denounce this theology as in reality, whatever it may be in profession, hostile to infant baptism, and unfriendly, therefore, to the whole idea of educational religion as it has been based upon it in the Reformed church from the beginning. Without the conception of baptismal grace going along with the baptism of infants, there can be no room properly for confirmation; and the catechetical training which is employed to prepare the way for this, may easily come then to seem a hinderance rather than a help, to the true conversions of the young to God. Then it will be well, if baptism falls not into general contempt, and so be brought to sink finally more and more into neglect altogether. To what a pass things have already come in this respect throughout our country, by reason of the baptistic spirit which is among us, and the general theological tendency we are now considering, we will not now take time to decide. Those who have eyes to see, can see for themselves.[38]

For Nevin, the real issue underlying the loss of infant baptism was the loss of baptismal efficacy and the loss of a proper understanding of the Church as the living body of Christ. Nevin argued infant baptism presupposes an objective force in the sacrament itself. It presupposes that Christ is at work by his Spirit in the ordinances entrusted to the Church.[39]

According to Nevin, children of Christian parents were not conceived or born as Christians in the full sense; rather they were made Christians at the font:

> What do good men mean when they tell us, that children of professing Christians are Christian likewise, members of the Church and heirs of all its grace by their mere natural birth? . . . Our birth relation to pious parents may give us a right to be taken into the Church; but it can never of itself make us to be in the Church as our *born* privilege.[40]

Prior to baptism, the children of believers were entitled to all the rights and privileges of the covenant promise, but those blessings did not actually become their true possession until baptism. Grace was bestowed not naturally, through conception by regenerate parents, but supernaturally and sacramentally, through the new birth of baptism.

Nevin could make a very good case that the Reformed church had traditionally held a substantially higher view of baptismal efficacy than nineteenth century American Presbyterians would tolerate. While an in-depth study would be needed to prove this claim, the prima facie evidence certainly points to its plausibility. Let's take a brief look.

Baptismal Efficacy in the Reformed Tradition: The Lost Legacy

Beginning with the prince of Reformed theologians, John Calvin, the Reformed church had strongly emphasized the sacraments as effectual means of salvation and assurance. In Calvin's Strasbourg catechism, he asks the student, "How do you know yourself to be a son of God in fact as well as in name?" The answer is, "Because I am baptized in the name of God the Father, and of the Son, and of the Holy Ghost."[41] In his Geneva catechism, he asks, "Is baptism nothing more than a mere symbol [i.e., picture] of cleansing?" The answer: "I think it to be such a symbol that the reality is attached to it. For God does not disappoint us when he promises us his gifts. Hence, both pardon of sins and newness of life are certainly offered and received by us in baptism."[42]

In response to the Council of Trent—a context in which we may be sure Calvin was very sensitive about appearing to attribute more to baptism than he thought fitting—he wrote:

> That this may be more clear, let my readers call to mind that there is a two-fold grace in baptism, for therein both remission of sins and regeneration are offered to us. We teach that full remission is made, but that regeneration is only begun, and goes on making progress during the whole of life.[43]

For Calvin, regeneration began at the font. The Christian life took its source and shape from the baptismal rite. Of course, baptism was not a complete salvation in itself; the one baptized had to grow in faith and repentance, living out the grace received in baptism. But as the foundation and touchstone of the Christian life, baptism was of unparalleled importance.

Early on in his discussion of baptism in the *Institutes,* Calvin claims,

> We must realize that at whatever time we are baptized, we are once for all washed and purged for our whole life. Therefore, as often as we fall away, we ought to recall the memory of our baptism and fortify our mind with it, that we may always be sure and confident of the forgiveness of sins.[44]

Further on in the *Institutes,* he explains that new life begins in baptism and is continued at the Table:

For as in baptism, God, regenerating us, engrafts us into the society of his church and makes us his own by adoption, so we have said, that he discharges the function of a provident householder in continually supplying to us food to sustain and preserve us in that life into which he has begotten us by his Word.[45]

Later, he wrote,

But as baptism is a solemn recognition by which God introduces his children into the possession of life, a true and effectual sealing of the promise, a pledge of sacred union with Christ, it is justly said to be the entrance and reception into the Church. And as the instruments of the Holy Spirit are not dead, God truly performs and effects by baptism what He figures.[46]

Calvin was very congenial to Luther's high view of baptismal efficacy. At one point, he subscribed to Melanchthon's Augsburg Confession, a Lutheran document. In debate with the feisty Lutheran Joachim Westphal, he defended himself saying, "Having distinctly asserted that men are regenerated by baptism, just as they are by the Word, I earlier obviated the impudence of the man, and left nothing for his invective to strike at but his own shadow."[47] Westphal claimed Calvin had denied baptismal regeneration. Calvin said his "alleged denial" was a "fiction". Thus, the Lutheran critique that viewed Calvin as an extreme "spiritualist" was refuted.

Also in response to Westphal's criticisms, Calvin wrote,

[Westphal] says, that the effect of baptism is brought into doubt by me, because I suspend it on predestination, whereas Scripture directs us to the word and sacraments, and leads by this way to the certainty of predestination and salvation. But had he not here introduced a fiction of his own, which never came into my mind, there was no occasion for dispute. I have written much, and the Lord has employed me in various kinds of discussion. If out of my lucubrations he can produce a syllable in which I teach that we ought to begin with predestination in seeking assurance of salvation, I am ready to remain dumb. The secret election was mentioned by me in passing, I admit. But to what end? Was it either to lead pious minds away from hearing the promise or looking at the signs? There was nothing of which I was more careful than to confine them entirely within the word. What? While I so often inculcate that grace is offered by the sacraments, do I not invite them there to seek the seal of their salvation? [48]

For Calvin, Christ is the mirror of election, and, of course, Christ is clearly seen in His ordinances. Assurance is not to be found by tracing out the eternal decrees (as though such a thing were possible); rather, Calvin would have us start with the covenantal administration of baptism and work back to the decree.

Towards the end of his life, in one of his last sermons, he told his congregation:

> So then we must ever come to this point, that the Sacraments are effectual and that they are not trifling signs that vanish away in the air, but that the truth is always matched with them, because God who is faithful shows that he has not ordained anything in vain. And that is the reason why in Baptism we truly receive the forgiveness of sins, we are washed and cleansed with the blood of our Lord Jesus Christ, we are renewed by the operation of his Holy Spirit. And how so? Does a little water have such power when it is cast upon the head of a child? No. But because it is the will of our Lord Jesus Christ that the water should be a visible sign of his blood and of the Holy Spirit. Therefore baptism has that power and whatsoever is there set forth to the eye is forthwith accomplished in very deed. [49]

For Calvin, sacramental efficacy was a matter of God's covenant faithfulness. If God's word is true the sacraments must be effectual means of salvation.

Martin Bucer, Calvin's close friend and mentor, is often regarded as the "most dedicated, and certainly the most prolific, champion of paedobaptism among the leading Reformers." [50] Bucer's views matured towards higher and higher conceptions of baptismal efficacy. By the late 1530s, he rejected any distinction between a "Spirit baptism" and a "ritual baptism," maintaining instead that the Spirit worked *through* the water ritual. He explained his view of instrumental efficacy: "Christ commended baptism as the means whereby participation in himself and heavenly regeneration should be imparted and presented through the Church's ministry." Elsewhere he wrote, "By [baptism] we are first consecrated to and ingrafted into the Father, the Son, and the Holy Spirit." "The sacraments of God are precisely what they are said to be since they really confer what they signify—the covenant of the Lord, the cleansing of sins, communion in Christ." In his much celebrated *Brief Summary of Christian Doctrine and Religion Taught at Strasbourg*, a document which functioned as something of a personal theological testament, Bucer stated:

> We confess and teach that holy baptism, when given and received according to the Lord's command, is in the case of adults and of young children truly a baptism of regeneration and renewal in the Holy Spirit, whereby those who are baptized have all their sins washed away, are buried into the death of our Lord Jesus Christ, are incorporated into him, and put on him for a new and godly life and the blessed resurrection, and through him become children and heirs of God.[51]

High views of baptismal efficacy were not limited to the Continental Reformers. John Knox's 1560 *Scots Confession* states:

> And so we utterly condemn the vanity of those who affirm the sacraments to be nothing else than naked and bare signs. No, we assuredly believe that by Baptism we are engrafted into Christ, to be made partakers of his righteousness, by which our sins are covered and remitted.

In other words, the sacraments instrumentally and efficaciously applied the grace they signified.

Westminster divine Cornelius Burges wrote a dense, thoroughly-argued treatise *The Baptismal Regeneration of Elect Infants* in 1629. Burges argued infant baptism was God's ordinary means of granting new life and forgiveness. Of course, the new life begun in baptism had to be cultivated through careful parental and pastoral nurture, or it could whither and die. Only the elect received new life in an indestructible sense. He wrote:

> Elect infants do ordinarily receive the Spirit in baptism, as the first efficient principle of future actual regeneration . . . It is most agreeable to the institution of Christ, that all elect infants that are baptized . . . do, ordinarily receive, from Christ, the Spirit in baptism, for their first solemn initiation into Christ, and for their future actual renovation, in God's good time, if they live to years of discretion, and enjoy the other ordinary means of grace appointed of God to this end.[52]

Burges argues his whole case carefully from Scripture, but perhaps the most interesting part of his work is chapters 5–8, in which he demonstrates that his position on baptismal regeneration is found in the Church fathers, the Reformed Confessions, the writings of the Continental divines, such as Calvin, Bucer, Musculus, and Zanchius, and the writings of several British theologians.

Reformed theologian Emanuel V. Gerhart, working alongside Nevin and Schaff, carefully surveyed fifteen Reformed Confessions in an 1868 article published in *The Mercersburg Review*. Gerhart marshaled weighty evidence in dealing with what he perceived to be the vital sacramental questions of the day:

> The principal and most important aspect of the question now at issue in the Reformed Church of America, including the Episcopal, Presbyterian, Congregational, Reformed Dutch and German Reformed Churches is whether Holy Baptism is the Sacrament of Regeneration? Has Christ ordained this Sacrament for the remission of sins, and the communication of a new spiritual life by the Holy Ghost? Is it the act of God, in which he translates the subject from the state of nature into the state of grace, from the kingdom of the Devil into the kingdom of Christ? Does a person, who is a child of the Devil through the fall of Adam and the inheritance of original sin, become, by Baptism, a member of the mystical body of Christ and thereby a child of God? These several questions are but different forms of presenting one general question, namely: Does Baptism take away the guilt and pollution of sin and communicate the new life of the Spirit in Christ Jesus?
>
> We answer in the affirmative; and maintain that the doctrine we hold concerning the objective, saving efficacy of this Sacrament is the true Protestant and Reformed doctrine. Our opponents, comprising four-fifths, if not nine-tenths, of the ministry and laity belonging to the Reformed family of churches answer in the negative, and maintain that the doctrine of baptismal regeneration is neither Reformed nor Protestant, but Romish.[53]

Gerhart exegeted the Confessions, demonstrating that they affirm the notion that God ordinarily works through the duly constituted means of Word and sacrament to apply salvation and that they reject the idea of "abstract saving grace" conferred apart from the divinely ordained means:

Non-sacramental grace, or the notion that the Holy Ghost by an immediate operation regenerates and saves men, is not recognized by the
Confessions . . . [S]aving efficacy is predicated of a *Sacrament* proper; not
of the natural element itself, not of supernatural grace as such, neither of
one which is a Sacrament; but of supernatural grace mystically conjoined
with the natural element in the divine institution.[54]

It is the complete sacrament—the physical, ritual sign *plus* the
working of Christ and the Holy Spirit—that is salvific. Again:

The Confessions teach accordingly that *we receive forgiveness of sins and
are born again of the Spirit, through the Sacrament of Baptism* . . . Through
all of them runs the same general idea, namely, that God forgives our
sins, and communicates a new and spiritual life by the Holy Ghost
through the Sacrament of Holy Baptism.[55]

In an earlier study of baptismal efficacy, Gerhart concluded the
Westminster Confession taught, "the baptismal transaction assures the
person baptized . . . that . . . he is as certainly baptized into Christ,
regenerated by the His Spirit, and forgiven through His blood, as he is
externally washed with water."[56]

Gerhart recognized that baptismal grace has a conditional aspect—
it must be received and maintained in faith—and is therefore defectible.
While this does not negate the objective efficacy held forth in the sacrament, it does require us to guard against the danger of apostasy, lest
we be found to have received the grace of God in vain (cf. 2 Cor. 6:1).
According to Gerhart, this is what the Westminster Standards are driving at with their language of "improving" one's baptism:

Baptism is and remains always the sign and seal of divine grace, just as the
Word is the same power of God whether Paul proclaims it to Timothy or
to Felix. Or just as natural birth makes the child a member of the family,
and invests it with all the rights of a child, whether as it grows up it
honors father and mother, or dishonors them . . .

Whether or not baptism issues in a godly life and eternal salvation,
depends also on the will and character of the subject. A baptized person
must improve the grace conferred in baptism. This he may fail to do.
Like the prodigal son, he may leave his Father's house, and waste his

inheritance in riotous living. Or like Esau, he may sell his birth-right for a mess of pottage . . . These being dead branches on the true Vine, are cut off and cast into the fire . . .

Baptism . . . puts the baptized person in a state of grace, a position from which he can watch and pray, worship God acceptably, be nourished by the body and blood of the Lord, grow in faith and knowledge, and fight against sin and Satan in the full armor of the Gospel. But it does not make salvation from sin certain unconditionally.[57]

In Gerhart's view, the Reformed doctrine of baptism taught saving grace was really and truly conferred through the sacrament. And yet there was nothing magical about baptism. It did not guarantee one's eschatological salvation. Apostasy remained a live danger for the covenant people. The waters of baptism must be mixed with persevering faith in order to result in final redemption.

In a more recent study, focused on the Westminster Confession, David F. Wright, Senior Lecturer at the University of Edinburgh, concurs with Gerhart's assessment of the confessional teaching.

What then about the efficacy of baptism according to the Westminster Confession? Its central affirmation seems clear: 'the grace promised is not only offered, but really exhibited and conferred by the Holy Ghost' (28.6). It is true that a variety of qualifications to this assertion are entered . . . But these qualifications serve in fact only to highlight the clarity of the core declaration, which is set forth . . . in the preceding chapter on sacraments in general . . . The Westminster divines viewed baptism as the instrument and occasion of regeneration by the Spirit, of the remission of sins, of ingrafting into Christ (cf. 28.1). The Confession teaches baptismal regeneration.[58]

Wright acknowledges this strong position is qualified elsewhere in the Confession:

But if the Assembly unambiguously ascribes this instrumental efficacy to baptism, it is not automatically enjoyed by all recipients: it contains 'a promise of benefit to worthy receivers' (27.3), who from one point of view are 'those that do actually profess faith in and obedience unto Christ, but also the infants of one or both believing parents' (28.4), and from another angle, 'such (whether of age or infants) as that grace belongeth unto, according to the counsel of God's own will, in his appointed time'

(28.6). But it would surely be a perverse interpretation of the Confession's chapter on baptism if we allowed this last allusion to the hidden counsel of God to emasculate its vigorous primary affirmation of faith.[59]

Most Presbyterians today focus on the qualifiers of baptismal efficacy in the Confession, rather than its central thrust. Indeed, the qualifiers are often treated as negating its plain statements. While it would be going too far to say the Confession necessitates belief in baptismal regeneration, there can be no question such a view of baptismal efficacy is included in its parameters, if determined by original authorial intent.

The Reformed Church, in pristine condition, believed in grace that is both sovereign and mediated. Sacramental grace, in fact, was understood to be the great anti-Pelagian weapon, since it proved that salvation had to come from the outside, not from any resources latent within the human heart. Thus, sacramental efficacy was viewed not as a competitor with the great Reformation principle of *sola gratia*, but as its corollary. The Reformed emphasis on sacramental objectivity complemented and reinforced the Reformed commitment to the utter graciousness of the gospel.

This is just a sampling of available evidence that could be cited. Certainly each one of these theologians' and confessions' understanding of baptismal efficacy is deserving of a more careful and thorough inquiry.[60] There are various nuances and qualifications we have not entered into. These were not the only views put forward by the Calvinistic branch of the Protestant Reformation, though they were dominant early on in the movement. Many Reformed theologians believed, indisputably, that God worked efficaciously through the water of baptism to regenerate and justify believers. The details may be a mystery to us, but the fact of baptism's instrumental efficacy is clearly taught. It is also undeniable that we have drifted far from our Reformed heritage at this point.

Nevin, it seems, was correct, to link the decline of paedobaptism to a broader sacramental trend—the decline of baptismal efficacy. The paedobaptist question hangs, at least in part, on the question of baptismal efficacy. As the forces of Revivalism and the Enlightenment undermined higher, more traditional views of sacramental efficacy, paedobaptism was bound to decline. Without a robust understanding of what *God* does in baptism, the grounds on which paedobaptism rested became very tenuous. If baptism is about a human action or experience, infants are, almost by definition, excluded and the Baptist position must prevail. But if it is primarily about God's action, there is no bar to paedobaptism. So in what sense is baptism God's act and in what sense is it a human act? What does God do in baptism and what do we do? We must now turn our attention to a biblical discussion of these questions.

Biblical-Theological Considerations

Many in the American Reformed church today remain suspicious of high views of baptismal efficacy.[61] The basic biblical-theological issues can be boiled down to three areas of discussion. While we cannot give each question its full due, we can at least sketch out initial answers, suggest some tentative conclusions that will strengthen the case for paedobaptism, and offer profitable trajectories on which the debate may run in the future.

> 1. What is the relationship between the sign and thing signified in the sacrament of baptism?

God's promise assures us there is a basic, fundamental unity between the sign and the thing signified. The water and the Spirit cannot be divided. This was the view of the sixteenth century Reformers:

> A . . . major principle of this reform was to make clear the unity of water and Spirit. The Reformers insisted that according to Scripture there was one baptism. To divide the sacrament into a baptism of water and a baptism of the Spirit . . . was misleading. The prayer for the Holy Spirit [in sixteenth century Reformed liturgies] was intentionally put before the baptismal washing to make clear the unity of water and Spirit. Baptism with water is a sign of both the washing away of sins and the pouring out of the Holy Spirit . . . Reformed Churches should not in their liturgical practice give ground to a separation of the baptism with water and the baptism of the Spirit.[62]

The Reformed Confessions clearly teach that a Sacrament includes *both* the sign *and* the thing signified. Sacraments are not merely signs;

they are signs *conjoined* with the gracious work of Christ and the Spirit. Westminster Confession chapter 27 makes this clear:

> 27.2. There is in every sacrament, a spiritual relation, or sacramental union, between the sign and the thing signified: whence it comes to pass, that the names and effects of the one are attributed to the other.

> 27.3. The grace which is exhibited in or by the sacraments rightly used, is not conferred by any power in them; neither doth the efficacy of a sacrament depend upon the piety or intention of him that doth administer it: but upon the work of the Spirit, and the word of institution, which it contains, together with a precept authorizing the use thereof, a promise of benefit to worthy receivers.

The Shorter Catechism is even more to the point, defining a sacrament as a sign wherein "Christ, and the benefits of the new covenant, are represented, sealed, and applied to believers." The sacrament is constituted by *both* the material sign *and* Christ with his New Covenant benefits. The two are so closely related that we may collapse them together in our sacramental language. The claim "Baptism saves" really means "Christ saves *through* baptism."

This view of sacramental causality is usually referred to as *instrumental efficacy.* The physical elements have no force in themselves; but Christ and the Spirit work *through* them to apply salvation. Just as a surgeon uses a scalpel, so the Lord uses His sacraments. And just as when the surgery is over, we don't praise the scalpel, but the one who wielded it skillfully, so in our salvation we give full credit to God, not to His means. But the real instrumental force of the means must not be denied. The sacraments are indeed efficacious means of salvation, but only because God has promised to make them so.

Thus, the Westminster standards teach that in baptism, the thing signified—which is nothing less than union with Christ, regeneration, and forgiveness—is truly sealed (WCF 28.1), conferred (WCF 28.5), applied (WSC 92) and communicated (WSC 88). Baptism is an "effectual means of salvation" (WSC 91). It is subconfessional, then, for Presbyterians to view baptism as a mere picture of something received in another way. It is also inadequate to suggest baptism is merely a strengthening and assuring ordinance, rather than a saving ordinance.

To state it yet another way, in Westminster's theology there is no such thing as a baptism that does not confer grace, just as there is no such thing as a salvific "spiritual baptism" that takes place apart from the physical sign of water. This linkage of sign and thing signified is the standard view of the Reformed confessions, as Gerhart explains:

> If anything be certain beyond the shadow of a doubt, it is that Baptism, according to all the Confessions, is the mystical conjunction of the blood and Spirit of Christ with the outward washing of water, established and perpetuated through all time by the Word of God, which conjunction or union is so real that the sign takes the name of the thing signified, and so essential that either one part without the other, the sign without the thing signified, or the thing signified without the sign, would not be Baptism.[63]

In other words, baptism is a work of both water and the Spirit (cf. John 3:5). Water alone is not a baptism; it is an empty symbol. Nor is the work of the Spirit apart from the means of water a baptism. The sacrament includes both. Baptism is more than just a sign; it is also the grace signified. In Augustinian terms, it is *both* the visible sign *and* the invisible grace. We distinguish the sign and thing signified in order to avoid ascribing any autonomy to the creaturely means, but we must never drive a wedge between them.

There is a long and venerable tradition in the Reformed church of modeling sacramental theology after Christology. The early church fathers insisted that in the incarnation there was a real, personal joining of humanity to the second person of the Trinity. To separate the natures is to lapse into Nestorianism; to mix them is to fall prey to Eutychianism. Similarly, in sacramental theology, there is a sacramental union of the creaturely element and the active presence of Christ. Christ has joined Himself to these elements, even as deity joined itself to humanity in the incarnation. To separate the sacrament from Christ's power and presence is to fall into a kind of sacramental Nestorianism; to not retain the physical integrity of the creaturely elements (e.g., transubstantiation) is to become a sacramental Eutychian.

Medieval Roman views may have attributed efficacy to the sign itself in a mechanical way rather than viewing the sign as the instrument through which the Spirit applied Christ's redemption. But

modern Reformed views have generally allowed the pendulum to swing
too far back the other way. We are very much children of Revivalism
and the Enlightenment, as we have already seen. Thus, we often treat
baptism as a picture or symbol of grace that is actually received in some
other, non-sacramental fashion. For example, some have compared the
sacrament to a street sign or billboard.[64] But such a definition is terribly incomplete. Baptism does more than picture the absent grace of
Christ. Calvin repeatedly claimed the sacraments perform what they
picture; that in them, God accomplishes what he signifies. The sign is
not the thing signified, but neither can the thing signified (ordinarily,
at least) be had apart from the sign. They are distinguishable, but inseparable, components of a sacrament. Moreover, if baptism is a kind of
street sign, why give it to infants who would seem to be incapable of
benefiting from it? The logic of infant baptism is tied to its efficacy.

Ever since the nineteenth century, Reformed theology has been
increasingly plagued with a false "spiritualism" that borders on gnosticism. We have divorced what God has joined together, the sign and the
grace signified. Nowhere is this more evident than in Southern
Presbyterianism. Schenck records one rather striking illustration:

> Dr. Latimer of Union Theological Seminary in Virginia further confused
> the issue of the significance of infant baptism. He made a distinction
> between ritual baptism and real baptism. Real baptism was related to the
> invisible church, ritual baptism to the visible church. "As the first re-
> moves an obstacle, otherwise insuperable, out of the way of spiritual
> fellowship with God, and introduces the subject of it as an actual mem-
> ber of the family of God, so the latter removes an obstacle which hinders
> outward fellowship with God, and introduces the subject of it to the
> privileges of that body of men who profess the true religion and separate
> themselves from the world as the people of God." The obstacle in the
> first instance was a "corrupt nature," in the second instance a "ceremonial
> defilement, symbolical of that real pollution."[65]

A more consistent departure from the teaching of Westminster
would be hard to imagine. The sign and thing signified have been
utterly pried apart, nullifying the "sacramental union" the Confession
desired to uphold. A sign all by itself is no sacrament. A sacrament, by
definition, includes the bestowal of the thing signified. Thus, there can

be no such thing as an "inner" baptism that takes place apart from an outward sign, just as there can be no "outer" or "ritual" baptism that is a sign only, without any accompanying work of the Spirit. God does not (in Calvin's words) "mock us"; the sign of baptism is the sure bearer of Christ's salvation.

This has also been a problem in Dutch Reformed theology, particularly among the followers of Abraham Kuyper. While Kuyper was an eminently capable man, his theology was deficient at several points. Nowhere are his shortcomings more evident than in his bifurcation of baptism into "true baptism" and "pseudo baptism." J. Kamphuis explains, using Kuyper's own words:

> Kuyper did not hesitate to speak about a "deceptive" appearance. For there are "true partakers of the Covenant" and "those who are partakers of the Covenant in appearance only." This has some consequences whenever a sacrament is administered to the latter. "As often as this sacrament is distributed to non-elect people" the Lord God "retracts His grace from it, so that they do not receive the real sacrament as yet." Kuyper formulates it in an even clearer and more frightening way when he says: "Sometimes there is a pseudo-baptism, just like when there can be a psuedo-birth among men, so that no baptism took place or no child is born." For the Covenant of grace as the real covenant is 'hidden' "in the relationship with the external church." But "the Covenant is not in it, but it is hidden beyond . . . that church."[66]

In other words, sometimes God hands out counterfeit promises. Sometimes a child really gets baptized, other times he just gets water on the head. There is no way to know if a child has received "real baptism" until he grows up. There is no way to know if he is only in the external Church or in the real "hidden" Church. Kuyper failed to come to grips with the immense and unsolvable pastoral problem his view caused: namely, if some baptisms are false, all baptisms are under suspicion. Just as when counterfeit bills are being circulated, no bill is trusted, so when some baptisms are true and others false, every baptism becomes the subject of doubt.

Kuyper sought to answer this difficulty with his doctrine of presumptive regeneration: we presume the regeneration of covenant children until they prove otherwise. Kuyper even offered presumptive regeneration as the basis of the practice of paedobaptism. But a presumption is not the same thing as a promise, and cannot provide a sturdy enough foundation for the comfort of the parents should the child die in infancy, or for the duties of the parents with regard to covenant nurture should the child grow to maturity. Only if we can have confidence that *all* the baptized have received the favor of God can we have the assurance and gratitude we need to do what we've been called to do.

For Kuyper, some children receive the outward sign of baptism, while others receive the outward sign *and* the inner reality. But to split the sacrament in two this way is deeply problematic both philosophically and biblically.

A pressing need in Reformed sacramental theology right now is a rethinking of the whole notion of "sign." For too long, we have assumed we know what a "sign" is without much biblical reflection. "Sign" certainly does not mean "picture"; it does not even mean "symbol" in any simple sense. Biblically, if we turn to Exodus and John we find that signs are powerful, transformative, saving actions of God. They have transcendent, symbolic value, but no cleavage between the sign and its effect can be maintained. The mighty acts performed by God in freeing the people of Israel from bondage in Egypt—including the Red Sea crossing, a typological baptism (1 Cor. 10:2ff.)—are called "signs and wonders" (Ex. 7:3). Likewise, in John's gospel, the miraculous acts of Jesus are called "signs." Given the sacramental character of John's gospel, it is not surprising many students of the fourth gospel believe John is deliberately associating some of these miracles with baptism.[67] A complete biblical-theological study of signs remains to be written.

Moreover, some scholars have drawn profitably from "speech act theory" in developing a theo-sociological account of signs. Just as speech acts are often performative (e.g., "I now pronounce you husband and wife"), not merely descriptive, so sacraments may be thought of as "performative ritual acts." They change one's standing, identity, privileges, and responsibilities, not only in the gaze of men, as it has been said, but also in the gaze of God. Given the traditional Augustinian and Reformed view of sacraments as "visible words," this should prove a fruitful avenue for further study.[68]

2. What is the relationship of baptismal efficacy to faith?

Baptismal efficacy raises a red flag for many in the Reformed community. In part, this is due to the specter of *ex opera operato* from the Medieval Church and is very understandable. We must carefully guard against any view that would lead people to believe that simply because they have been baptized, all is well no matter how they live their lives. In this sense, baptism does not automatically guarantee salvation. We must combine the waters of baptism with a living faith.

What then is the relationship of baptism to faith? If faith is demanded, how does this requirement qualify our notions of baptismal efficacy? It is easy to draw caricatures here, so we must be careful. For example, I know of no theologian in history, Roman Catholic or otherwise, who has taught baptism *automatically guarantees* final salvation, come what may. By contrast, at the same time, the Reformed confessions do bind us to believe in a certain limited version of *ex opera operato*: Everyone baptized, no matter their subjective heart condition, is joined to the "visible church" at the time of their baptism—automatically and without exception, right then and there, you might say (cf. WCF 28.1). So baptismal efficacy, and its relation to faith, is something that deserves careful and nuanced consideration. We must avoid making hasty and sloganized judgments.

Perhaps it is best to consider baptism in analogy with preaching. Preaching, the Reformers taught us, is the very Word of God, albeit in a qualified sense.[69] It has been a staple of Reformed theology from the beginning to insist that God is at work whenever and wherever His Word is preached. That Word, considered objectively, is pure blessing. And it is always effectual (Isa. 55:11). But just what it effects is dependent on the varied responses of the listeners (2 Cor. 2:14ff.). It brings salvation, if met with faith in the hearer. If not, it intensifies judgment.

Baptism is similar. Its efficacy is inherent and objective, yet conditional. It is always a blessing to receive God's heavenly rain (cf. Heb. 6:7–8). But if the one baptized rejects what God offers and gives in baptism—namely, Christ himself—then those waters of life become waters of drowning and judgment. Baptism is what it is, even apart from our response, just as in the case of preaching. A sermon doesn't become false simply because it isn't believed. It does not stop being the

Word of God. Similarly, a baptism doesn't cease to be a means of real grace just because the one baptized doesn't exercise faith. The nature of the sacrament as such remains unaffected. This is Calvin's point, again and again: He insists that the "force and truth" of the sacrament do not hinge on

> the condition or choice of him who receives it. For what God has or-
> dained remains firm and keeps its own nature, however men may vary.
> For since it is one thing to offer, and another to receive, nothing prevents
> the symbol consecrated by the Lord's Word from being actually what it
> is called, and from keeping its own force. Yet this does not benefit a
> wicked or impious man. But Augustine has well solved this question in
> a few words: "If you receive carnally, it does not cease to be spiritual, but
> it is not so for you."[70]

Word and sacrament have an objective efficacy. They retain their integrity, completely apart from our subjective response. But what a sermon or baptism becomes *to you* does depend on your response. How will you receive your baptism? Will it be a means of rich, salvific bless-ing? Or will it only make hell that much hotter for you? Will you continue in the grace of baptism or fall from it? The choice is yours. But note that Scripture consistently attributes apostasy not to the with-holding of grace on God's part (as though some baptisms didn't "take"), but the abuse of grace on man's part.[71]

Sadler is helpful in explicating the covenant efficacy and condi-tionality of the sacrament of baptism:

> It may be well here to say a word or two respecting the unworthy recep-
> tion of Baptism by an adult . . . Baptism, *no matter what the state of the*
> *heart of the recipient,* at once brings the baptized into contact (if I may use
> the expression) with the highest powers of the unseen world. In some
> infinitely mysterious way the human graft there and then comes into
> contact with the new stock of humanity—the Second Adam.
>
> If there be faith in the person baptized, he, at once, begins to partake of
> the root and fatness of the Divine olive-tree, which, *if he yields his will to*
> *it* (Rom. 11:22–24; John 15:1–8), subdues to itself the whole inner
> man (1 John 3:6–9). If he has not faith, the saving efficacy of the grace
> of Christ enters not into him; *nevertheless he is, all the same, brought into*

contact with the True Vine, BUT TO HIS CONDEMNATION. His unbelief is the obstacle to the grace of the Savior flowing into him. Christ would, but cannot, heal him, because of his unbelief (Mark 6:5-6). Till that is removed, the goodness of the Divine Olive cannot renew him. If God, after such sin, still vouchsafes to grant him repentance unto life, then the grafting takes beneficial effect. The grafting, I say, which he has already undergone, *for he has not to be grafted in anew.* He has not to be baptized over again, no matter what the circumstances of unbelief and impenitency which attended his original baptism; for that would imply that a thing done in the name and by the authority of the ever-blessed Trinity had been an empty form.[72]

Michael Horton explains the Word/sacrament analogy in fuller fashion, drawing out the two sided nature of the means of grace:

The Sacraments do not give us something different from the Word; rather, both conspire to give us Christ. We have no trouble when Scripture tells us that "the Word of God is living and powerful" (Heb. 4:12), or that the Gospel is "the power of God unto salvation" (Rom. 2:16). When we say that someone was converted by hearing a sermon, we are not attributing saving efficacy to language, or ink and paper in their own right. Rather, we are claiming (whether we realize it or not) that God has graciously taken up these human things and, by uniting them to the heavenly treasures, has made them effective himself. Precisely the same is true of the Sacraments. If one rejects the Gospel as it is given in the preaching of the Word and in the Sacraments, it remains the Gospel, still the power of God unto salvation, but " . . . for everyone who believes, to the Jew first and to the Greek." Apart from faith, one is no more saved by Baptism and the Lord's Supper than he or she is by the preached Gospel . . . If anyone fails to believe, he has not made the Word and Sacrament ineffective; he has simply refused to accept that which was truly offered to him, objectively, by God.[73]

On the one hand, we do not suggest that baptism's efficacy depends on our faith. Its efficacy depends on the goodness and trustworthiness of God who stands behind its administration and promises to work in and through it. On the other hand, we insist that the blessings delivered over to us in baptism can only be received with the open hand of faith. Baptism is the way God gives us Christ; faith is the human instrument that receives Christ through the physical means.

The Westminster Shorter Catechism (91) ties together both sides wonderfully: "The sacraments become effectual means of salvation . . . only
by the blessing of Christ, and the working of his Spirit in them that by
faith receive them."

The deep resources of Reformed theology have not yet been fully
tapped into in developing a complete model of sacramental efficacy.
Our covenant theology opens the door to viewing various events and
rituals of the Old Testament as types of the New Covenant sacraments.[74]
For example, the flood and exodus events are interpreted in the New
Testament in baptismal categories (1 Pet. 3:18ff., 1 Cor. 10:2ff.). Note
that these redemptive historical baptisms were clearly efficacious. In
the case of the flood, the world is cleansed and regenerated. The covering of the earth with water once again recalls the primordial conditions
of Genesis 1:2, from which dry land emerges. A dove fluttered above
the flood waters, just as the Spirit hovered above the creation waters.
Through the entire ordeal, Noah himself has become a New Adam,
and thus receives a new Adamic commission when he steps off the ark
(Gen. 9:1ff.). But participation in this Noahic regeneration did not
guarantee final salvation. True, eight lives were saved in all, as Peter says
(1 Pet. 3:20); but apparently one, Ham, apostatized and came back
under the curse (Gen. 9:18ff.). True, baptism now saves, as Peter claimed
(1 Pet. 3:21); but that salvation is not finished apart from persevering
faith.

Baptismal typology is also present in the Red Sea crossing. The
Israelites—including their babies!—were rained on from the glory cloud
as they passed through the sea bed (Ps. 77:17). This baptism formed
Israel into God's new creation (cf. Isa. 51:13ff.) and defeated her Satanic oppressor Pharaoh (Isa. 51:9). Clearly, it was a baptism with salvific
efficacy, though once again many of those redeemed in the Red Sea
baptism failed to persevere in faithfulness and thus perished in the
wilderness (Heb. 3–4).[75]

Likewise, the Levitical washings may be interpreted as typological
forerunners of New Covenant baptism.[76] Baptisms formed part of the
prescribed cleansing regiment for leprosy, corpse defilement, and other
forms of uncleanness. Interestingly, under the Levitical system, babies
were probably baptized shortly after birth since they contracted uncleanness from their mother (cf. Ezek. 16:4, 6). Paedobaptism was

already practiced in some form long before the New Covenant went into effect![77] And of course, these baptisms were efficacious in an Old Covenant fashion, removing defilement and restoring access to the cultic system. Their efficacy pointed to the more powerful baptism of the New Covenant.

To take another example from the Levitical system, Peter Leithart has shown the priestly ordination service of Leviticus 8 is fulfilled in New Covenant baptism.[78] Much of the New Testament's imagery for baptism is drawn from this complex rite.[79] Again, this priestly baptism was efficacious, at the level of Old Covenant realities, pointing ahead to the greater power of New Covenant baptism. Aaron and his sons did not have priestly access to the tabernacle prior to their baptismal ordination; afterwards they did. So the ritual effectively accomplished a change in status, privilege, and responsibility.

This entire network of typological precursors to baptism needs to be explored in greater depth. Carefully studying these sacramental models will undoubtedly shed great light on baptismal efficacy and related questions. We have been far too simplistic about this matter in the past. A fully covenantal, typological hermeneutics has not been allowed to form and inform our sacramental theology.

3. What is the relationship of paedobaptism to conversion?

What then of infants? What can a tiny, unreasoning child receive from God in the sacrament of baptism? We've already touched on this question above, including the much-vexed issue of infant faith, but a few more things need to be said to round out the discussion and point to an important area of future research and further study.

It is standard in paedobaptist circles to argue for the baptism of infants out of the Old Covenant system. Because there is no explicit command in the New Testament, we are left to the broader principles and patterns of Scripture. In the Old Covenant, we continually find that the children of covenant members are themselves brought into the covenant on the basis of God's transgenerational promise, and therefore participate in the sacramental life of the people of God. Paedobaptists allow for an eschatological intensification in the power of the sacraments, but the basic structure of sacramental administration carries over from the Old Covenant to the New.

Paedobaptists are often quick to point out the benefits received by parents when their children are brought for baptism. They are assured that God loves their children and has adopted them into covenant relation with himself.[80] This much is usually not disputed. The more pressing question, of course, is what can infants themselves benefit from receiving covenant signs and seals?

Some have argued that the benefit of baptism is delayed altogether; that is, infants are baptized into *future* blessings they will probably receive later in life if and when they repent and believe.[81] Covenant children are regarded as outsiders, for the most part, until they can make a mature profession. Occasionally credobaptists and even some paedobaptists will argue infants are constitutionally incapable of being regenerated. This is simply not the traditional Reformed view.

Calvin's position reveals some of the complexities involved. At times, Calvin speaks as though covenant children already belong to God from the moment of conception; their baptism, then, simply ratifies their pre-existing membership in God's covenant.[82] At other times, as we have already seen, he ties regeneration and justification to the moment of baptism. Infants receive an age appropriate portion of that grace that will later be theirs in a fuller fashion.[83] In still other places, he speaks of baptizing infants into "future repentance and faith" (even though he acknowledges the seed of both is already present in the infant due to the Spirit's secret work).[84] In this context, Calvin puts the emphasis on baptism's prospective efficacy, looking ahead to the child's spiritual maturity. There is an element of truth in each of these positions, though Calvin never quite showed how his various statements fit together into a total package. Perhaps we can do so for him.

This seems to be the full picture: the covenant child from the moment of conception is not without a promise from God even though the covenantal blessings have not yet been bestowed upon him, properly speaking. We might say the unbaptized child of the covenant is *betrothed* to the Lord from conception onwards. But the *marriage*— that is, the actual covenant bonding—takes place at baptism. Or, to put it in more theological terms, God is already in the process of drawing the child to himself from the moment of conception. The examples of David (Ps. 22:9–10)[85] and John the Baptist (Luke 1:41) show God's *in utero*, pre-sacramental work. But this work isn't complete until the child receives the sign of initiation. The child remains in a liminal, transitional state until then. The threshold into union with Christ, new life in the Spirit, and covenant membership in the family of God is actually crossed when the child is baptized.[86] From baptism forward, the child is expected to grow in faith and repentance unto maturity as he is nurtured in the Church and in the home.

This organic model allows us to do full justice to biblical teaching on baptismal efficacy, but also keeps us from saying that baptism is *absolutely* necessary for salvation in each and every case. It is *ordinarily* necessary, but there are exceptions, such as when a child of the covenant dies before baptism was possible.[87]

If the position sketched out here is true to Scripture and the Reformed faith, we have plenty of work to do in the future. An entire area of practical theology remains relatively unexplored. We must come to grips with what the baptismal status of covenant children means practically, especially the way their standing should shape the ecclesial and familial nurture we give them.

In the mid-nineteenth century, Gerhart charged that Presbyterian ministers "do not know in what light to look upon the baptized children of the Church: do not know whether they belong to the Devil or to the Lord, whether they are in a state of condemnation or a state of grace, whether they are in the kingdom of light or in the kingdom of darkness." Schenck explained the precariousness of this position:

> But, if the minister did not know what these children of Christian parents were, how could he have been able to treat them properly? Would he and his church have been able to perform the duties of their office toward the child clearly and efficiently? These questions Dr. Gerhart had in mind when he referred to the Presbyterian minister as a "workman in the garden of the Lord," and then asked, "are these little ones," that is, the children of believing parents, "living plants, or are they poisonous weeds? If he cannot answer that question, how shall he go to work? The question lies at the very threshold of the pastor's office; and we ask, how can a man take that first step intelligently and consistently who does not know what a baptized child is?"[88]

Almost 150 years later, we still have not answered Gerhart's question with one voice. In the meantime, countless covenant children baptized in infancy, but never taught about the blessings and responsibilities received therein, have walked away from the Church. The pastoral and parental tasks elude us because we do not understand the nature and status of the child we are dealing with. It has been noted by many that the strongest argument against paedobaptism has been the failure of paedobaptist parents to raise their children in and for the Lord.

Unfortunately, most of the work done on covenant nurture has been done by liberal leaning theologians like Horace Bushnell.[89] One of the most pressing needs of the contemporary Reformed Church is a well-formulated account of the relationship of paedobaptism to Christian parenting. Is there such a thing as "growing up Christian"? What does it mean for our children to be of "the kingdom of heaven" (cf. Matt.19:14)? Can we call our children to live as those dead to sin and alive to God because they have been baptized (cf. Rom. 6:1ff.)? Should we expect our baptized children to know the Lord from their earliest days? Can parents trust the Lord to work savingly in their child at the font? Or do we expect a datable, experiential conversion to occur sometime in the future when the child reaches years of maturity? Which paradigm—covenant nurture or revivalistic conversionism—do we apply to our children?

If baptized children are to be received as the children of God and treated accordingly, as John Murray says,[90] then our task is obvious. I want to address that task, as I see it, very practically and forthrightly, though I realize this is only an initial foray into a vast realm that needs to be charted out.

Within the circle of the covenant community, we must learn to parent out of faith, not fear. We must train our children to understand what God has done for them in making them a part of His covenant and kingdom even in their infancy. We must train our children in such a way that their whole lives will be a grand "Amen!" to their baptisms. Alfred North Whitehead once quipped the whole history of philosophy was simply a giant footnote to Plato; I doubt that's right, but I am sure that the whole Christian life may be seen simply as a footnote to one's baptism. The importance of baptism to one's identity and assurance can never be overestimated. Understanding infant baptism, therefore, is critical to faithful Christian parenting. This is not to say baptism in isolation guarantees salvation, and parents must guard themselves and their children against Pharisaical presumption (cf. Matt. 3:7ff.). But God never intended baptism to stand on its own. Rather, as we combine the waters of baptism with the obedience of faith, authentic life in the Church, and godly family nurture, we find that God has already given us, including our children, every blessing in Christ.

Such an approach to parenting, of course, cuts against the grain of our modern Western individualistic sensibilities, shaped as they have been by Revivalism and the Enlightenment. Some have objected to paedobaptism because it imposes a religious identity on the child without his consent. It certainly does stamp a religious identity onto the child, but this is just what God requires of us in passages like Deuteronomy 6:1–25, Ephesians 6:4, and Proverbs 22:6. Nothing could be more gracious than socializing and enculturating our child into the life of God's kingdom. Besides, a religious identity will inescapably be imposed upon our child. The only question is, Will it be a Christian identity, as the Bible requires? Or some non-Christian identity?

We must reject the unscriptural notion that our children are neutral in relation to God until they reach some mythical age of accountability. We must teach our children what God has done for them in Christ's death and resurrection and what He applies to them through the means of grace in the life of the Church. We are not to try to convert our baptized children, as though their spiritual experience had to fit the revivalistic paradigm; rather, we teach them to persevere in the faith and grace that they have *already* received in baptism. We are not to treat them as outsiders until they are old enough to make a profession of faith; rather, we enfold them into the life of the body of Christ from their earliest days. When they're young and a thunderstorm scares them at night, we comfort them with their baptism, reminding them that their heavenly Father will care for and protect them. When they're in junior high and lonely, we remind them they've been joined in their baptism to the worldwide family of God. When they reach the temptations of the teen years, we graciously help them recall the obligations impressed upon them in baptism. "Be true to your baptism! Remember who you are!" we exhort them as they leave the house on a Friday night. When confronted with the wiles of Satan they learn to fight back as Luther did: "Away! I am baptized!" In this way, baptism shapes their self-understanding at every step, providing a sense of worth and accountability. We teach them the answer to the question of Jesus, "Who do men say that I am?" (Matt. 16:13). But we also teach them the answer to the inverse question, "Who does Jesus say that I am?" We teach them that Jesus said, referring to covenant children, "of such is the kingdom of God" (Matt. 19:14). We train them in such a way that they cannot forget to whom they ultimately belong—that they are not their own, but have been bought with the precious blood of the Son of God. They have been graciously claimed by the Triune God and marked with His name.

It is totally incongruent to baptize a child on the basis of God's covenant promise and then doubt the reality of that promise until the child is older. This practice undercuts everything infant baptism means. It is an insult to our heavenly Father who wants our children to know that He loves them and it turns the means of grace into means of doubt and confusion. A baptized person is a Christian until and unless he apostatizes. Let us learn to treat our baptized children as the Christians that they are. This is what it means to receive little ones in Jesus' name (Luke 18:16).

Counting and treating our baptized children as Christians is not a matter of pretending or presuming. It is more than a "judgment of charity." When we tell our children that God is their Father and that Jesus is their Savior, we are telling them something true and helping them internalize their covenant identity. We are speaking to them as Scripture speaks to them. True, baptized children can renounce their Father and become prodigals; they can reject Jesus as their Husband and become adulterers. But having once passed through the waters of baptism, however unfaithful their actions are to that newly granted baptismal identity, they are still the actions of baptized persons. They have been sanctified by the blood of the covenant, even if they later choose to reject that blood and covenant (Heb. 10:29). Baptism is an act with eternal consequences for the faithful and the unfaithful. Covenant members who fall from grace can only expect God's harshest judgment. Just as the promises of salvation are for us and for our children, so the warnings of apostasy are for us and for our children as well.

But apostasy is not our expectation for our covenant seed. As we trust in God's promises concerning our children and as we nurture them through teaching, discipline, and prayer, we may be confident that God will preserve them. Christian parents must continually instruct and remind their children of the status, roles, privileges, and responsibilities that their baptisms have laid upon them. Our children must learn that the Christian story, lifestyle, rituals, and most importantly, the Christian Savior, all belong to them. In baptism they were incorporated into Christ's body, inducted into the royal priesthood of the Church, and initiated into the new creation. They must know that these things define who they are and how they are to live. By God's grace, they will grow up never knowing a day when they did not love their heavenly Father. When they do stray into sin, we must "grab them by their baptisms," as Philip Henry used to say, and gently bring them to repentance through loving discipline.

If this is the basic approach we should take, we have a lot to learn in the Reformed community. We obviously have not done these things well, as the current state of our churches reveals. We need to cultivate parents who are skilled in covenant nurture. May God give us grace to pursue this task of paedobaptism-based parenting, with the glorious goal of keeping our beloved covenant offspring in the Shepherd's fold all their days![91]

Beginning the Reformed Discussion Anew

The Reformed tradition remains varied and vibrant, as the contemporary debates show. While we all agree infants born of Christian parentage ought to be baptized, we are not in full agreement about the nature and efficacy of baptism. It is important to understand this is an intramural discussion. A careful study of Reformed history shows a diversity of positions have been taken, and have even coexisted somewhat peacefully under the Reformed umbrella. As the issue of baptismal efficacy is discussed within the Reformed camp, we should be careful to display charity and humility at all times.

But it should also be noted that this debate is too important to ignore or put off. While we should be patient towards one another, it must be recognized that the stakes are rather high. Weighty theological, exegetical, and practical issues come into play. If the historical thesis of this essay is right—namely, if paedobaptism declined in America largely because of declining views of sacramental efficacy—then we have a great deal to gain by recovering and rearticulating in fresh ways a high view of sacramental grace, as taught by our fathers in the faith. If the biblical-theological considerations offered here are accurate, then today's Reformed church should have an openness and humility, compelling her to study the Scriptures and her own confessions to learn again things that have been forgotten, or perhaps to learn new things not yet discovered. Some have said the time for discussion of these matters is passed and the case is closed.[92] I say: Let the discussion begin!

Notes - Chapter 3

[1] This article is entitled "The Neglect of Infant Baptism" and appeared in *Biblical Repertory and Princeton Review*, 1857, pp. 73–101. It is discussed in James Hastings Nichols, *Romanticism in American Theology: Nevin and Schaff at Mercersburg* (Chicago: The University of Chicago Press, 1961), pp. 238ff. and John Payne, "Nevin on Baptism" in *Reformed Confessionalism in Nineteenth Century America: Essays on the Thought of John Williamson Nevin*, ed. Sam Hamstra, Jr. and Arie J. Griffeen (Lanham, MD: Scarecrow Press, 1995), pp. 125ff. The Hodge quotations and statistics come from these two sources.

[2] On this trend, see *The Failure of American Baptist Culture*, ed. James B. Jordan, Christianity and Civilization, No. 1 (Tyler, TX: Geneva Divinity School, 1982).

[3] On problems already inherent in the First Great Awakening, see Peter J. Leithart, "Revivalism and American Protestantism" in *The Reconstruction of the Church*, ed. James B. Jordan, Christianity and Civilization No. 4, (Tyler, TX: Geneva Divinity School, 1985), pp. 46ff.

[4] Quoted in Ann Douglas, *The Feminization of American Culture* (New York: Noonday Press, 1977), p. 37.

[5] Nathan O. Hatch, *The Democratization of American Christianity* (New Haven: Yale University Press, 1989), p. 89.

[6] Quoted in Hatch, *The Democratization of American Christianity*, p. 89.

[7] Quoted in Leithart, "Revivalism and American Protestantism," p. 67.

[8] Douglas, *The Feminization of American Culture*, p. 165.

[9] Payne, "Nevin on Baptism," p. 126.

[10] Quoted in Hatch, *The Democratization of American Christianity*, p. 179.

[11] Ibid., Hatch p. 174.

[12] On Revivalism's shift to experientialism, see Philip J. Lee, *Against the Protestant Gnostics* (New York: Oxford University Press, 1987), p. 143f.

[13] Nichols, *Romanticism in American Theology*, p. 239.

[14] Payne, "Nevin on Baptism," pp. 127ff. compares the revivalistic method of crisis conversion to the more organic model of covenant nurture. More on this below.

[15] Lewis Bevens Schenck, *The Presbyterian Doctrine of Children in the Covenant: An Historical Study of the Significance of Infant Baptism in the Presbyterian Church in America* (New Haven: Yale University Press, 1940), p. 70.

[16] Peter De Jong *The Covenant Idea in New England Theology 1620–1847* (Grand Rapids, MI: Eerdmans, 1945), p. 97. De Jong shows the experientialism of Puritanism (which was only exacerbated by revivalism) eventually overthrew the Calvinistic principle of the church membership of children.

[17] As baptism degenerated into a "mere ceremony" and baptized children were no longer regarded as occupying a special position in the covenant, New England Congregationalism continually lost members to newly formed Baptist churches. DeJong,

The Covenant Idea, chronicles this slide into anti-paedobaptism. See especially pp. 147, 157, 171.

[18] There are numerous helpful studies on the rise of Reformed scholasticism. See, for example, Bryan D. Spinks, *Two Faces of Elizabethan Anglican Theology: Sacraments and Salvation in the Thought of William Perkins and Richard Hooker* (Lanham, MD: Scarecrow Press, 1999). J. I. Packer, in his fine study of the Puritans, *A Quest For Godliness: The Puritan Vision of the Christian Life* (Wheaton, IL: Crossway Books, 1990), claims that Puritan preaching was driven by a committment to the primacy of the intellect. "It was a Puritan maxim that 'all grace enters by the understanding'" (p. 281). While we should appreciate the Puritan emphasis on the preached Word, such a maxim is patently unbiblical. It not only rules out the sacraments as means of grace, but it also excludes infants, the senile, and the mentally deficient from being recipients of God's grace. Thankfully, many Puritans did not subscribe to this maxim and preserved the soteric function of the sacraments, alongside the Word.

[19] M. F. Sadler, *The Second Adam and the New Birth* (London: G Bell and Sons, 1892), pp. 217–18, 285. A wonderfully contemporary anti-Enlightenment, anti-ideological exposition of biblical faith is found in Peter Leithart, *Against Christianity* (Moscow, ID: Canon Press, 2003).

[20] There is ample biblical evidence for infant faith, e.g., Psalm 22:9–10 and Matthew 18:6. Calvin believed in infant faith as a real, though mysterious, possibility: "But how (they ask) are infants, unendowed with knowledge of good and evil, regenerated? We reply that God's work, though beyond our understanding is still not annulled," *Institutes of the Christian Religion*, ed. John T. McNeil (Philadelphia: Westminster Press, 1960), 4.16.17. Calvin rejected the argument that claimed infants could not be regenerated because they cannot understand preaching (4.16.19) and cites as examples of spiritual life in infancy the cases of John the Baptist (4.16.17) and Jesus (4.16.18). More on this below.

[21] This reverses the paradigm of Jesus, who made little children the norm for adults. See Matthew 18:3–4. In one sense, all baptisms, properly understood, are paedobaptisms since we all come into the kingdom as children. Biblically, faith is first and foremost the heart's posture of trust, and only secondarily a matter of assent to intellectual propositions. While covenant children must manifest a growing, dynamic faith, in accord with their increasing mental abilities, there is no reason to doubt they have faith in some sense even from the womb.

[22] Of course, Reformed antipathy to the sacraments was not due solely to the Enlightenment. It also stems from an (over)reaction to Roman Catholicism. But Enlightenment rationalism had an undeniable influence.

[23] Adolf von Harnack, *What is Christianity?* (London: Ernest Benn, 1958), trans. Thomas Bailey Saunders, pp. 49–50.

[24] *Against Christianity*, p. 81.

[25] The social contract theory tells a story that is so patently absurd it is hard to believe it ever gained credence in the first place. Social contractualists, in brief, assume that men, by nature, are isolated individuals existing in a state of war with one another. They then voluntarily enter into a social compact with each other, establishing the "state." They consent to give up some of their individual liberties to enter into common life. Biblically, however, the hostility that exists between men is not "natural" at all; rather, it comes in as a result of the fall. Moreover, the story as told by social contract theory makes human community peripheral to human life, as though we were by nature isolated atoms. The theory claims the individual precedes the society. It would be hard to imagine anything more obviously false. Human beings, from the very point of conception onwards, already exist in community! Community is not something *added to* human life as a tacked-on, optional extra; it is constitutive of human life. As John Zizoulas has so aptly put it, being *is* communion; that is, *to be* is *to be in communion*. God exists only in community as Father, Son, and Spirit, a unity in Trinity. Mankind is made in the image of this communal God. The inescapability of community is seen, furthermore, if we ask how these isolated individuals could enter into social compact with one another unless they *already* shared a common socialization so that they spoke the same language, employed the same customs or rituals, and so forth. In short, the theories of Hobbes and Locke, so integral to modern Western democracies, simply don't square with the way the world actually works. Their metanarratives go against the grain of human life. Society always has (at least) temporal priority over the individual. There are certain "givens" in human life that are simply not a matter of individual choice or consent. The stories Hobbes and Locke tell, as the mythical foundations of their theories, are non-sense. This critique of social contract theory derives from several sources. See especially Peter Leithart, "The Politics of Emma's Hand," *First Things* 51 (March 1995), pp. 16–17, and William Cavanaugh, *Theopolitical Imagination: Discovering the Liturgy as a Political Act in an Age of Global Consumerism*, (Edinburgh and New York: T and T Clark, 2002), pp.15ff.

[26] For more on the conflict between the Enlightenment's emphasis on individual choice and the practice of paedobaptism, see Peter Leithart, "The Sociology of Infant Baptism" in *Christendom Essays*, edited by James B. Jordan (Niceville, FL: Transfiguration Press, 1997). Leithart shows how the Baptist movement, among other things, aided and abetted the secularization of public life and the privatization of religion. Paedobaptism and Christendom stand or fall together.

[27] Benjamin B. Warfield, *The Plan of Salvation*, (Avinger, TX: Simpson Publishing, 1989). A few years earlier than Warfield, Abraham Kuyper presented similar thoughts in his 1898 Princeton lectures:

> [Calvinism] does not seek God *in* the creature, as in Paganism; it does not *isolate* God *from* the creature, as Islamism; it posits no *mediate communion* between God and the creature, as does Romanism; but proclaims the

exalted thought that, although standing in high majesty above the creature, God enters *into immediate fellowship with the creature,* as God the
Holy Spirit. This is even the heart and kernel of the Calvinistic confession of predestination . . . There is no grace but such as comes to us
immediately from God.

From *Lectures on Calvinism: Six Stone Foundation Lectures* (Grand Rapids: Eerdmans,
1931), p. 21. Like Warfield, Kuyper's emphasis on *sola gratia* is to be commended,
but his juxtaposition of *sovereign* grace and *mediated* grace is hardly faithful to Calvin.
A truly Calvinistic soteriology requires a Calvinistic sacramentology and vice versa.
[28] William Willimon, *Remember Who You Are* (Nashville: The Upper Room, 1980), pg.
33. James White, *Introduction to Christian Worship: Revised Edition* (Nashville:
Abingdon Press, 1990), pp. 182–4, explains further:

> [T]he Enlightenment . . . found repugnant the very notion that God
> would intervene in present time or use physical objects and actions to
> accomplish the divine will. Slowly, for some Protestants, these views
> eroded the traditional Catholic and Reformation view that God acts to
> accomplish God's purposes through sacraments. The desacralizing ten-
> dencies played down God's role in the sacraments and magnified
> humanity's . . . For a vast segment of Protestantism, the two sacraments
> became simply pious memory exercises . . . Today there is a real split in
> Protestantism between those who follow Luther, Calvin, and Wesley in
> the traditional view that God acts in the sacraments, using them as a
> means of grace for divine self giving, and those who follow the desacralizing
> tendencies of the Enlightenment which saw the sacraments as some-
> thing humans do in order to stimulate memory of what God has already
> done. This split is at least as great as that between the Reformers and their
> Roman Catholic contemporaries.

Douglas Wilson suggests the influence of the Enlightenment has reshaped the way
some conservative Presbyterians read their pre-Enlightenment Reformed confessions:
"It is our conviction that certain epistemological developments since the Enlightenment have caused many *modern* conservative Calvinists to read their confessions in a
spirit alien to that which produced them." *Reformed Is Not Enough: Recovering the
Objectivity of the Covenant* (Moscow, ID: Canon Press, 2002), pp. 7–8. A major goal
of the present work is to learn to read the classic Reformed confessions as if Revivalism
and the Enlightenment never happened.
[29] For details, see my "Reworking the Covenant of Works" essay in *The Auburn Avenue
Theology, Pros and Cons,* edited by E. Calvin Beisner (Ft. Lauderdale, FL: Knox
Theological Seminary, 2004) pp. 118-148. The doctrine of a meritorious covenant

of works was a latecomer to Reformed theology, only crystallizing in the late sixteenth century after Calvin's death. The early Reformers were not averse to the idea of a pre-fall covenant, but did not posit a non-gracious, meritorious relationship between Adam and his heavenly Father.

[30] Quoted in Nichols, *Romanticism in American Theology,* p. 95.

[31] Ibid., p. 255.

[32] Ibid., pp. 253–4. See also Schenck, *The Presbyterian Doctrine of Children in the Covenant,* pp. 85ff. Schenck clearly identifies revivalistic trends in Southern Presbyterianism.

[33] James Henley Thornwell, *The Collected Writings of James Henley Thornwell,* Vol. 4: Ecclesiastical, (Banner of Truth Trust, Carlisle, PA, 1986), pp. 341–348.

[34] Nichols, *Romanticism in American* Theology, pp. 92–3. For a survey of the anti-sacramental nature of American piety in general, see Lee, *Against the Protestant Gnostics,* pp. 177ff.

[35] Lee, *Against the Protestant* Gnostics, p. 183. Lee's whole book is a stunning expose of North American "Gnosticism."

[36] Quoted in Nichols, *Romanticism in American Theology,* pp. 237–8.

[37] John Nevin, "The Old Doctrine of Baptism," *Mercersburg Review,* April 1860, pp. 214–215. Other Reformed theologians also lamented the decline of paedobaptism and traced its neglect back to a faulty understanding of the sacrament itself. See Schenck, *The Presbyterian Doctrine of Children in the Covenant,* pp. 80ff. Schenck summarizes:

> Uncertainty in regard to the status of children in the Church was doubtless one great cause of inattention to the ordinance. Although people generally may not have reasoned it out logically, they came to feel, at least, that if the significance of baptism for the infant was a present uncertainty . . . the infant's baptism was not so important. If parents themselves looked upon their children as having no more relation to the covenant of God and the Church of Christ than children born out of the covenant and never baptized, if this was their theory and practice, it is not surprising that there was a growing inattention to the sacrament. The question arose in many minds, to what purpose is baptism administered to children? Why bring children to an ordinance in the Church of which the Church herself makes nothing when it is over? If our children are in precisely the same position as others, why baptize them? Certainly parents would not long continue to practice an empty form upon their children, simply because they had been taught the observance of it. If the Church had no assurance that the infant children of believers were truly the children of God, if it did not treat them as Christians under her special love and watchfulness, if it ignored practi-

cally their baptism, this was reason for the decline of the ordinance (pp. 81–2).

Apart from an efficacious view of baptism, the question "Why baptize infants?" became progressively more and more difficult to answer coherently. The credobaptists won the day by default.

[38] From John Williamson Nevin, "Vindication of the Revised Liturgy: Historical and Theological" found in *Catholic and Reformed: Selected Theological Writings of John Williamson Nevin* edited by Charles Yrigoyen, Jr. and George H. Bricker. (Pittsburgh, PA: Pickwick Press,), pp. 399–400.

[39] See Payne, "Nevin on Baptism," pp. 134, 141, 144.

[40] Quoted in Nichols, *Romanticism in American Theology*, p. 244.

[41] A complete English version of this catechism, *Instruction in Christian Doctrine for Young Children*, has been made available by Joel Garver at http://www.lasalle.edu/~garver/calcat.html.

[42] John Calvin, *Catechism of the Church of Geneva, Being a Form of Instruction in the Doctrine of Christ*. My version has no publication information.

[43] Quoted in Schenck, *The Presbyterian Doctrine of Children in the Covenant*, pg. 9. Note that Calvin used the term regeneration in a broader sense than it is usually used today. A significant amount of confusion over issues such as "baptismal regeneration" could be removed if we understood the latitude certain key terms have had in theological discourse.

[44] John Calvin, *Institutes of the Christian Religion*, 4.15.3.

[45] Ibid., 4.17.1.

[46] John Calvin, "Second Defense of the Pious and Orthodox Faith Concerning the Sacraments, in Answer to the Calumnies of Joachim Westphal," in *Selected Works of John Calvin*, ed. Henry Beveridge and Jules Bonnet, trans. Henry Beveridge, (Grand Rapids: Baker, 1983), 2:222.

[47] Ibid., 2:342.

[48] Ibid.

[49] John Calvin, *Sermons on Deuteronomy: Facsimile of 1583 Edition*, (Carlisle, PA: Banner of Truth Trust, 1987), p. 1244, language modernized.

[50] David F. Wright, "Infant Baptism and the Christian Community in Bucer," *Martin Bucer: Reforming Church and Community*, ed. David F. Wright, (Cambridge: Cambridge University Press, 1994), p. 96.

[51] All Bucer quotations from Wright, "Infant Baptism and the Christian Community in Bucer," p. 98ff. For more on the development of Bucer's baptismal theology, see John W. Riggs, *Baptism in the Reformed Tradition: An Historical and Practical Theology* (Louisville, KY: John Knox Westminster Press, 2002), pp. 30ff.

[52] Cornelius Burges, *The Baptismal Regeneration of Elect Infants* (Oxford, 1629), pg. 21.

[53] E. V. Gerhart, "Holy Baptism: The Doctrine of the Reformed Church," *Mercersburg Review*, April 1868, pp. 181–2.

[54] Ibid., p. 198.

[55] Ibid., pp. 216, 218.

[56] Quoted in Nichols, *Romanticism in American Theology*, p. 255.

[57] Gerhart, "Holy Baptism: The Doctrine of the Reformed Church," pp. 220–3. Gerhart further illustrates the possibility of a real apostasy from baptismal grace:

> Baptism renders salvation possible . . . [But] it does not remove the danger of failure. It does not impose on the baptized person the necessity of becoming an earnest Christian and persevering in the Christian life. He is not forced to walk in the way of actual salvation . . . .
>
> [W]e may illustrate the same idea by an analogous fact in human life. A young man may be endowed with extraordinary powers of mind, qualifying him to become a profound scholar, an eminent statesman, or a great artist. Yet he may not become either one or the other. The real possibilities may never be realized. To become what he is potentially, he needs opportunity or occasion, education, and above all, the will to act. Wanting in these, particularly in will, he may live and die as though, for all practical purposes at least, he were not thus endowed.
>
> Because endowed with extraordinary natural powers, it does not follow, necessarily, that he will become an eminent and influential man. The result is conditional. It depends upon himself . . .
>
> So is a man born into the kingdom of Heaven by the Sacrament of Holy Baptism, endowed with divine grace, which is new life in Christ Jesus. He is a babe in Christ. As such, there is in him the real possibility of a complete normal development of spiritual life, including the fruits of the Spirit, the resurrection from the dead, and glorification with Christ in Heaven . . . [H]e may fail to become, in fact, in the kingdom of Heaven what he is potentially, in virtue of his new birth of the Spirit; just as the design of God may never be realized when he endows a person, by natural birth, with the powers of genius.
>
> Hence it does not follow that a person must be saved because he is born of the Spirit in Holy Baptism; just as a man must not rival the greatness of Napoleon or Washington, Homer or Shakespeare, because he is by nature a genius.
>
> Nor does it follow that a person is not really born of the Spirit into the Kingdom of Heaven by Baptism, because he lives in sin, and is lost; just as we cannot infer that a man is not by nature a genius, merely because he accomplishes nothing that is great and good, and lives in obscurity and vice (pp. 223–4).

[58] David F. Wight, "Baptism at the Westminster Assembly" in *The Westminster Confession in Current Thought: Calvin Studies,* No. 7. (Davidson College, NC, 1996) pg. 80.

[59] Ibid., p. 81.

[60] For more, see three of my essays: "Baptismal Efficacy and the Reformed Tradition: Past, Present and Future" available at http://www.hornes.org/theologia/content/rich_lusk/baptismal_efficacy_the_reformed_tradition_past_present_future.htm; "Calvin on Baptism, Penance, and Absolution" available at http://www.hornes.org/theologia/content/rich_lusk/calvin_on_baptism_penance_absolution.htm; and "Baptismal Grace and Reformed Theology: Past Positions, Present Possibilities, and Future Prospects" (forthcoming).

[61] Consider, for example, the outcry following the Auburn Avenue Pastor's Conferences in 2002 and 2003, in which PCA Pastor Steve Wilkins espoused a high view of baptismal efficacy, including a qualified form of "baptismal regeneration." (Tapes from the conferences are available from Auburn Avenue Presbyterian Church, Monroe, LA.) A micro Reformed denomination, the RPCUS, even officially concluded such a view was heretical, calling Wilkins and others to repentance. (See http://www.rpcus.com/aapc.htm for details.) Given the flexibility of the term "regeneration" within the Reformed tradition, as well as the number of theologians in the Reformed heritage that have been willing to use baptismal regeneration language, such a charge is shocking and ill founded. Debate among Reformed theologians over these matters is nothing new, as Brooks Holifield's remarkable study *The Covenant Sealed: The Development of Puritan Sacramental Theology in Old and New England 1570–1720* (New Haven: Yale University Press, 1974) reveals. At the very least, the whole matter deserves far more open discussion than has been allowed to this point. A primary purpose of this essay is to facilitate such discussion. While I will be presenting my own views (obviously), I understand that they may need to be substantially revised in the future. I am hopeful that a thorough dialogue over the issue of baptismal efficacy will develop in the Reformed world until we reach full agreement with one another.

[62] Hughes Oliphant Old, *The Shaping of the Reformed Baptismal Rite in the Sixteenth Century* (Grand Rapids: Eerdmans, 1992) pp. 284–5. Old's entire study is critical to understanding early Reformational baptismal theology and praxis.

[63] Gerhart, "Holy Baptism: The Doctrine of the Reformed Church," p. 216; see also pp. 188, 198, 212.

[64] See, e.g., G. I. Williamson, *The Shorter Catechism for Study Classes Vol. 2* (Phillipsburg, NJ: Presbyterian and Reformed, 1970), p. 97f.

[65] Schenck, *The Presbyterian Doctrine of Children in the Covenant*, pp. 87-88. Brooks Holifield's *The Gentlemen Theologians: American Theology in Southern Culture 1795–*

1860, (Durham, NC: Duke University Press, 1978), pp. 155ff., traces out the disintegration of sacramentalism in the antebellum South.

[66] J. Kamphuis, *An Everlasting Covenant* (Launceston, Australia: Publication Organization of the Free Reformed Churches of Australia, 1985).

[67] See, e.g., Oscar Cullman, *Early Christian Worship*, (Bristol, IN: Wyndham Hall Press, no date).

[68] See, e.g., Richard P. Flinn, "Baptism, Redemptive History, and Eschatology: The Parameters of Debate," in *The Failure of American Baptist Culture*, ed. James B. Jordan, pp. 129ff.

[69] See Ronald Wallace, *Calvin's Doctrine of the Christian Life*, (Edinburgh and London: Oliver and Boyd, 1959), p. 206f.

[70] John Calvin, *Institutes of the Christian Religion*, 4.14.16. Cf. Martin Luther's Larger Catechism: "For my faith does not constitute baptism but receives it."

[71] This does not deny the sovereignty of God. Obviously, how humans respond to preaching and the sacraments is ultimately determined by God's all-ordering decree. But it has been a hallmark of the best Augustinian and Reformed theology to emphasize human responsibility as well (cf. WCF 9). It is at this level that preaching and the sacraments function.

[72] Sadler, *The Second Adam and the New Birth*, pp. 174-5.

[73] Michael Horton, "Mysteries of God and Means of Grace" available at http://www.christianity.com/partner/Article_Display_Page/0,,PTID307086|CHID560798|CIID1413562,00.html.

[74] For those interested in pursuing Reformed typology, consult James B. Jordan *Through New Eyes: Developing a Biblical View of the World* (Brentwood, TN: Wolgemuth and Hyatt, 1988); Christopher J. H. Wright, *Knowing Jesus in the Old Testament*, (Downers Grove: InterVarsity, 1992); and Edmund Clowney *The Unfolding Mystery: Discovering Christ in the Old Testament*, (Phillipsburg, NJ: Presbyterian and Reformed, 1988). Baptismal typology is vastly underdeveloped in Reformed theology. We have made so much of the baptism/circumcision link (cf. Col. 2:11f.), we have overlooked other equally valid Old Covenant connections to baptism. Baptism should not be simplistically equated with circumcision. Baptism fulfills a host of Old Covenant rituals and events in addition to circumcision. The meaning of circumcision is rolled into baptism, but much else is as well. We have to do justice to this broader spectrum of Old Covenant types in order to have a well rounded biblical theology of baptism.

[75] N. T. Wright has suggested exodus typology also underlies Paul's baptismal theology in Romans 6. See his essay "New Exodus, New Inheritance: The Narrative Structure of Romans 3–8" in *Romans and the People of God*, ed. Sven Soderlund and N. T. Wright (Grand Rapids: Eerdmans, 1999), pp. 26–35.

[76] These Old Covenant washings are categorized as baptisms in Hebrews 9:10.

[77] A. Andrew Das, *Baptized into God's Family: The Doctrine of Infant Baptism for Today* (Milwaukee: Northwestern Publishing House, 1991), pp. 76f., 110.

[78] *The Priesthood of the Plebs* (Eugene, Oregon: Wipf and Stock, 2003).

[79] For example, the Levitical ordination involved an investiture ceremony, so Paul says in Galatians 3:27 that baptism is a "clothing" event. In Hebrews 10:19–22, washing is linked with drawing near to God's presence; the same structural pattern of washing and then drawing near is found in Leviticus 8–9.

[80] See, e.g., Calvin, *Institutes of the Christian Religion*, 4.16.9, 4.16.32.

[81] See, e.g., R. C. Sproul's discussion of infant baptism in *Essential Truths of the Christian Faith*, (Wheaton: Tyndale House, 1992), pp. 227ff. Some interpret the Westminster Confession in this fashion since 28.6 states, "The efficacy of baptism is not tied to that moment of time wherein it is administered." Some argue this means one may be baptized as an infant, but not receive baptism's benefits until later in life. But such an interpretation, while possible, is unlikely given the historical background of the Confession's writing. In light of the Reformational debate over postbaptismal sin and penance, as well as the consistent teaching of earlier Reformed Confessions and theologians, it seems more likely the Confession is teaching baptism's efficacy is not limited to the moment of administration. The point, then, would not be that one's baptism may not take effect until long after the time of administration; rather, the sense would be that baptism's efficacy, beginning at the moment of administration, extends through the whole of one's life. The Reformers argued that the additional sacrament of penance was not necessary to deal with postbaptismal sin, since baptism already cleansed us once and for all. The Belgic Confession (34) states, "Neither does this Baptism only avail us at the time when the water is poured upon us and received by us, but *also through the whole course of our life*." Likewise, the Scots Confession (21) says, "For baptism once received *continues for all of life*, and is a *perpetual sealing of our adoption*." The French Confession (35) teaches the same: "[A]lthough we are baptized only once, yet the gain that it symbolizes to us *reaches over our whole lives and to our death*, so that we have *a lasting witness that Jesus Christ will always be our justification and sanctification*." Finally, Cornelius Burges, in *The Baptismal Regeneration of Elect Infants*: "There is no ordinance set up by Christ in his church, more useful and comfortable unto a Christian, *throughout the whole course of his militant condition*, than sacred baptism, the laver of regeneration and of the renewing of the Holy Ghost . . . I deny not future actual efficacy of baptism after the act of administration, but I only plead for some efficacy *when it is administered*" (1, 112). Burges claimed Calvin for support of this view (cf. 159, 169). All emphases in above quotations mine.

[82] Calvin, *Institutes of the Christian Religion*, 4.15.20: "God pronounces that he adopts our infants as his children, before they are born, when he promises that he will be a God to us, and to our seed after us. This promise includes their salvation."

[83] Ibid., 4.16.9, 4.16.19:

[T]he children receive some benefit from their baptism . . . I ask, what the danger is if infants be said to receive now some part of that grace which in a little while they shall enjoy to the full? For if fullness of life consists in the perfect knowledge of God, when some of them, whom death snatches away in their very first infancy, pass over into eternal life, they are surely received to the contemplation of God in his very presence. Therefore, if it please him, why may the Lord not shine with a tiny spark at the present time on those whom he will illumine in the future with the full splendor of his light?

[84] Ibid., 4.16.20.

[85] Note that David's prenatal experience is embedded in Israel's hymnbook. Every Israelite would have sung these words in a corporate setting. David's experience of trust in God before birth was not unusual but normative for the covenant community.

[86] The status of pre-baptized and baptized children of the covenant was hotly debated from Calvin's day onwards. It continued to be a divisive issue in the Reformed chuches of the Puritan era. The Westminster divines wisely left the issue ambiguous, affirming that children of the promise are in the covenant in one respect prior to baptism, and put in the covenant in another respect at baptism (WLC 166). In one sense, covenant children are "natural branches"; in another sense they must be "grafted in" (cf. Rom. 11).

[87] The *ordinary necessity* of baptism for salvation is simply the teaching of the Westminster standards. See Shorter Catechism 85: "diligent use of all the outward means" is necessary to "escape God's wrath and curse due to us for sin." The Confession teaches that there is no ordinary possibility of salvation outside the visible Church and baptism is the mode of entrance into the visible Church (25.2, 28.1).

[88] Gerhart and Schenck quotations from Schenck, *The Presbyterian Doctrine of Children in the Covenant*, pg. 156; cf. pp. 80ff.

[89] Horace Bushnell, *Discourses on Christian Nurture*, (New York: Scribner, 1861). But see also "Charles Hodge on Christian Nurture" available at http://www.modernreformation.org/mr01/janfeb/mr0101hodgesb.html.

[90] John Murray, *Christian Baptism*, (Philipsburg, NJ: Presbyterian and Reformed, 1980), p. 56; cf. pp. 58ff.

[91] Two books that make helpful inroads in developing this kind of plan for covenant nurture are Douglas Wilson, *Standing on the Promises* (Moscow, ID: Cannon Press, 1997) and Willimon, *Remember Who You Are*. See also Peter Leithart, "The Sociology of Infant Baptism." Obviously, Leithart's work has influenced my thought forms and language on this issue very deeply.

[92] See, e.g., these RPCUS documents: "Heresy Ad-Hominem" available at http://www.rpcus.com/mcdade1.htm and "Message from the Moderator Regarding the Auburn Avenue Controversy" available at http://www.rpcus.com/otis1.htm.

Chapter Four
What's for Dinner?
Calvin's Continuity with the Bible's and
the Ancient Church's Eucharistic Faith

Mark Horne

Sometimes the best way to get at the truth is to begin by telling a lie. With that in mind, consider the following falsehood:

> Once upon a time, God made two creatures named Adam and Eve. Adam and Eve were pure spiritual beings without bodies and without passions. They did not need to sleep. More importantly they did not need to eat, burp, chew, swallow, pass gas, relieve themselves, or do any of the other gross and "carnal" things which are associated with physical food. All they did was meditate on the nature of God without any of the distractions and temptations which beset us because we are imprisoned in this material environment. They were simply disembodied minds, without anything to do but contemplate God.

> But somehow these two spirits sinned. As punishment, Adam and Eve were cursed by God to dwell in physical bodies which needed food and drink in order to live. Furthermore, their relationship to God was no longer a purely mental or spiritual affair, involving pure contemplation of God. On the contrary, Adam and Eve were now reduced to gross physical symbols through which God maintained His relationship with them. God set apart special food by which Adam and Eve were given merely symbolic communion with Him.

Now, the story you just read is utterly false. But more than that, it is positively perverse. What do I mean by perverse? According to my story, among other problems, Adam and Eve were cursed for their sin by being given food as a symbolic means of communion with God. That's not simply inaccurate, it is exactly the opposite of what actually took place when Adam and Eve sinned. Adam and Eve were given sacramental food, the fruit of the Tree of Life, when God first created them in knowledge, righteousness, and holiness. After they sinned, their punishment was to be banned from the Tree of Life by the Cherubim and the flaming sword. In other words, it was because of sin that Adam and Eve were reduced to purely non-material communion with God.

Before I comment any further on this lie, however, I'd like to give you another story. After all, anyone who tells one lie usually finds himself forced to tell more lies to cover for the first. Thus, consider the following:

> Once upon a time, thousands of years after Adam and Eve, Jesus met with His twelve disciples in an upper room during the Old Testament feast of Passover. The disciples noticed that Jesus was not eating anything. So, after they talked among themselves, Peter was selected to ask Jesus about his behavior.
>
> "Lord, why are you not eating with us?"
>
> Jesus answered and said, "Truly, truly, I say unto you, no longer shall you take part in carnal meals when you worship God, for you are not of the flesh but of the Spirit."
>
> And Peter said, "But what shall we do if we do not eat and drink the Passover meal?"
>
> Jesus replied, "From now on, he who would be My disciple, must go off by himself away from his brethren and must close his eyes and simply contemplate the Father, or meditate on Me and My work."

Here again, not only is this second story false, but it is completely backwards. Jesus did not reject the Passover feast nor the other sacramental celebrations of the older covenants as the means by which God is to be worshiped. Rather he built on them and transfigured them at the Last Supper. Jesus could have established a special form of private meditation or Bible reading if He had wanted to, but instead He instituted a public feast.

What was the point in writing these false stories which are antithetical to the Word of God? Quite simply this: I want you to ask yourself: Would any outside observer of Evangelical churches be able to figure out which stories we believed? Would they be able to tell from watching a random worship service that we affirm that God created Adam and Eve as physical beings for sacramental communion with Him through the Tree of Life? Would they be able to tell that we affirm Jesus instituted a communion meal?

In other words: Which stories do we really believe—the ones in the Bible or the ones I just made up?

A Quick Glance at the Ancient Church

Whatever accusations might be made about the ancient Church after the Apostles, no one doubts they preserved this aspect of the Apostolic Faith. Indeed, it kept them from many other errors.

In the second century heretics arose who propagated the sorts of false stories with which I began this essay. They were called gnostics. The gnostics believed that matter was evil and salvation consisted of escaping from the "prison" of creation. Thus, they denied that the Father of Jesus had created the world, for the creator was an evil being. Of course, they also denied the incarnation and the resurrection of Jesus. According to them, all that mattered was knowing certain mysteries so that one could escape the material universe.

Against these heretics God raised up Saint Irenaeus. Like the Apostle John, Irenaeus insisted on the reality of the incarnation and the physical resurrection of our Lord as being the sum and substance of our salvation. Like the Apostle John, Irenaeus found these truths manifested and applied in the practice of the Lord's Supper. Against those who denied the resurrection of believers, Irenaeus wrote:

> [H]ow can they say that the flesh, which is nourished with the body of the Lord and with His blood, goes to corruption, and does not partake of life? Let them, therefore, either alter their opinion, or cease from offering the things just mentioned. But our opinion is in accordance with the Eucharist and the Eucharist in turn establishes our opinion. For we offer to Him His own, announcing consistently the fellowship and union of the flesh and Spirit. For as the bread, which is produced from the earth, when it receives the invocation of God, is no longer common bread, but the Eucharist, consisting of two realities, earthly and heavenly; so also our bodies, when they receive the Eucharist, are no longer corruptible, having the hope of the resurrection to eternity.[1]

For Irenaeus, any attempt to reduce Christianity to mere knowledge and non-material realities is a subversion of it. Christianity is not immaterial but rather quite physical. It is based on the incarnations— God taking on flesh and blood and bone of a real human being. It is based on the resurrection of Jesus Christ, and of those who are united to Him by the Holy Spirit. It is based on the manifestation and application of these realities in the practice of the Lord's Supper. If Christianity was the kind of "spiritual" religion which the gnostics claimed that it was, then the Church would not worship God by means of the Eucharist.

Later, one of the famous liberals who infected the ancient Church was the monk Pelagius. To Pelagius, the life of Jesus was superfluous. Man did not, in the fall of Adam, become cursed with corruption and death. On the contrary, there was no fleshly solidarity between Adam and his children which conveyed to them his sin and deadly curse. Thus, there was no need for a Spiritual solidarity between a New Adam and His children which conveyed to them his righteousness and life-giving glory. On the contrary, the only influence which Adam had on the rest of the human race was that of a bad example. Likewise then, the New Adam might help those who excepted his teaching, and give them an extra push in the right direction by "grace," but there was no new life needed for those "dead in their sins" because no one was really so bad off as all that.

Against this heretic, Aurelius Augustine restated the teaching of Scripture that all mankind was doomed in Adam and needed a new life from Christ. Ingeniously, Augustine pointed out that even though this had perhaps not been yet formulated in an official Church creed, it was and had been, nevertheless, the official position of the Church as far back as the New Testament.

> Those who say that infancy has nothing in it for Jesus to save are denying that Christ is Jesus for all believing infants. Those, I repeat, who say that infancy has nothing in it for Jesus to save, are saying nothing else than that for believing infants, infants, that is, who have been baptized in Christ, Christ the Lord is not Jesus. After all, what is Jesus? Jesus means Savior. Jesus is the Savior. Those whom he doesn't save, having nothing to save in them, well for them he isn't Jesus. Well now, if you can tolerate the idea that Christ is not Jesus for some persons who have been baptized

then I'm not sure your faith can be recognized as according with the sound rule. Yes, they're infants, but they are his members [1 Cor. 12.27], they're infants, but they receive the sacraments. They are infants, but they share in his table, in order to have life in themselves [John 6.53][2].

Augustine here assumes that both friend and foe, orthodox and heretic alike will admit that children have been fed at the Table from infancy as far back as anyone can remember in the history of the Church. How could the Church have done any differently unless they believed their children either do not need salvation or are incapable of salvation? The Apostle Paul says clearly that "since there is one loaf, we who are many are one body; for we all partake of one loaf" (1 Cor. 10.17). If the Church had denied the Eucharist to children then the Church would have been declaring that children are cut off from Christ. If Christianity was the kind of self-help religion which the Pelagians claimed that it was, then the Church would not give the baptized children of Christians the Eucharist.

My intention, however, is not to expound and explain the faith of the ancient Church. I am assuming we can all agree, more or less, on that point. Rather, my intention is to show that the Reformed faith, especially in John Calvin and in the Westminster Confession and Catechisms, is in basic continuity with the ancient Church as well as with the Apostolic Church.

The Thesis

Jesus Christ's exalted human life—His resurrection life—is *really present* to believers in their participation in the Lord's Supper. His flesh is meat indeed and His blood true drink. This does *not* mean that physical particles of His body are located within the elements. That is most certainly not the case. Jesus Christ's human life—His resurrection life—is *spiritually* present in the practice of the Lord's Supper—that is, He is present *by the Holy Spirit* as the medium of communication.

This does *not* mean that believers *only* participate in the Holy Spirit. As John Calvin put it, "I am not satisfied with those persons who . . . make us partakers of the Spirit only, omitting mention of flesh and blood" (*Institutes*, Battles, 4.17.7[3]).

And again:

> Paul, in the Epistle to the Romans (Rom. 8:9-11), shows that the only
> way in which Christ dwells in us is by his Spirit. By this, however, he
> does not take away that communion of flesh and blood of which we now
> speak, but shows that it is owing to the Spirit alone that we possess Christ
> wholly, and have him abiding in us (Beveridge, 4.17.12).

In Communion, *by the presence and power of the Holy Spirit*, believers *truly participate* in Jesus' transfigured humanity, which sits at the
right hand of the Father.[4] Our new life in Christ is thus strengthened
and renewed.

Jesus, Our New Life

To understand the Reformed or, to distinguish it from other views
within the tradition, Calvinistic view of the Lord's Supper, we need to
begin with John Williamson Nevin's observation that "Christianity is a
life, not a doctrine"[5] (*Mystical Presence*, p. 216). This slogan may be
met with some suspicion due to the strange turn of events in the recent
history of the controversy between true Christianity and Liberalism or
Modernism. At that time, many who were on the Liberal/Modernist
side of the struggle used the slogan for their own ends. They had the
temerity to use the saying as a way of dismissing their Evangelical opponents who, they said and implied, are only concerned about "dead"
doctrine and not the more important "life" of Jesus.

However these words *condemn* Modernism, rather than vindicate
it. What do Liberals and Modernists ultimately find in Jesus beyond a
"great moral teacher"? In its purer and more consistent expressions,
Liberalism only gives us a *dead* Christ with nothing left but a moralis-
tic way of life. When they say that Christianity is "a life, not a doctrine,"
what they really mean is that even the teachings of a Jesus long ago
decayed in the grave are hardly worth analyzing, and that all that can
be hoped for is that the feeling one gets upon contemplating certain
ideals or pious sayings is worth more than anything else. To translate
the phrase: for Liberals, Christianity is a groundless feeling and groundless tradition, not a doctrine.

Yet we Evangelicals and other believers have grasped (and, more
importantly, been grasped by) the living and reigning Christ Jesus "who

is the blessed and only Sovereign, the King of kings and Lord of lords; who alone possesses immortality and dwells in unapproachable light; whom no man has seen or can see" (1 Tim. 6:16). Doctrine is indispensable, just as thoughts are necessary for a human person to live, but just as a human person is not reducible to ideas, so Christianity is not merely a doctrine. Rather, it is the resurrected life of the Son of God. If Christianity were merely doctrine, then we would still be without God and without hope in the world. We are not merely ignorant, awaiting further information or instruction in order to rescue us from our plight. Rather, we are dead in our transgressions and sins and by nature children of wrath. We need life from the One who alone possesses immortality. Thus Paul writes of his prayer for the Ephesians that they will understand how it is that they possess this resurrection glory:

> I pray that the eyes of your heart may be enlightened, so that you may know what is the hope of His calling, what are the riches of the glory of His inheritance in the saints, and what is the surpassing greatness of His power toward us who believe, in accordance with the working of the strength of His might which He brought about in Christ, when He raised Him from the dead, and seated Him at His right hand in the heavenly places, far above all rule and authority and power and dominion, and every name that is named, not only in this age, but also in the one to come. And He put all things in subjection under His feet, and gave Him as head over all things to the Church, which is His body, the fullness of Him who fills all in all. And you were dead in your trespasses and sins, in which you formerly walked according to the course of this world, according to the prince of the power of the air, of the spirit that is now working in the sons of disobedience. Among them we too all formerly lived in the lusts of our flesh, indulging the desires of the flesh and of the mind, and were by nature children of wrath, even as the rest. But God, being rich in mercy, because of His great love with which He loved us, even when we were dead in our transgressions, made us alive together with Christ (by grace you have been saved), and raised us up with Him, and seated us with Him in the heavenly places, in Christ Jesus, in order that in the ages to come He might show the surpassing riches of His grace in kindness toward us in Christ Jesus (Eph. 1:18–2:7).

The pattern of the Gospel here is quite clear: Paul prays we will understand God's grace and power to us and states that this was exercised toward Christ Jesus by raising Him from the dead. Thus, by being united with Christ by faith ("us who believe") His resurrection and ascension are ours. Christ took upon Himself our curse from God that He might share with us the blessing He received from God. This is Paul's repeated doctrine (Rom. 6:3–10; 8; Gal. 2:20; Phil. 3:7–11; Col. 2:9–14; 3:1–4; etc). John Calvin writes, while commenting on the Lord's Supper:

> Hence it follows, that we can confidently assure ourselves, that eternal life, of which he himself is the heir, is ours, and that the kingdom of heaven, into which he has entered, can no more be taken from us than from him; on the other hand, that we cannot be condemned for our sins, from the guilt of which he absolves us, seeing he has been pleased that these should be imputed to himself as if they were his own. This is the wondrous exchange made by his boundless goodness. Having become with us the Son of Man, he has made us with himself sons of God. By his own descent to the earth he has prepared our ascent to heaven. Having received our mortality, he has bestowed on us his immortality. Having undertaken our weakness, he has made us strong in his strength. Having submitted to our poverty, he has transferred to us his riches. Having taken upon himself the burden of unrighteousness with which we were oppressed, he has clothed us with his righteousness (Beveridge, 4.17.2).

Just as Paul makes Jesus the first to have the power of God exercised in Him (Eph. 1:19, 20), Calvin argues that Christ Himself is an "Heir" of eternal life, one who has "entered" the kingdom of heaven. Jesus is the Savior, but He is the Savior precisely by suffering the humiliation of the curse and being the preeminent and original "Saved One," who has been rescued by the Father. *In Him*, we are rescued too. *In Him* we are received into new life at the Father's right hand. As He was justified by the Spirit (1 Tim. 3:16), for those of us in Him by the Spirit there is no condemnation (Rom. 8:1ff.). Thus Paul writes to the Corinthians in his first letter, "by [God's] doing you are in Christ Jesus, who became to us wisdom from God, and righteousness and sanctification, and redemption" (1:30). All the benefits of the new creation are ours in Him who is the new creation having undergone the judgment deserved by the old. The reason the Corinthians have Christ as wisdom, righteousness, sanctification, and redemption is because they have communion with Him by the power of the Spirit: "God is faithful, through whom you were called into communion [*koinonia*] with His Son, Jesus Christ our Lord" (1:9; cf. 6:11, 17; 12:12–13). Jesus can share all He has received and accomplished in our place because He can share Himself.

Peter's first sermon thus proclaims, "This Jesus God raised up again, to which we are all witnesses. Therefore having been exalted to the right hand of God, and having *received from the Father the promise of the Holy Spirit*, He has poured forth this which you both see and hear"— the Holy Spirit (Acts 2:32–34). Thus, the Apostle Paul writes that all the promises of salvation and glory have come to us in and through Jesus Christ to whom and in whom all those promises have been ful- filled: " . . . as many as may be the promises of God, in Him they are yes" (2 Cor. 1:20). As Paul makes clear as he continues to write, the promise is ultimately resurrection life.

In the Apostle John's first epistle, we see this contrast between doctrine and life clearly demonstrated. John is, no doubt, quite con- cerned about correct doctrine and correct behavior: "every spirit that confesses that Jesus Christ has come in the flesh is from God" (4:2b); "everyone who loves is born of God and knows God" (4:7b). These are important tests, but they are only tests which verify whether or not life is present. After all, why is John concerned with defending the Incar- nation and our union with Him in our regeneration? Because without that life, no amount of correct knowledge or moral behavior can do us any good.

> What was from the beginning, what we have heard, what we have seen with our eyes, what we beheld and our hands handled, concerning the Word of Life—and the Life was manifested, and we have seen and bear witness and proclaim to you the eternal Life, which was with the Father and was manifested to us—what we have seen and heard we proclaim to you also, that you also may have fellowship with us; and indeed our fellowship is with the Father, and with His Son Jesus Christ (1:1–3).

The life which the Apostles saw, heard, and even handled was none other than the incarnate life of the Son of God. More specifically, they handled His resurrected life of not only spirit but flesh and bone: "See My hands and My feet, that it is I Myself; touch Me and see, for a spirit does not have flesh and bones as you see that I have" (Luke 24:39). Just as it is the fact of the incarnation and resurrection which begins John's first epistle, it is the fact of our sharing in that incarnate life which concludes his epistle:

> And the witness is this, that God has given us eternal Life, and this Life is in His Son. He who has the Son has the Life; he who does not have the Son of God does not have the Life. These things I have written to you who believe in the name of the Son of God, in order that you may know that you have eternal Life . . . And we know that the Son of God has come, and has given us understanding, in order that we might know Him who is true, and we are in Him who is true, in His Son Jesus Christ. This is the true God and eternal Life (5:11–13, 20).

For John, Christianity is a life. Or better, it is *the* Life. The heretics who deny that Christ came "in the flesh" are the ones left with nothing but doctrines. Man cannot be saved by mere doctrine, just as a dying man cannot be saved by an explanation of how one's heart should normally beat. What we need is new life, and that new life is found in Jesus Christ. This is Paul's doctrine no less than John's. "For if while we were enemies, we were reconciled to God through the death of His Son, much more, having been reconciled, we shall be saved by His life" (Rom. 5:2). These twin truths: that God has bestowed all salvation with every related blessing on Jesus *and* that we must be united to Christ to receive them ourselves by receiving and being united to Christ himself are best summed up by Calvin:

> We must now see in what way we become possessed of the blessings which God has bestowed on his only-begotten Son, not for private use, but to enrich the poor and needy. And the first thing to be attended to is, that so long as we are without Christ and separated from him, nothing which he suffered and did for the salvation of the human race is of the least benefit to us. To communicate to us the blessings which he received from the Father, he must become ours and dwell in us. Accordingly, he is called our Head, and the first-born among many brethren, while, on the other hand, we are said to be ingrafted into him and clothed with him, all which he possesses being, as I have said, nothing to us until we become one with him (Beveridge, 3.1.1).

This is the view set forth in the Westminster Confession and Catechisms. The most obvious mention of union with Christ is in chapter 26 of the Westminster Confession of Faith, "Of the Communion of Saints": "All saints, that are united to Jesus Christ their Head, by his Spirit, and by faith, have fellowship with him in his graces, sufferings, death, resurrection, and glory: and, being united to one another in love, they have communion in each other's gifts and graces" (26.1). This chapter follows the chapter on the Church, indicating the divines were following the pattern of the Apostles and Nicene Creed. The statement gives us several essential teachings for a Reformed and biblical understanding of Christ's presence in the Lord's Supper:

- *We are united to Jesus, the incarnate Son of God, through His human nature.* The Confession does not explicitly elaborate on how we are united to Christ, but in paragraph 3 it does eliminate from consideration the idea that we might be partakers of His deity: "This communion which the saints have with Christ, doth not make them in any wise partakers of the substance of his Godhead . . . of which to affirm is impious and blasphemous." This only leaves Christ's human nature as the source of our union, which *may* be meant in the reference to Christ as "our head"— implying our identity with His body.

- *We are united to Jesus by the Spirit.* Our union is not with the Spirit only but with Jesus Christ in His human nature. The Spirit, however, is the medium of that union and the One who communicates Christ to us.

- *We are united to Jesus only by faith.* This chapter does not stress the uniqueness of faith as the instrumental human response, but that has already been established extensively in the Confession and, as we will see, is reiterated in the Catechisms. Only believers are savingly united to Christ. Though union with Christ is a sovereign work of the Spirit, it happens through a human response to the Spirit that is itself a gift of the Spirit. The only analogy I know of to even begin to do justice to all the biblical data in this matter is John Williamson Nevin's referral to a piece of iron and a magnet. A magnet attracts iron and holds it. Yet, a magnet does this by magnetizing the iron so that it has itself magnetic properties. Likewise the Spirit sovereignly works in our lives and draws us into union with Christ. In so doing we are transformed into those who cling to Christ by faith, for the Spirit immediately gives us justifying faith. Thus, union with Christ is both by the Spirit and by faith.

• *We are united through Christ to one another.* Perhaps you are not surprised to realize that the communion of the saints is not primarily their communion with one another but their union with Christ and through Him as members of one another.

• *We are united to Christ in our whole person, body and soul.* I list this point last not because it is of little importance but because it is not explicitly mentioned in the chapter on the Communion of the Saints. But it is explicitly singled out in the answer to question 68 of the Westminster Larger Catechism, that our bodies "even in death continue united to Christ," implying we can be even more certain they are united to Christ, with our souls, in this life.

From its placement in the Confession and the brevity of the description, the importance of union with Christ does not seem that great. But this is a false impression which is easily corrected by examining the application of redemption as it is set forth in the Catechisms, especially in the area of soteriology.

The elect are saved by the work of Christ only because Christ Himself is united to them and they to Him. "We are made partakers of the redemption purchased by Christ by the effectual application of it to us by His Holy Spirit" (SC 29). Redemption is effectually applied, and we are made partakers of that redemption, simply because Christ is applied and we are made partakers of Him. "The Spirit applieth to us the redemption purchased by Christ by . . . uniting us to Christ" (SC 30). Union with Christ results in all that is necessary for salvation: justification, adoption, and sanctification (SC 32). Indeed, to be "elect" means to be chosen for union with Christ (WCF 3.6).

God planned in eternity to save those He had chosen for glory and then He saves them "in time by the Holy Ghost" (LC 57). God's decision in eternity to elect some to glory does not itself constitute the salvation that He has predestined them to receive (for that would confound God's planning to do something with His actually doing it). Thus, the Divines rejected the idea of eternal justification:

> God did, from all eternity, decree to justify all the elect, and Christ did, in the fullness of time, die for their sins, and rise for their justification; nevertheless, they are not justified, until the Holy Spirit doth, in due time, actually apply Christ unto them (WCF 11.4).

The Confession is following John Calvin here who wrote that justification is the Spirit's gift:

> In like manner, by means of him [the Holy Spirit] we become partakers of the divine nature, so as in a manner to feel his quickening energy within us. Our justification is his work; from him is power, sanctification, truth, grace, and every good thought, since it is from the Spirit alone that all good gifts proceed (Beveridge, 1.13.14).

This union to Christ by the Spirit is so essential to our salvation that justification, adoption, and sanctification are simply manifestations of union with Christ that the elect have once they are regenerated (LC 69). Indeed, the only reason faith justifies is because faith by the Spirit unites us to Jesus Christ: "The Spirit applieth to us the redemption purchased by Christ, by working faith in us, and thereby uniting us to Christ in our effectual calling" (SC 31).

This union is truly with Christ through His human life and nature without being *material.* Jesus, no doubt, passed many particles through His body as He lived His thirty-three years on this earth. You may even have a molecule in your nose as you read these words that Jesus sneezed out of Himself at the age of four. So what? A living physical body cannot exist without physical particles but it is not reducible to those particles. The life of a tiny seed may grow into a massive tree and count as one life from germination to maturity, and yet have, over the years, not one single particle remaining within the confines of the tree that was in the original seed (cf. *Mystical Presence*, 151, 156).

Adam and Eve were created as the first and only human life from which all further humanity has grown as branches of a tree from a seed or even a forest from one original seed. Against all attempts at self-salvation, the Bible tells us that our only hope is for God to provide a new "tree" or "vine," a new humanity, a new creation; and to transplant us from the dying and condemned life of the old Adam into the vindicated life of the new Adam.

Thus the Holy Spirit is essential to the entire transaction. In the old creation the Spirit gave the good gift of life and took it away by His sovereign power:

> O Lord, how many are your works!
> In wisdom you have made them all;
> The earth is full of your possessions.
> There is the sea, great and broad,
> In which are swarms without number,
> Animals both small and great.
> There the ships move along,
> And Leviathan, which you have formed to sport in it.
> They all wait for you,
> To give them their food in due season.
> You give to them, they gather it up;
> You open your hand, they are satisfied with good.
> You hide your face, they are dismayed;
> You take away their spirit, they expire,
> And return to their dust.
> You send forth your Spirit, they are created;
> And you renew the face of the ground (Psalm 104:24–30).

The Spirit as the Giver of Life is at work in and through what the world interprets as automatic biological processes. Obviously, this means that the Spirit uses means. Starvation results in death but plenteous food and water results in abundant life—yet this is all attributed to the sovereign work of the Spirit either withdrawing or renewing.

The Spirit gives us each our natural life but that natural life is given us by means of Adam's flesh and bone. We come into the world in solidarity with him and we thus share his condemnation and sin and lack of original righteousness. "When Adam had lived one hundred and thirty years, he became the father of a son in his own likeness, according to his image" (Gen. 5:3a). God sent His Son as a new Adam to deal with the first Adam's sin and to obey in his and our stead. By the Spirit, sinners are saved—called, justified, sanctified, and adopted—when they are made one with Christ so that they are flesh of His flesh and bone of His bone (Eph. 5:29–32; Gen. 2:23).

With this possible misunderstanding out of the way, and despite the brevity of this discussion, it should be clear, and could easily be demonstrated more fully, that Jesus Christ is the sum and substance of our salvation. The New Testament, Calvin, the Westminster Confession and Catechisms (as well virtually all other Reformed Standards, and the testimony of the Patristics which I have bypassed here), all give a solid witness that we are saved by being united to the new humanity of Jesus Christ. He is the Second Adam and in Him we have a new creation.

The Church, Christ's Body

It is noteworthy that Paul's statements regarding union with Christ, in addition to functioning as suitable prooftext for individual soteriology, are aimed at describing the institutional Church.

> For even as the body is one and yet has many members, and all the members of the body, though they are many, are one body, so also is Christ. For by one Spirit we were all baptized into one body, whether Jews or Greeks, whether slaves or free, and we were all made to drink of one Spirit (1 Cor. 12:12–13).

> For just as we have many members in one body and all the members do not have the same function, so we, who are many, are one body in Christ, and individually members one of another (Rom. 12:4–5).

> And He gave some as apostles, and some as prophets, and some as evangelists, and some as pastors and teachers, for the equipping of the saints, for the work of service, to the building up of the body of Christ; until we

all attain to the unity of the faith, and of the knowledge of the Son of God, to a mature man, to the measure of the stature which belongs to the fullness of Christ (Eph. 4:11–13; comma inserted between "saints" and "for").

If then you have been raised up with Christ, keep seeking the things above, where Christ is, seated at the right hand of God. Set your mind on the things above, not on the things that are on earth. For you have died and your life is hidden with Christ in God. When Christ, who is our life, is revealed, then you also will be revealed with Him in glory. Therefore consider the members of your earthly body as dead to immorality, impurity, passion, evil desire, and greed, which amounts to idolatry. For it is on account of these things that the wrath of God will come, and in them you also once walked, when you were living in them. But now you also, put them all aside: anger, wrath, malice, slander, and abusive speech from your mouth. Do not lie to one another, since you laid aside the old self ["man," i.e., Adam] with its evil practices, and have put on the new self ["man," i.e., Adam] who is being renewed to a true knowledge according to the image of the One who created him—a renewal in which there is no distinction between Greek and Jew, circumcised and uncircumcised, barbarian, Scythian, slave and freeman, but Christ is all, and in all (Col. 3:1–11).

It is no accident that the Apostles Creed was developed, or that the Nicene Creed was formulated, in such a way to put the Church visible as an article of faith next to the Communion of the Saints as the same. The Westminster Divines were wise to follow this historic pattern because it genuinely Pauline. While God's plan for the Church is not yet visible to us[6] (WCF 25.1) the present Church is not simply a natural institution but is "the kingdom of the Lord Jesus Christ, the house and family of God, out of which there is no ordinary possibility of salvation." In the passages listed above, Paul is obviously speaking of the Church we can see, a Church with ministers that is entered through baptism, in which we are required to treat each other in a certain way, and ignore certain divisions, because we are members of one another through Christ our Head. As the Book of Church Order puts it in its "great" and "preliminary principles,"

> Our blessed Saviour, for the edification of *the visible Church, which is His body*, has appointed officers not only to preach the Gospel and adminis-

ter the Sacraments, but also to exercise discipline for the preservation both of truth and duty (Office of the Stated Clerk of the General Assembly of the Presbyterian Church in America, Preface, II, emphasis added).

The Church is not a natural voluntary society, but a supernatural community. Thus, ministerial preaching is not merely human advice or the reminder of divine truth, but the actual voice of the Lord to His people: "The Preaching of the Word of God Is the Word of God" (Second Helvetic Confession, ch. 1). No wonder the Church's sacraments are not merely human rituals either! "A sacrament," Presbyterians teach their children, "is an holy ordinance instituted by Christ, wherein, by sensible signs, Christ, and the benefits of the new covenant, are represented, sealed, *and applied* to believers" (SC 92; emphasis added).

The Lord's Supper:
An Effectual Means of Salvation for Believers

If believers are saved by being united to Christ and being made one body with Him, and the Church is thus corporately the body of Christ by the power of the Spirit, then when the members "come together as a Church" (1 Cor. 11:18) and celebrate the Lord's Supper in corporate worship, on the basis of the promise of Christ's presence, how could they fail to be strengthened and renewed in the heavenly—while human—life of Jesus Christ? According to the Westminster Larger Catechism:

> That we may escape the wrath and curse of God due to us by reason of the transgression of the law, he [God] requireth of us repentance toward God, and faith toward our Lord Jesus Christ, and the diligent use of the outward means whereby Christ communicates to us the benefits of his mediation (#153). The outward and ordinary means whereby Christ communicates to his Church the benefits of his mediation, are all his ordinances; especially the word, sacraments, and prayer; all which are made effectual to the elect for their salvation (#154).

While the Catechisms allow that the whole of life can and should be a means of grace, they especially single out corporate worship (private prayer would also be a means of grace, but the emphasis, in the context of the preached word and the sacraments, falls on public prayer).

When being renewed by God's Spirit in God's presence as a corporate body, we come to the center of God's ongoing action toward us to strengthen and nourish us in salvation.

Here I am going to be forced, regretfully, to compound one controversial idea with another. Though Calvin asserted that communion should be at least weekly, the Westminster Standards do not prefer it, and Presbyterian tradition, despite a recent recovery of more biblical moorings, has not favored it. I am not going to offer any argument here, except to say that I'm forced to mention it because, otherwise, problems arise. If we make the Lord's Supper the culmination of worship on the Lord's Day with the Lord's people gathered in His presence, then the relationship between union with Christ, the working of the Spirit in the body of Christ, and a congregation's corporate renewal all fit together quite well. But if we make the Lord's Supper an occasional extra then we will almost certainly degenerate into one of two errors. On the one hand, we will come to regard the Lord's Supper as an empty gesture—a thing which is a dispensable part of human life, enacted at best simply because it is an ordinance that divine authority forbids us to abandon. On the other hand, if it is allowed to represent some sort of strange force outside of the normal worship and the normal context of the outward means, it will come to be seen superstitiously as having some extra power not found in the Word or the prayers. We are better off seeing the real presence of Christ in His Supper as the normal presence He promises us when we gather together for normal worship.

In any case, the Scriptures and Calvin and the Presbyterian standards are clear that Christ is really present to believers so that they partake of His flesh and blood with all His benefits at the Lord's Table. Calvin's testimony could be reproduced from any number of places but here I'll quote from his *Short Treatise on the Holy Supper of our Lord Jesus Christ*:

> 10. All the Treasures of Spiritual Grace Presented in the Supper.
>
> We can therefore say, that in it the Lord displays to us all the treasures of his spiritual grace, inasmuch as he associates us in all blessings and riches of our Lord Jesus. Let us recollect, then, that the Supper is given us as a mirror in which we may contemplate Jesus Christ crucified in order to

deliver us from condemnation, and raised again in order to procure for us righteousness and eternal life. It is indeed true that this same grace is offered us by the gospel, yet as in the Supper we have more ample certainty and fuller enjoyment of it, with good cause do we recognize this fruit as coming from it.

11. Jesus Christ is the Substance of the Sacraments.

But as the blessings of Jesus Christ do not belong to us at all, unless he be previously ours, it is necessary, first of all, that he be given us in the Supper, in order that the things which we have mentioned may be truly accomplished in us. For this reason I am wont to say, that the substance of the sacraments is the Lord Jesus, and the efficacy of them the graces and blessings which we have by his means. Now the efficacy of the Supper is to confirm to us the reconciliation which we have with God through our Savior's death and passion; the washing of our souls which we have in the shedding of his blood; the righteousness which we have in his obedience; in short, the hope of salvation which we have in all that he has done for us. It is necessary, then, that the substance should be conjoined with these, otherwise nothing would be firm or certain. Hence we conclude that two things are presented to us in the Supper, viz., Jesus Christ as the source and substance of all good; and, secondly, the fruit and efficacy of his death and passion. This is implied in the words which were used. For after commanding us to eat his body and drink his blood, he adds that his body was delivered for us, and his blood shed for the remission of our sins. Hereby he intimates, first, that we ought not simply to communicate in his body and blood, without any other consideration, but in order to receive the fruit derived to us from his death and passion; secondly that we can attain the enjoyment of such fruit only by participating in his body and blood, from which it is derived.[7]

This is Calvin's consistent doctrine, in keeping with his consistent teaching on union with Christ. Of note are two commonalties between the statement and the Westminster Confessions.^^

First, Calvin teaches that in the Lord's Supper, God *confirms by conjoining*. He emphasizes that the Lord's Supper is to "confirm" promises and states that the only way our faith is so confirmed in the promises is for God to "conjoin" the substance to the symbol. The Westminster Divines followed Calvin, stating that sacraments were instituted to "to confirm our interest in him," and yet also insisted that the reality was conjoined with the signs in the sacraments for them to accomplish this. Thus, the sacraments actually apply Christ to believers (SC 92) and, in the Lord's Supper, "worthy receivers are, not after a corporal and carnal manner, but by faith, made partakers of his body and blood, with all his benefits, to their spiritual nourishment, and growth in grace."

This brings us to the second point. Calvin is emphatic that we do *not* simply receive Christ's benefits but that we receive Christ Himself in the Lord's Supper: "Hence we conclude that two things are presented to us in the Supper, viz., Jesus Christ as the source and substance of all good; and, secondly, the fruit and efficacy of his death and passion." The Westminster Divines follow Calvin consistently in this. Whether they say it is "Christ and the benefits of the new covenant" as in the case of the Sacraments in general (SC 92), or "our ingrafting into Christ, and partaking of the benefits of the covenant of grace" with regard to baptism (SC 94) or "his body and blood, with all his benefits" in the Lord's Supper, they consistently keep hold of Calvin's principle that we get none of Christ's benefits without Christ Himself.

Conclusion

To show testimony from a different confessional tradition, Question 76 of the Heidelberg Catechism explains, "What is it then to eat the crucified body, and drink the shed blood of Christ?":

> It is *not only* to embrace with a believing heart, all the sufferings and death of Christ, and thereby to obtain the pardon of sin and life eternal; *but also besides that,* to become more and more *united to his sacred body, by the Holy Ghost,* who dwells both in Christ and in us; so that we, although Christ is in heaven, and we on earth, are, notwithstanding, "flesh of his flesh and bone of his bone"; and that we live and are governed forever by one Spirit, as members of the same body are by one soul (emphasis added).

Zacharius Ursinus, the primary author of the catechism, expounds this answer in his *Commentary on the Heidelberg Catechism* by saying, "to eat the crucified body and to drink the shed blood of Christ . . . is to believe—to obtain remission of sins by faith—to be united with Christ, and to become partakers of his life."[8]

Ursinus insists that the material symbols used in the sacrament are accompanied by "the things signified" which are "spiritual, invisible, and heavenly." He considers an objection: "But the body and blood of Christ consist of that which is material and earthly." Ursinus replies: "The things signified are here called spiritual, *not as it respects their substance; but as it respects the manner in which they are received,* because they are received *through the working of the Holy Ghost,* by faith alone, and not by any of the members of our body.[9] Like Calvin, Ursinus maintains emphatically that, though the flesh and blood of Christ are received through the power the Holy Spirit, nevertheless, not only is the Spirit received, but also the flesh and blood of Christ. As Calvin put it earlier, 'Jesus Christ gives us in the Supper the proper substance of his body and blood, in order that we may possess it fully, and possessing it have part in all blessings" (*Short Treatise*, ch. 17).

We Christians confess a New Man who is Lord of Heaven and Earth, having been raised from the dead, God incarnate. This is not a mental technique for manipulating reality, but simply confession of how reality has now been changed: "We trust in one holy, catholic, and apostolic church," to quote the Nicene Creed more literally than is common. The Church was brought into existence through the death and resurrection of Christ communicated to a people through the Holy Spirit. The Lord's Supper is an objective means by which the Church is renewed and strengthened—an objective means by which believers are renewed and strengthened in their union with the glorified human life of Jesus.

Notes - Chapter 4

[1] *Against Heresies*, 4.18.5, Schaff, ed., p. 486.

[2] *The Works of Saint Augustine*, trans. Edmund Hill, ed. John E. Rotelle, 11 vols, Part III—Sermons (New Rochelle, New York: New City Press, 1992), 5:261; emphasis added. Thanks go to Tommy Lee for this quotation from his paper, "The History Of Paedocommunion: From The Early Church Until 1500." It can be found at http://www.reformed.org/sacramentology/tl_paedo.html.

[3] Henceforth, I will designate which translation of Calvin's *Institutes of the Christian Religion* I am quoting by using the names of the translators, Battles or Beveridge.

[4] To see a Lutheran attempt to deny Calvin believed and taught this, see "Honoring the Lord and His Supper: An Exegetical Refutation of the Reformed Doctrine of the Lord's Supper" by Brian R. Kom available at http://www.wls.wels.net/library/Essays/Authors/K/KomReformed/KomReformed.pdf.

Kom is, in my view, rather selective in his quotations from Calvin. This seriously skews his analysis and misdirects his critique. Kom's paper, in my opinion, suffers some other defects. Let me give three examples:

1. Kom quotes Francis Pieper (p. 14) that the Reformed view, "Christ's body and blood are not present in the Lord's Supper, but as far removed from it as is heaven from earth." But this formula is so ambiguous that it is hard to see how it does not encourage equivoca-tion. Does "in the Lord's Supper" refer to the rite or the elements? If Pieper is referring to the elements abstracted from the sacrament, then I would agree with his statement. But I deny that this is an accurate exposition of the view of Calvin, Nevin, or Mathison. I highly doubt it could be the view of Letham. Christ is present by the Spirit to believers.

2. Kom also quotes Pieper approvingly about how the nature of Christ's body dictates that he is "absent" in this way. But the throwaway arguments used to ignore actual exegesis. To claim the Holy Spirit is the bond of union between Jesus Christ and his people is hardly something lacking direct Biblical support. Calvin's eucharistic views flowed organically from his soteriology in which believers are saved because they are united to Christ by the Holy Spirit only through faith. This, not allegations about the properties of Christ's human nature, are the foundation of Calvin's view. I am not denying he held the view attributed to him. I am denying that argumentative strategy can be simply equated with the origin of the view.

3. Kom seems unaware that Nevin criticized Calvin's view that believers were raised up to Christ by the Spirit. I can only assume he thinks this as the essential way in which Calvin's view holds together. On the

contrary, the real presence can be defended without recourse to such an idea (as I do in this essay).

I might add that in Kom's review of Reformed Theology in general, he seems to exemplify the mindset of Lutheran sectarianism. He insists on classifying virtually all non-Lutheran Evangelicals as "Reformed." The "Reformed Dogmatician" (!) Millard Erickson, a Baptist, is treated as if he had any relationship to Presbyterian theology. (Would it be fair for me to sample Kom's views as Roman Catholic because of a shared view of the "local presence"?) I will grant that Kom had plenty of ammunition if he had stuck to Reformed sources. I simply want to register my complaint at being classified in this way. It is not accurate and Kom would not appreciate such treatment from others.

[5] *The Mystical Presence and Other Writings on the Eucharist*, vol. 4 of Lancaster Series on the Mercersburg Theology, Bard Thompson & George H. Bricker, ed. (Philadelphia, Boston: United Church Press, 1966). Henceforth: *Mystical Presence*. Unhappily, I am using an edition that is not readily available outside a library. A reproduction of *The Mystical Presence: A Vindication of the Reformed or Calvinistic Doctrine of the Holy Eucharistic* is available from Wipf & Stock. It uses different pagination.

[6] The meaning of the invisible Church is rather commonly misunderstood as a present reality in space of time rather than a mental concept in God's mind, despite the definition in the Confession. See my "Of the Church: An Exposition of Chapter XXV of the Westminster Confession of Faith" at http://www.hornes.org/theologia/content/mark_horne/of_the_church.htm.

Part of the problem, I believe, is the choice of prooftexts for the paragraphs on the invisible and then the visible Church which require us to believe that Paul jumped from one to the other in his letter to the Ephesians without giving any warning to his readers (Eph. 1:10, 22–23; 5:23, 27, 32; 2:19; 3:15). In my opinion it would be better to use Romans 9:6 by analogy along with the general prooftexts for predestination.

[7] John Calvin, "Short Treatise on the Lord's Supper," in *Selected Works of John Calvin: Tracts and Letters*, trans. and ed. by Henry Beveridge, vol. 2 (Edinburgh: Calvin Translation Society, 1849), pp. 168–170. Available online at http://www.hornes.org/theologia/content/john_calvin/short_treatise_on_the_holy_supper_of_our_lord_jesus_christ.htm.

[8] John Calvin, *Commentary on the Heidelberg Catechism*, G. W. Willard, tr. (Phillipsburg, NJ: P&R, reprint n.d., 1852), p. 382.

[9] Ibid, p. 347; emphasis added.

Chapter Five

Merit Versus Maturity:

What Did Jesus Do for Us?[1]

James B. Jordan

When I was in theological seminary in the late 1970s, it was fairly common for men to express reservations about the traditional Reformed doctrine called "the covenant of works." The gist of that doctrine was that Adam was somehow supposed to earn something while he lived in the garden of Eden, that something being "eternal life." Because of his sin, Adam fell into death, and so did all of his posterity. Jesus, however, lived a sinless life as a new Adam, and by His merits earned eternal life, which is now given to all who are in union with Him.

That there were to be two stages in human existence is clear from Romans 5, which tells us repeatedly that what we have in Christ is "much more" than what Adam lost.[2] Hence, there is an Adamic stage of human life and then a glorified stage, which Adam failed to attain. Paul makes the same affirmation in 1 Corinthians 15:44: "If there is a natural body, there is also a Spiritual body," which means that the existence of a "natural body" implies the future existence of a "Spiritual body."[3] Paul assumes that it is clear from the creation account that there are two stages of human existence. The purpose of this essay is to clarify what is involved in those two stages.

What, then, is the nature of these two stages of life? On the face of it, the two stages would seem to be childhood and maturity. Indeed, this is the language Paul uses to describe the change of ages brought about by Jesus (Gal. 3:23–4:11). A person does not become a mature adult by "earning" or "meriting" it by doing good works. Rather, a child is supposed to grow up to be an adult, unless he dies before attaining mature age. Adam came under death as a child, and hence did not attain maturity and glory. It is the thesis of this paper that maturation rather than meriting is the proper way to understand the two phases of human life.

The notion of a "covenant of works" had become problematic in conservative American Presbyterian theology by the late 1970s for several reasons. First, there were the criticisms put forth by John Murray. For Murray, there was an "Adamic administration" but not a "covenant" with Adam.[4] A series of taped lectures on "The Adamic Administration" by Murray was in circulation, as was his article on "Covenant Theology" in *The Encyclopedia of Christianity.*[5]

Contact with conservative continental Reformed theology, which, unlike Presbyterianism, does not have a confessional tie to the phrase "covenant of works," also served to open up the discussion. Most professors at the various conservative Presbyterian seminaries in America at that time had taken advanced degrees in the Netherlands, and so had been exposed to continental views. The first volume of S.G. De Graaf's *Promise and Deliverance* was published in English in 1977.[6] My seminary contemporaries and I read:

> We are accustomed to speaking of this covenant as the covenant of works. However, we should not take this name to mean that man was expected to earn eternal life as a reward for doing good works, as though eternal life was man's payment for services rendered. Because man owes everything he has to God, we may never speak of man earning wages paid out by God. Therefore it might be wiser to speak of the covenant of God's favor. *Grace*, in general, also means favor, but in the Scriptures *grace* always has the special meaning of favor that forgives guilt. We could express the difference by saying that God made a covenant of favor with Adam and a covenant of grace with Christ. The only demand made of Adam was that he choose consciously for the favor given him by God if he and his posterity were to abide forever in that favor.[7]

As can be seen, a rejection of the idea of a covenant of meritorious work was commonly entertained in Continental Reformed circles.[8]

Moreover, the phrase "covenant of works" was seen as problematic. What did it mean? Better, what did this phrase quickly communicate to people not rigorously schooled in systematic theology? It might mean that God had a Plan A, which was Pelagian, and by which people could "earn their way to eternal life by doing good works." Since Adam had not earned eternal life, Jesus came to do so, and now it is given to us by grace and received by faith. It almost seems as if that is the view. Murray summarizes Robert Rollock's opinions, delivered in 1596 and 1597, as follows: "The *promise* [of the Adamic covenant] is eternal life accruing to man, not on the basis of his original righteousness or integrity, but on the basis of good works performed in the strength of this integrity."[9]

This notion received a better and more moderate expression by Turretin, as summarized by Murray:

> The obligation which God assumed in this promise [of eternal life] was wholly gratuitous: God had no debt, strictly speaking, from which a right could belong to man. The only debt was that of his own faithfulness to the promise. And as for man, he could not, strictly and properly, obtain merit from his obedience and could not seek the reward as a right. The worthiness of works could bear no proportion to the reward of life eternal.[10]

Despite Turretin's strictures, this scheme is still fundamentally Pelagian in character: God graciously set up a system by which Adam would earn eternal life, though the reward earned was out of all proportion to the merits acquired through Adam's work.

If this be what the Bible teaches, then so be it. Simply charging it with "Pelagianism" or work-salvation is not enough. After all, no one was suggesting that we as sinners are capable of working out our own eternal life. The thought was that Jesus has earned it for us, and we receive it as a gift by faith alone.

There are, however, several problems with this theological scheme, despite the fact that what it seeks to affirm is quite true (to wit: the two-stage nature of human life). One problem is the notion of earning glorified eternal life through meritorious works. As I intend to show in this paper, nothing in the Bible teaches that Adam was supposed to earn glory. He was, rather, called to remain faithful and mature to the point of awareness that he needed a fuller kind of life from God, which God would freely give him at the proper time.

A second problem is the notion that the reward is "life" or "eternal life." This led many, if not most, Reformed theologians to maintain that Adam somehow knew that he was not to go to the Tree of Life until after the probation, which as we shall see is flatly contradicted by the text of Genesis 2. In fact, the reward is not life but glorification, and "eternal life" needs to be understood as not the mere perpetuation of original life, but as this new glorified life.

It is clear that Reformed theologians *have* understood eternal life as glorified life, but the matter has lain somewhat undeveloped and confused. Notice the unclarity of the Westminster Confession of Faith 19.1:

> God gave to Adam a law, as a covenant of works, by which He bound him and all his posterity to personal, entire, exact, and perpetual obedience, promised life upon the fulfilling, and threatened death upon the breach of it, and endued him with power and ability to keep it.

This statement is not so much wrong as incomplete and somewhat ambiguous. Where is faith in all this? Surely Adam was to put his faith and trust in God while he obeyed.[11] And what is the "life" that is promised? Mere continuance of life, or glorified life? To be sure, true obedience is faith-full obedience; and to be sure, the life promised is somehow eschatological and hence transfigured life. But the statement is at best confusing and at worst misleading.

Even more problematic is what we read in chapter 7.2–3 (emphasis added):

> 2. The first covenant made with man was a covenant of *works*, wherein life was promised to Adam, and in him to his posterity, upon condition of perfect and personal *obedience*.

> 3. Man by his fall having made himself incapable of life by that covenant, the Lord was pleased to make a second, commonly called the Covenant of *Grace*: whereby he *freely* offereth unto sinners life and salvation by Jesus Christ, requiring of them *faith in Him*, that they may be saved . . .

It seems clear that for Adam, "life" was not freely offered but was to be earned through "works," an obedience that is not expressly stated to be through faith. I submit that section 2 would better read: "The first covenant, into which God created Adam, freely provided initial life to him, and promised glorified life to him, and in him to his posterity, upon condition of perfect and personal faithfulness."

Considerations such as I have outlined were in the minds of the many men who, when being considered for ordination in the presbyterian churches, took and continue to take "exception" to the notion of a covenant of works.[12] As Murray wrote in *The Covenant of Grace*:

> Theology today must always be undergoing a reformation. The human understanding is imperfect. However architectonic may be the systematic constructions of any one generation or group of generations, there always remains the need for correction and reconstruction so that the structure may be brought into close approximation to the Scripture and the reproduction be a more faithful transcript or reflection of the heavenly exemplar.[13]

The purpose of this paper is to take up Murray's challenge and provide a better systematic construction of the nature of the Adamic Covenant and of how Jesus fulfilled it for us. My thesis is that what Adam was supposed to provide, and what Jesus provided for us, is maturity. That is to say, the new status that Jesus provides for us does not come about because He earned something Adam failed to earn, but because He persevered in faith toward the Father until He was mature, which Adam did not do.

Rich Lusk has helpfully stated the matter this way:

> The covenant of works construction strikes at the filial nature of covenant sonship. Adam was God's son, not his employee. He wasn't to earn anything. Eschatological life was a promised *inheritance*, not something to be merited. When Jesus is brought into the picture, the problems with the covenant of works are even greater. Jesus is God's Son in an even deeper sense. To reduce His relationship with the Father to an employer/ employee relationship, with Jesus earning wages, strikes at the heart of intra-Trinitarian relationships. The Son never has to earn the Father's love and to suggest otherwise seems virtually blasphemous. The sonship of Adam and, behind that, of the Logos, simply rule out covenant-of-works style theologies. Sons never merit anything from fathers, in the Trinity or in creation.[14]

An example from ordinary life will serve to illustrate what I mean. Let us consider granting a 17-year old, Tom, the privilege of driving the family automobile. We might say that Tom has earned the right to the keys, but that is not quite correct. The fact is that we as parents deem Tom mature enough to be granted the privilege of the keys. When Tom was six, he took out the garbage every night, and when he was eight he began doing the dishes for his mother. When he was twelve, he began mowing the lawn every week. But no matter how good a job Tom did of taking out the garbage when he was six, we would not have dreamed of letting him drive the car, because he was not old enough to do so.

Now let us consider Tom's evil twin, Zork. Zork tossed the garbage on the ground when it was his turn to take it out. He did a very sloppy job with the dishes, frequently breaking them. He just never got around to mowing the grass when it was his turn. Now he also is 17 years old, and is physically mature enough to drive. But he has proven too irresponsible to be allowed the privilege of the keys, so we refuse to let him drive the family car.

From this we see that good behavior is part of what prepares a person for mature responsibilities and bad behavior disqualifies a person from mature responsibilities. At the same time, however, specific acts of good behavior do not somehow earn "points" that can be cashed in for mature privileges. Also, good behavior is only part of the matter, for a child must grow up and become mature enough for such privileges, and this is a subtle and somewhat mysterious matter. It involves deep character building, as well as the subtle influences of time and age.

At this point, let us look a bit more closely at the event of giving Tom the keys. As Tom moves into his teenage years, he begins to want to drive the car. He also begins to see reasons why he should be allowed to do so. He senses that he lacks something he needs. So, when he is 15 he comes to his mother and father, and asks us if we will please let him start driving the car. We reply that he'll be allowed to drive when he is 17, and that he needs to be patient. Patiently waiting for something known to be good becomes part of the maturation process for Tom.

As Tom approaches 17, his mother begins to say to his father, "I wish Tom could drive. I'm tired of having to drive him everywhere he needs to go. He really needs to be able to drive himself. He's almost old enough. I'm looking forward to his 17th birthday."

On Tom's 17th birthday, he is presented with a set of keys. He also gets his driver's license, which is like a special garment that shows he is permitted to exercise authority behind the wheel of a car.

(Meanwhile, Zork stole the car when he was 16, and drove it in a joyride that almost wrecked it. When he became 17, we told him that he would need to prove himself for a while before we would grant him car-privileges.)

Now, we could call this whole process Tom's "meriting" the right to drive. But notice that growing up in physical size, an essential aspect of Tom's maturation, actually has nothing to do with anything Tom has personally merited. Growing up in physical size is something God did, not something Tom merited. Hence, Tom's personal "character merit" is only part of the matter.

Additionally, "character merit" is far more than a summation of individual "merits." It is not actually merit at all, but character *development*. Faithful acts of obedience are part of the building up of his character, but character-building involves far more than simply adding up good works. It is a deepening of the consciousness and a development of wider awareness. Again, it is something God does far more than it is something Tom himself does.

Individual merits and rewards do play a part in Tom's life, but within the period of his childhood. Tom may have earned his allowance week by week (while Zork forfeited his), but there is no accumulation of merits that adds up to being allowed to drive the car. Merits and rewards function within a particular "covenant" situation: If you do your chores, you'll get your allowance. But merits and reward do not directly lead to or imply that a person must be installed in a new "covenant," a new life situation, as someone privileged to drive the family car. No matter now many chores Tom faithfully has performed by the time he is 14 years old, he will still not be allowed to drive the car. Driving the car is not a reward given in response to some particular work, or even to the accumulation of thousands of good works, but is a privilege bestowed on a person morally and physically and psychologically mature enough to be given it.

I trust that this father-son analogy has exposed the inadequacy of speaking of "works" or "merits" that "earn" mature privileges. What is involved is maturation, not merit. The ultimate root of maturation lies in the nature of the Logos. As the Father is the "root" of *being,* so the Son is the "root" of *becoming.* The Son is always fully mature, and equal to the Father, but also always fully *maturing.* This maturation is brought about, in the Godhead, by the Spirit who proceeds from the Father to the Son. The Logos is the root of human life as developing through the Spirit's influence from infancy to full maturity. In the Godhead, the Son is always growing and also always fully grown; in creation, the images of God grow toward maturity.[15]

As the rest of this paper will show, the transformation promised to Adam and achieved by Jesus was not something to be "earned" like a weekly allowance or like a payment for the accumulation of many good works, but was a mature privilege to be bestowed on Adam when he was old enough to receive it. Moreover, the sin of Adam was not a failure to do a good work and earn a merit, but was a rejection of the whole God-given process of maturation, because Adam prematurely seized the privilege that God had held out as the end of that process of maturation. Hence, Adam did not fail to earn a "merit," but short-circuited the whole process of human development.

The Adamic Covenant[16]

Our concern here is with what precisely Genesis 2–3 tells us about the Adamic Covenant. I believe that part of the failure of traditional Reformed theology lies right at this point. There has been a tendency to move from certain assumptions, derived rightly or wrongly from the New Testament, to a rather cursory reading—too often a misreading—of the data of Genesis 2–3. If we are to follow Murray's advice, we must begin with a careful examination of this text.

What follows is by no means a full exposition of that text. I have done that elsewhere, drawing from it for this essay.[17] Our concern is with particular aspects of the text that bear on the question of merit versus maturity.

The first seminal text is Genesis 2:16–17:

> And Yahweh God commanded the man, saying, "From any tree of the garden, eating you may eat. But from the tree of the knowledge of good and evil, you shall not eat from it, for in the day that you eat from it, dying you shall die."

Prior to this we have read:

> And Yahweh God caused to grow from the ground every tree, being pleasant to sight and good for food; and the tree of life was in the middle of the garden, and the tree of the knowledge of good and evil (Gen. 2:9).

From these two texts it appears that the Tree of Life was not forbidden to Adam. In fact, being in the center of the garden right next to the Tree of Knowledge, it is pointed out to him. His attention is focussed on it as well as on the Tree of Knowledge.

What is set before Adam is a choice. He is free to eat of every tree, including the special Tree of Life. He is forbidden to eat of the Tree of Knowledge. Approaching the garden's center, he must choose which of the Trees to eat first. If he rejects the Tree of Knowledge and partakes of the Tree of Life, he will enter into a process of further life that will eventuate in eternal life. Having obeyed God in faith at the outset, he will set himself on a road of further faithful obedience.[18] If, however, he chooses to eat of the Tree of Knowledge first, he will die and not move any farther down the road to eternal life.

We notice that there is nothing of "merit" or "work" here. Adam will become hungry, and he will have to eat. This is a necessity, not a work that can possibly merit anything. The choice before Adam is whether or not to trust and fear God's word. In short, the choice before him is whether to exercise faith or not. It is not a religious "work" that Adam is called to, but faith. Adam is impelled to make a choice. He has received life from God, but now he is hungry. Will he go to the Tree of Life in order to receive more life from God, or will he use his hunger as an opportunity to seize what God has forbidden him? Will he eat in faith, or in rebellion?

This will become important as we go along: Adam's need to eat is caused by his lack or need; by his hunger. It is need and lack, perhaps even a feeling of weakness, that causes him to go to the trees of the garden for food, food freely provided as a gift from God. So far from earning this food, Adam is given it as a free gift because he needs it. As we shall see, this is precisely what is involved in Adam's glorification. He is to be given it not because he has earned it, but because he desperately needs it in order to deal fully with the serpent.

The Prohibition on the Tree of Knowledge

There is more, however, that must be taken into account, and here is where tradition fails us more radically. God said to Adam that when he ate of the Tree of Knowledge he would die. But later on, after Eve was drawn from Adam's side, God told the two of them:

> And God said, "Behold, I give to you [plural] every grain-plant seeding seed that is on the face of the whole earth, and every tree that has in it fruit of a tree seeding seed. For you it shall be for food" (Gen. 1:29).

As I shall argue more thoroughly below, this statement implies that eventually Adam would indeed eat of the Tree of Knowledge. There seems to be no other possible way to take this promise.

From this, Adam learned that someday God would give him permission to eat of the Tree of Knowledge, and that on that day he would die. The Tree of Knowledge, then, not the Tree of Life, was the eschatological tree, the tree of promise. The Tree of Knowledge would end Adam's first phase of life.

We must not let later statements of the Bible about death blind us to what is said here. After the fall of man, death is always an enemy, but it is not quite death itself that is evil. Rather, as Paul insists, "The sting of death is sin" (1 Cor.15:56). Not death per se, but sin, is the problem. Sin is what makes death painful and horrible.

What did Adam already know about death? Perhaps nothing. Perhaps he had never seen what death means. But this is not true. In fact, Adam had already "died" and been resurrected to a new and fuller life.[19] This happened during the process whereby Eve was made from his side. This is recounted for us in Genesis 2:21–22:

> And Yahweh God caused to fall a deep-sleep [*tardema*] upon the man, and he slept [*yashan*]. And He took one of his sides, and He closed the

flesh in its place. And Yahweh God built the side that He took from the man into woman, and He brought her to the man.

It is important to understand that "deep-sleep" is not ordinary sleep. It is something like a coma. Adam is sufficiently unconscious that flesh can be ripped from his side without awakening him.

The Hebrew verb and noun for deep-sleep (*radam* and *tardema*) is not related at all to the ordinary verb for sleep (*yashan*). We ask the question, then, why does the Hebrew use a completely different word? Why not just say "deep sleep," using the adjective "deep" to modify the ordinary noun for sleep?

An investigation of the usage of the verb translated deep-sleep will reveal that it has a special meaning associated with death and with covenant-making acts of God. The first instance of it is here, where we see God separate the woman from the man and then join them in covenant.

Deep-sleep is close to death and is the place where covenants are made; it is a sleep that precedes either full death or resurrection. The term occurs in Judges 4:21, where Sisera falls into deep-sleep just before his head is crushed. Building upon this incident is 1 Samuel 26:12, when David finds Saul in deep-sleep and is given opportunity to crush his head, but merely removes items from around his head instead. Coming back to life from deep-sleep, Saul renews covenant with David (1 Sam. 26:13–25).

Jonah, fleeing from God, is found in deep-sleep in Jonah 1:5–6 (the word is found in both verses). Soon he will be cast overboard and experience death and resurrection in the belly of the great fish, renewing his covenant with God therein.

Some, like Sisera, move from deep-sleep to the total sleep of death. The Egyptian army was, like Jonah, in deep-sleep in the Red Sea, but they were not raised to life again:

> The stouthearted were plundered;
> They slumbered their sleep;
> And none of the men of might have found their hands.
> At Your rebuke, O God of Jacob,
> Both chariot and horse were cast into deep-sleep (Ps. 76:5–6).

Such is the case also in Isaiah 29:10: "For Yahweh has poured over you a spirit of deep-sleep." Similarly, the sluggard in his laziness is moving into a deep-sleep condition near death, and may starve to death (Prov. 19:15). The same fate awaits him who deep-sleeps during harvest (Prov. 10:5).

The man who is in deep-sleep and is headed for death is not conscious, but the man who is in deep-sleep and is headed for resurrection may be in a vision. Eliphaz claims to have had a vision while in deep-sleep (Job 4:13), and Elihu states that God visits men with visions while they are in deep-sleep (Job 33:15). As we shall see, Abram also experienced a vision in deep-sleep.

The association of deep-sleep with death and resurrection is clearly seen in Daniel. In Daniel 8:18, Daniel is told that he is going to be shown the end. Immediately he falls into deep-sleep, but then is raised to stand on his feet to be shown the vision. Similarly, as soon as Daniel hears the Angel of Yahweh speaking to him in Daniel 10:9, he falls into deep-sleep, from which he is raised to hear the message. This event is a type of the death and resurrection of Israel that is prophesied throughout the message and especially in Daniel 12:2; cp. 10:9, 15. An identical death-resurrection sequence is found in Revelation 1:17, where John fell at Jesus' feet "as a dead man" and then was raised again. John's death and resurrection is a type of the death and resurrection of the Church described in Revelation.[20]

In our survey we skipped Genesis 15, because it perhaps gives the fullest picture of this kind of event. At the beginning of this chapter, Abram has become aware that though God has promised him the land, he does not possess it. The land has refused to yield anything to him, forcing him by famine into Egypt. Then, when he finally returned to the land, a civil war raged over it, during which it became clear to him that he was not in charge of the land at all. Yet, Abram had defeated Chedorlaomer and had delivered Lot. Now Abram is afraid Chedorlaomer will return, and God appears to comfort him. During the night God tells him that his seed will be like the stars and that he will possess the land. Abram asks for assurance, and God tells him to cut three animals in half and to kill two birds. During the next day, Abram does this. Birds of prey seek to devour the carcasses, but Abram drives them away. Notice this: The animals are dead, but not devoured.

They are, symbolically speaking, in deep-sleep, but not yet dead. They are dead, but not under the curse-judgment of the covenant. Then Abram himself falls into deep-sleep (Genesis 15:12). While in this condition, Abram sees God pass between the parts of the animals.

This event is often misunderstood today. God is not saying, "May I be ripped in half and devoured by the birds if I don't keep this covenant." Rather, God is making a covenant between the two parts of the animals, which signify Abram on the one hand and the land on the other. This symbolism is possible because both man and the animals are made of soil, so animals can represent both soil and man. God's fiery Spirit will reunite the two halves of the broken covenant. Adam was cursed from the soil, and up to now Abram has experienced that curse. Now, however, God will resurrect that relationship by His Spirit, and on the basis of the death-sacrifice of a representative. The land will remain uncooperative for 400 years, but then will become a new and more glorious "land flowing with milk and honey."

We see that the covenant is made through death and resurrection. When we apply this sequence to Jesus, we can see immediately what it means. Jesus is the animal torn in half, but not cursed in His death. He dies, but does not undergo corruption. The birds do not devour Him, though He is hanged up and made available to them by His crucifixion (compare 2 Sam. 21:9–10). As the dead animals represented the estrangement between Abram and the land, so the death of Jesus is necessary because of the estrangement between God and mankind. Being both God and man, Jesus in His death takes upon Himself both sides of the estrangement. Then God's Spirit raises Jesus from the dead, passing between the two halves and granting covenant renewal. As the Spirit moved between the divided animals in Abram's vision, creating a bond between Abram and the land, so now after Pentecost the Spirit moves between God and mankind, creating a bond between them. Just as Abram and the land were both glorified after this death and resurrection event (Abram's being multiplied like the stars, and the land's becoming a land flowing with milk and honey), so also a new and glorious covenant comes about between God and man through the resurrection of Jesus, so that humanity no longer lives under the curse of the law but in the glories of the Kingdom of God.

For Abram to appreciate this, Abram too must die. He must enter deep-sleep and then awaken. So must we. We must die to the old broken, cursed, shattered covenant in Adam and be raised into the new covenant in Christ. Then we are restored to God, to one another, and to the world. Then the soil no longer curses us. God Himself is the bond of the new covenant.

Let us notice that Abram in no way earns this new covenant. In fact, he humbly asks God for it because of his need and lack, because of his weakness. He has matured in understanding his need as a result of the failure of the land to cooperate with him in Genesis 12–14.

The instances we have looked at all happened after the fall of man, and thus deep-sleep carries with it the possibility of final death, or of resurrection to the new creation. Before the fall, however, it did not carry this precise meaning. Adam goes into deep-sleep, and "dies" to his state of being alone.[21] Then, from his side, God makes a partner for him. When Adam awakens, he is in covenant union with his wife. This covenant is made through blood, for it is not just a rib but a whole flesh-and-bone (and hence blood) piece of Adam that is made into Eve; as Adam says, "This is flesh of my flesh, bone of my bone." And, Adam also says that man must "die" to his old family to make a new one: "For this cause a man shall leave his father and mother and cleave to his wife."

Thus, dying to the old and moving by resurrection into the new is not just something that comes into being because of the fall of man. Human life involves such passages even apart from sin. After the fall, of course, such transitions become much more traumatic, and in the greatest transition what we must leave behind is an old world of sin and what we are raised to is a new world in God's kingdom.[22]

The formation of Eve from Adam's side is fulfilled when the soldier pierces Jesus' side and blood and water come out of it. Jesus has died, but is not to be cursed. In that place of deep-sleep, His bride is formed. The Church is created on the basis of the blood of Christ, and by the water of baptism that comes from His side. It is the Spirit, the para-clete, the "side-comer," who comes from Jesus' side in baptismal water, and it is the Spirit who forms the bride.

Now, this survey has shown us what Adam could have and would have understood. When he ate of the Tree of Knowledge, he would undergo another "death," but be raised to a more glorious existence on the other side of that death.

We are now in a position to begin to understand the promise entailed in the Adamic Covenant. Many older Reformed theologians, not finding any particular promise in the text, have supposed that the Tree of Life was the promise. We can now understand that the temporary prohibition on the Tree of Knowledge was both a promise and a threat. It was a promise of "good-death" and resurrection, if Adam waited until God gave him permission to eat of it. It was a threat of "bad-death" if he seized the fruit prematurely.[23]

It is now clear what Adam was called to do. He was called to accept God's gracious provisions. He was called to live by faith in God's Word alone, for there was no obvious and visible reason for him to avoid the Tree of Knowledge—If Adam lived by sight and not by faith he would only see a special tree that was "pleasant to the sight and good for food" (Gen. 2:9; 3:6). He was called to work in the garden day by day, eating of the Tree of Life, and growing in that life. He was called to patience and maturation, until he was ready to be granted access to the glorifying Tree of Knowledge. He would be ready for it when he was fully aware of his need for what it bestowed.

The Nature of the Tree of Knowledge

The full name of the eschatological tree is "Tree of the Knowledge of Good and Evil." What was the Tree of the Knowledge of Good and Evil? It was a real tree with real fruit, and somehow man's interaction with that tree and fruit would produce in him knowledge of good and evil. There are three aspects of this situation we need to understand.

First, Adam and Eve already knew the difference between good and evil, right and wrong, in a moral and spiritual sense. They were made in God's image and had His moral character imprinted on their persons. They were not somehow ethically neutral. Genesis 1:28 says that God blessed Adam and Eve, and verse 31 says that they were very good. The fact that they were blessed and pronounced good certainly eliminates the possibility that they were somehow in a state of ethical neutrality. The Tree of the Knowledge of Good and Evil was *not* designed to teach Adam and Eve right from wrong.

Second, some have suggested that man would mature in his understanding of good and evil, of right and wrong, by refraining from eating of the tree. The discipline of agreeing with God and saying "no" to something that is in itself "a delight to the eyes and good for food" would have the effect of gradually bringing man into an evermore self-conscious understanding of what good and evil, in the sense of right and wrong, are. God's initial programming of goodness into man would be reinforced by man's conscious decision to pursue the good, which would deepen his moral consciousness and bring him into a greater state of maturity. I agree that this may be part of the meaning of the Tree of Knowledge, but there are two errors sometimes connected with this interpretation.

The first error is the idea that eating the fruit of the tree had nothing to do with good and evil; rather, it was the avoidance of the fruit that would bring about an increased understanding of good and evil, of right and wrong. As we shall see, however, "knowledge of good and evil" has a particular meaning that must be associated with actually eating the fruit. The prohibition was temporary. Holding off from the Tree of Knowledge was a form of fasting. When God was ready, man would be allowed to eat and acquire "knowledge of good and evil" in a special sense. This will be developed as we go along.

The second error commonly encountered is that man somehow knew that he was not to eat of the Tree of Life until God was ready to let him do so. Passing the test of the Tree of Knowledge would lead to the reward of the Tree of Life. This is based on sheer supposition. As we have seen, Adam was invited to the Tree of Life from the beginning.

The third thing to understand concerning the Tree of Knowledge is that eating the fruit of this tree was a designed to effect a change in man's position. The phrase "knowledge of good and evil" has to do with rule and authority, the right to pass judgments, to right to act as a god under the authority of God. Evidence for this interpretation comes right from the context itself, for in Genesis 1 and 2 it is God who repeatedly passes judgments: "God saw that it was good"; "God saw that it was very good"; "It is not good for the man to be alone." Thus, for man to acquire knowledge of good and evil means, in context, that man would acquire the privilege of making judicial pronouncements.

Indeed, the rest of Scripture confirms this. Solomon prays to be given "an understanding heart to judge Your people, to discern between good and evil. For who is able to judge this Your weighty people?" (1 Kings 3:9). God grants this kingly request—we notice that Solomon does not assume that he already possesses this discernment—and immediately we see Solomon exercise just judgment (1 Kings 3:28).

Similarly, the wise woman of Tekoa said to David, "For as the angel of God, so is my lord the king to discern good and evil" (2 Sam. 14:17). In other words, man's judicial authority is a copy of God's. The angel of God has wisdom to "know all that is in the earth" (2 Sam. 14:20), and such knowing entails seeing: "My lord the king is like the angel of God, therefore do what is good in your sight" (2 Sam. 19:27). When Laban pursued Jacob, God appeared to him and told him not to pass judgment on Jacob: "Take heed to yourself that you do not speak to Jacob either good or evil" (Gen. 31:24).

Infants, such as Adam and Eve were, do not have the wisdom to know good and evil in this judicial sense (Deut.1:39), and sometimes the aged lose this capacity due to senility (2 Sam. 19:35).[24]

Thus, the Tree of the Knowledge of Good and Evil does not have primarily to do with moral knowledge but with judicial knowledge. According to Genesis 1:29, the fruit of every tree was made for man to eat. Hence, the prohibition on the tree of knowledge was temporary. Refraining from it involved fasting from something for which they were not ready, and this period of fasting was designed to work into their hearts the dispositions needed for proper exercise of judicial authority.

The author of Hebrews puts it this way: "For everyone who partakes of milk is not accustomed to the word of righteousness, for he is a babe; but solid food is for the mature, who because of practice have their senses trained to discern good and evil" (Heb. 5:13–14). What Hebrews says is applicable to Adam and Eve. Being newly created, as babies, they were naked. They had not yet had any experiences at all. Only through experience in the garden would they gradually have their senses trained to discern good and evil. They would not be learning right from wrong, but how to make good judgments. They were fed on milk-like "baby food," consisting of all the trees and particularly the Tree of Life. Once they had had their senses trained, which would come as a result of interaction with the wicked serpent, they would acquire a knowledge of good and evil, and be ready for the Tree of the Knowledge of Good and Evil—"solid food."

Further confirmation of this understanding is found in Genesis 3:4–7 and 22:

> And the serpent said to the woman, "Not dying you shall die. For God is knowing that in the day of your eating from it your eyes will be opened and you will be like God, knowing good and evil."

> And the woman saw that good was the tree for food, and that pleasant was it to the eyes, and desirable was the tree for gaining wisdom . . .

> And the eyes of both of them were opened, and they knew that they were naked . . .

> And Yahweh God said, "Behold, the man has become like one of us, knowing good and evil. And now lest he send out his hand and take also from the tree of life and eat and live forever . . . "

Several aspects of these statements call for our attention. First, it is clear that what the serpent said was not wrong, save in his flat contradiction of God's threat-promise of death. God Himself says—and there is no irony to be imported into this statement—that the man has become like God, and has acquired knowledge of good and evil, has acquired judicial authority. Moreover, the serpent rightly said that their eyes would be opened when they ate of the fruit, for that is in fact just what happened.

Adam and Eve were already made in the "likeness" of God (1:26), so how could they become more "like" God? And of course they were able to see, for Eve saw that the fruit was good to eat and a delight to the eyes (as was true of all the garden's trees; 2:9). Obviously, the opening of the eyes and the matter of becoming "like God" have particular meanings, and once again, the rest of the Bible helps us understand what these are.

Concerning the opening of the eyes, we have already seen from Genesis 1 that the special sense of sight involved judging and evaluating things: "God *saw* that it was *good.*" It is, in a word, kingly sight. The following passages in the Bible can be consulted for more information on this: 2 Samuel 19:27; Psalm 11:4; Jeremiah 32:18–19; Isaiah 44:9; Ezekiel 5:11; 7:4; 20:17.

Concerning God-likeness, we find that rulers and judges are called gods (*elohim*) in Exodus 21:6; 22:8, 28; Psalm 82, and John 10:34.

Hence these expressions conform to the meaning of "good and evil." We can summarize what the Tree of the Knowledge of Good and Evil bestows as saying that it bestows kingship, the right to pass godly judgments as those mature in God-likeness.

Adam had made himself a king. He had prematurely seized the robe of authority, instead of waiting patiently for it to be bestowed upon him.[25] We can contrast David, who refused steadfastly to seize the kingdom from Saul, and who repented when he cut off a corner of Saul's kingly robe. We can contrast Jesus, who refused any crown until the Father bestowed it upon Him at His ascension. We can remember that a defining mark of true faith is patient waiting: "And thus, having patiently waited, [Abraham] received the promise" (Heb. 6:15).

Shame and Glory

Genesis 2:25 says: "Now the two of them were naked, the man and his woman, and they did not sense shame." The nakedness of Adam and Eve requires several comments. First of all, against those who think that nakedness is what God intended for humanity as a permanent estate, we have to notice that God Himself is robed in a glory cloud whenever He appears in the Bible. Human beings, as the images of God, would also wear garments of glory and beauty. After all, we do not dress only to cover our private parts. We wear clothes of color and design (beauty), to express ourselves, signify our office or work, and impress others (glory). Eventually, Adam and Eve would also wear garments of glory and beauty. When they became "like God" in the fuller sense, they would, like God, be robed in glory.

Second, Adam was naked because he was a newborn babe. As we have seen, the concept of the "knowledge of good and evil" is associated with the robe of office, of rule and authority. Adam did not yet have the capacity for this. He was a newborn babe, partaking only of milk, as Paul writes in Hebrews 5:13–14. The fact that Adam sinned as a baby, and not as a mature adult having full knowledge of the truth, is what made it possible for God to redeem him (Gen. 3:22; Heb. 6:4–6).

Third, Adam and Eve were naked to each other because they were married. The married couple are clothed together in one garment, not two separate ones. There were no barriers between them because they were not ashamed before one another. If a married couple cannot get openly naked with each other, there is a problem that needs to be resolved.

Once Adam and Eve had sinned, they felt shame before God, so they hid from Him, and before one another, so they created clothing to put a barrier between themselves. Formerly they had been surrounded together by leaves. Now each makes his own garment. Formerly they walked openly in the garden. Now they hide from God under the leaves of a tree.[26]

When God interviewed Adam, the man said that he was afraid because he was naked, and therefore hid himself. Clothing is a barrier, and thus reduces fear. Lecturers usually prefer to stand behind a podium, because it protects them from their hearers, whom they fear ("How will these people receive what I have to say?"). Only an accomplished speaker can do without one.

Shame is not guilt. Shame means a feeling of weakness and impotence. Adam and Eve felt shame because they had seized adult privileges, seized the right to rule, but did not have the inner maturity to exercise these privileges. They felt weak and impotent. They needed the "prop" of garments to make up for their inner immaturity and powerlessness.

The true garment is glory added to nakedness. We see this in the transfigured and resurrected body of Jesus. Jesus left behind His garments on the cross and in the tomb, but He was not naked. His new body shone with glory. The garments of glory and beauty given to sinful man are only a symbolic anticipation of the transfigured glory-body that is to come. These garments, these "coverings," make up for what is lacking in the immature human consciousness.

In his 1975 book, *Naked and Not Ashamed* (privately published), Lowell Noble writes:

> Insight into the meaning of shame can be gained by contrasting it with honor. Honor and shame are two sides of the same coin. Dishonor is a

synonym of shame. Honor refers to upright character, integrity, glory. While honor may be involved in acts of right and wrong, it goes far beyond what the law requires. Honor involves the integrity of one's being in the way he lives and in the way he respects others.

The loss of honor is disgraceful, shameful. Therefore, a person attempts to cover up, to hide, so as to avoid painful exposure. The shameless person has no sense of honor; he engages in disgraceful behavior openly.

Even though there is a painful negative element in an experience of shame, the importance of shame must not be restricted to the negative aspect. An experience of shame exposes what is wrong with the goal of showing what is right and moving a person in that direction. A person can refuse to move towards honorable behavior and again revert to hiding behind his mask to try to cover his shame. The function of anticipated shame is to keep a person doing what is honorable. Anticipated shame serves as a powerful force for social control.[27]

As Noble notes, shame involves loss of glory. In the Bible, glory is beautiful clothing; consider the glory cloud around God. Thus, when a person loses glory or "face," and experiences shame, he moves instantly to cover or re-cover himself as fast as possible. Since the glory-covering exists as people as well as physical clothing (as the glory cloud around God consists of myriads of angels and saints), a person loses glory or face when he is betrayed and/or abandoned by those around him. If he is excommunicated from the Church, or otherwise isolated, he must act to find a new social group to act as his clothing. Thus Cain, expelled from God's community, went forth and created a city for himself. Thus those who leave the true Church become active in founding or promoting false ones.[28]

Shame also involves the loss of a sense of integrity. Integrity is the inner side (what Noble calls "honor"), while glory is the outer side.[29] The Biblical word for integrity is "holiness." God is holy (has integrity), and so we must be holy as He is holy. Holiness does not mean "set apartness," because it makes no sense for God to command, "You be set apart as I am set apart." Rather, holiness means inner integrity, both the metaphysical integrity of being a unique person and being personally inviolate, and the moral integrity of being in conformity to God's image.

Hence, when a person's integrity is violated, he feels shame. If his beard is torn off, or if his clothing is ripped, or if people praise others more than they do him, he loses glory and feels shame (2 Sam. 10:4–5; 1 Sam. 15:27–30 [Samuel tore Saul's robe here]; 1 Sam. 18:6–9). If his or her body is raped (2 Sam. 13:12–19), or his house is broken into and robbed, or if he commits a sin, or if he does a poor job of something, he loses integrity and feels shame.

Both sides of this experience (loss of glory, loss of integrity) are expressed by the term "nakedness." A person feels naked and exposed if any of these things happen to him. Thus, in Leviticus 18, it is a violation of a person's holiness to expose his or her nakedness. Forbidden sexual invasions of another person's body defile holiness and expose nakedness.

When we feel naked and ashamed, we can do either of two things. We can draw close to God and let Him restore us, or we can try to recover ourselves, try to keep with the old situation by getting our glory back. Consider an example. When the people sang, "Saul has slain his thousands, but David his myriads," Saul lost glory and felt burning shame. He could have gone before God, poured out his heart, and adjusted to the new situation. Out of his sense of loss (death) would have come a *new* life. Then he would have felt good that God had given him a young warrior—indeed, his adopted son—to help the kingdom. He would have acquired a new a sense of personhood and worth—integrity—and would not have felt ashamed and exposed. But this is not what Saul chose to do. Instead, he tried to kill David, and thereby get the original glory back for himself. He tried to turn the clock back, instead of moving into God's future.

Oddly enough, we feel shame sometimes even when we have done nothing wrong. Ravished women, for instance, usually feel intense shame. Why is this? It is because we are sinners; that is, we carry original sin, basic sin, in our inner parts (flesh) always. When we are overcome with guiltless shame, this is a sign that we need to "make our calling and election sure" by returning to the fact that we are fully justified. "There is therefore now no condemnation [no shame] to those who are in Christ Jesus." God graciously provides times of guiltless shame in order to draw us closer to Him, so that we become more secure in the knowledge of our justified position with Him.

When God restores us, He first declares us just before Him (justification), and then restores our holiness and integrity (sanctification), in order that He might then give us glory and glorious covering (glorification). Sinful man, however, seeks glory without first seeking justification and sanctification (integrity).

To seek one's own glory results in that glory's turning into shame (Hos. 4:7; Jer. 9:23f. & 1 Cor. 1:26–29). This is what happened to Adam and Eve. The Tree of Knowledge, as we have seen, is the Tree of Eldership, Rule, and Glory. By seizing it, they sought their own glory, and found only shame. They did not need justification, for they were sinless, but they had not matured in holiness (integrity) when they seized glory. Being inwardly weak and immature, they could not bear up under the "weight" of glory (2 Cor. 4:17). It is no accident that the Hebrew word for glory (*kabhod*) literally means "heavy."

Then, instead of drawing near to God, admitting fault, and receiving justifying forgiveness and sanctifying integrity from Him in their new situation, they tried to re-cover themselves. The Garden had been their common garment, and they sought to reinforce that covering with the leaves of the trees of the Garden. Thus, *they sought to deal with shame without dealing with guilt and sin.* When God slew an animal and gave them animal skins to clothe them, He was moving them into a new future. God dealt with their guilt, and provided glory to them, but a new glory—a new covering appropriate to their new situation.[30]

As we have seen, the Bible has a huge amount to say about shame, and we have only touched on it here. Paul writes, "All have sinned and fallen short of the glory of God." He did not write, "fallen short of the righteousness of God." Paul refers back to Adam and Eve, and to the basic problem of integrity and glory.

Our theology deals largely with justification and sanctification, and hardly at all with glorification. We tend to postpone glorification until the resurrection. This is a serious defect in our theology, which blinds us to a great deal that is in the Bible. As Paul says, believers grow "from glory to glory" (2 Cor. 3:18).

Shame is not the root but the fruit of sin. Shame is pain that alerts us that something is wrong, but we must not try to deal directly with shame by trying to re-cover ourselves and recover our former glory or situation. Rather, we must deal with our guilt and sin, and then the shame is removed, enabling us to move into a *new* life-situation.

Investiture

We have seen that Adam was not called upon to merit anything at all. He was not called upon to do any works that would earn anything. He was called upon to remain faithful to God day by day, and patiently wait until God deemed him mature enough to be given kingly prerogatives.

We have seen that if Adam had chosen the right path and gone to the Tree of Life first, he would have been sealed into a path of maturation that would lead to the death and transfiguration promised in connection with the Tree of Knowledge. For Adam to eat of the Tree of Life after his sin, however, would seal him in a path of death and destruction, and this God graciously prevented his doing.

All the same, having prematurely usurped the right to pass kingly judgments, Adam found that God honored his decision. First God called upon Adam to judge himself, and Adam failed miserably, blaming God Himself ("the woman You gave to be with me") and his wife ("she gave me from the tree").[31] Adam comes to renewed faith only when he accepts God's statement that the woman will be the mother of all living, of all future life in the Messiah to come (Gen. 3:15, 20).

Second, God sent Adam into the wider world, and then expelled him (3:23–24). Evidently Adam was reluctant to leave the garden.[32] He wanted to ascend to a throne, but now realized that he was far from ready for this responsibility.

The contrast between the garden and the outer world has been established in 2:8–14. The garden was quite properly a kindergarten, a place where Adam could grow from childhood to kingly maturity. The garden was the place of an easy life, with free food. It was a place of learning how to cultivate and guard. Cultivating and guarding the outer world would require more wisdom to deal with greater difficulties that Adam would joyously overcome as he developed from initial glory (from the Tree of Knowledge) to final glory.[33] The outer world was the place into which the Tree of Knowledge would usher him when he was mature enough to go there. Had Adam not sinned, he might have returned sabbath by sabbath to the garden and its central sanctuary. Because of his sin, to protect him, God did not permit him back into the garden, but, honoring Adam's eating of the Tree of Knowledge, did send him out into the kingly world.

God graciously did not send the child Adam into the world unprepared. God's slaughter of the animal to provide royal tunics (Gen. 3:21) for Adam and Eve had the twin meaning of investing them as king and queen, and also of covering their sin until the Messiah should come and remove it. We must now consider the meaning of the royal tunics.

The fact that Adam and Eve became aware of their nakedness when they ate from the Tree of Knowledge means that investiture with some kind of garment was part of the meaning of that Tree. The garment made by Adam and Eve was inadequate. They sought to re-cover themselves in garden materials (leaves). Their nakedness was already covered by the garden's vegetation as a whole, but now they sought to bind that garden-covering around themselves more fully. Each sought his own garment, thus breaking their one-flesh union.

The Tree of Knowledge has to do with death. If Adam and Eve had waited for God to let them eat from the Tree, they would have passed through a "good-death" into a more glorious existence, either consisting of or (more likely) pointing forward to the glorious garment of the transfigured resurrection body that Jesus displayed after His resurrection.

Adam and Eve did not pass through "good death" and thus did not receive glorification as a result of eating from the Tree of Knowledge. Having eaten of the Tree of Knowledge, they became aware that they needed garments, and that they did not have them. God is quite emphatic about this: The fact that they knew they needed garments was proof that they had eaten of the Tree of Knowledge (Gen. 3:11), for God knew that it was too early in their lives for them to become aware of such a need before eating from the Tree.

The Tree of Knowledge is the Tree of Death. Since Adam and Eve ate from it, there needs to be some kind of death. If God now brings death to Adam and Eve, it will be a "bad death" from which they will not rise in glorious garments. Like human beings, and unlike plants, animals have the "breath of life," and so an animal is put through death in order to provide glorious garments for Adam and Eve.[34]

Living in the garden, Adam and Eve were already surrounded by and clothed by plants. The transition through which the Tree of Knowledge took them results in their being clothed by animals. The fact that

God bestows this garment shows us again that the Tree of Knowledge involved investiture by God: When Adam and Eve were ready, God would bring them to the Tree of Knowledge, take them through death and resurrection, and clothe them in royal garments.

The word "tunic" (*k-thoneth*) indicates a garment of privilege. It is used eight more times in Genesis—in Genesis 37:3 for the tunic Jacob made for Joseph as a sign of his authority, and then seven more times in 37:23–33 in the story of the brothers' attack upon Joseph. The seven-fold use of the term in this passage indicates that it was the garment as a sign of authority that was a large part of what provoked the brothers.

The same kind of garment was worn by the daughters of King David (2 Sam. 13:18, 19). It was also worn by Hushai the Archite, who tore it (2 Sam. 15:32). Hushai is called "David's Friend," a title indicating that he was David's chief counsellor. Compare Abraham as God's Friend, and Jesus' statement that we are no longer His servants but His friends because He has told us everything (Jas. 2:23; John 15:15; Gen. 18:17ff.; 1 Kings 4:5). When Hushai tears his garment, it is a sign that the royal house and the kingdom have been torn.

Tunics were included in the garments of the priests of Israel (Ex. 28:4, 39, 40; 29:5, 8; 39:27; 40:14; Lev. 8:7, 13; 10:5; 16:4). These tunics were made of pure linen, which is vegetable fibre, in contrast to the tunics of animal skins placed upon Adam and Eve. The pure linen garments are said to be "holy," and the multicolored sash that bound it (Ex. 39:29), with the other outer garments, are said to be "for glory and beauty." Since the colored yarns were made of wool, from animals, there is a link to God's covering Adam and Eve in garments of rudimentary glory.[35]

Leviticus 16 delineates the ritual of the Day of Covering (which is the accurate translation; not "Day of Atonement"). On this day, the Cover (not "Mercy Seat") of the Ark of the Covenant was covered by blood sprinkled on it. That Cover represented the firmament between heaven and earth,[36] and blood put upon it meant that God viewed the world through the blood of a propitiatory offering. The world of God's people, Jew and Gentile (16:29–31), was covered by this blood, under the protection of this blood, which averted His wrath. The High Priest wore only special linen garments while doing this ritual. At the end of the ritual, the High Priest would put back on his garments of glory and beauty, and thus he was re-covered as God's High Priest. In other words, the High Priest was restored to a position of glory and rule on the basis of the shed blood of the animal sacrifices, and this was signified by his being re-covered with garments made of both vegetable and animal fibers.

In short, on the Day of Covering, the High Priest (representing all God's people) replayed the events of Genesis 3. First he was covered in linen, vegetable. Then animals were killed. Then he was covered in glorious linen + wool, animal skins. His glory garments also included a third element, minerals (gold and gemstones). The implications of this will concern us later on.

With all this information in mind, we can see that God was honoring Adam and Eve as royalty, with a kind of glory, when He gave them tunics. They had made aprons from vegetable leaves to cover their shame, but God does something much more than give them better aprons. He gives them glory.

We might see all this as somehow ironic or sarcastic on God's part: "Well, you've made yourselves kings by seizing the forbidden fruit before you were ready for it, so now I'll dress you with royal garments." But we have seen that Adam has repented and has accepted God's word by calling Eve the mother of all future life. It is true that there is no going back. Adam and Eve cannot return to being babies in the garden. They have indeed made themselves kings prematurely; but when they repent God promises to enable them to grow into being true kings in spite of their sin. By the blood, they are covered. And by the blood, the covering they receive is a sign of privilege and glory.

Moreover, as with Joseph, Hushai, the priests, and the Davidic princesses, the tunic is a sign of princely rule under a father or king. It is a sign of authority, but authority that is in submission to higher authority.

It should be noted also that the seamless garment stripped from Jesus at His crucifixion was a tunic, the Greek word being equivalent to the Hebrew (John 19:23–24). The temporary royal covering provided for Adam by God is now removed from Jesus, so that He is naked like Adam in the garden. Passing through the death of the Tree of Knowledge (i.e., the cross), Jesus is raised in the fullness of what glorious garments meant: a glorified body.

Adamic Maturation

We are now in a position to reflect more fully on what Adam's time in the garden was supposed to bring about. We have seen that everything about the Tree of Knowledge has to do with death and resurrection into a kingly status. To review: The Tree of Knowledge is associated with:

1. a new opening of eyes to pass judgments;
2. a knowledge of judicial matters, good and evil;
3. becoming more like God;
4. being invested in a royal tunic;
5. being sent out into the wider world from the garden;
6. empowerment.

In the garden, Adam was not supposed to earn anything, but he was supposed to grow in awareness of what he lacked. This had already happened once. Adam's naming the animals did not merit him anything, but it taught him that he lacked a helper. Then he was ready to go through a death and resurrection experience and receive a more glorious life with a wife.

This and precisely this is what the rest of the story is about. Just as God brought animals to Adam to name, so God allows an animal into the garden for Adam to deal with. Genesis 2:15 outlines Adam's course of education: he was (first) to cultivate and (second) to guard the garden. The first animal experience taught him that he needed a helper for his work of cultivation. The second animal experience was to teach him that he needed royal authority to help him guard the garden.

The statement in Genesis 3:6 that the woman gave "to her husband with her, and he ate," can only mean that Adam was present during the conversation. The phrase "with her" is meaningless otherwise. Moreover, the paragraph that narrates the fall is bookended by the statement in 2:24, "and the man and his wife were both naked and were not ashamed," and 3:7, "and the eyes of them both were opened and they knew that they were naked."[37] The whole paragraph is chiastically structured:

A. Shameless nakedness (2:25)
  B. Crafty wisdom of serpent (3:1a)
    C. Serpent asks about eating (3:1b)
      D. Woman speaks of death (3:2–3)
    C' Serpent promises about eating (3:4–5)
  B' Humanity adopts crafty wisdom of serpent (3:6)
A' Shameful nakedness (3:7a)

From this structure we also see that Adam was present throughout the event.

Adam was to guard the garden, and Eve is now in the garden. He is to guard her. That, of course, is what he fails to do. We remember that Eve has gotten her knowledge about the forbidden fruit from Adam. The serpent challenges Eve, and then explicitly denies God's word. The conversation has been nothing more than an educational experience up to that point, as the serpent asks Eve to think about things. But when he contradicts God, it is clearly Adam's duty to step in. He must rebuke the serpent and protect his wife.[38]

This is the holy war. Adam's weapon will be his words, as we see in Jude 9: Michael fought with Satan by saying "The Lord rebuke you." Adam could say that and score a temporary victory. But Adam could not drive the serpent from the garden, and he was certainly not ready to combat the serpent in the outer world.

The reason is that during our childhood, humanity was under angelic tutors (Heb. 1–2; Acts 7:53; Gal. 3:19), and was lower than the angels (Ps. 8:5). From this weak position, Adam would not have been able to deal with the serpent, for Satan was behind the serpent. It is at this point that Adam would have begun to realize that just as he needed a helper to do his work of cultivation, so now he needed power and glory to do his work of guarding. He must be elevated over the angels, crowned with glory and honor (Ps. 8:5b; 1 Cor. 6:3). We may readily suppose that it would have been at this point that Adam would become conscious of his nakedness, and of the need for glorious and judicially-empowering clothing. Adam would bring his problem before Yahweh, and Yahweh would point him to the Tree of the Knowledge of Good and Evil.

Jesus rebukes Satan, but Satan returns again and again. After His resurrection, however, Jesus can both bind Satan and also give the power to crush Satan to all His people in union with His glorification (Rom. 16:20). Jesus, as New Adam, shows what Adam's own situation was. Unlike Adam, Jesus constantly protected His bride: "I guarded them, and not one of them perished but the son of Perdition [Satan]" (John 17:12). When the son of Perdition came with soldiers to the garden (note!) of Gethsemane, Jesus protected the disciples: "If you seek Me, let these go their way" (John 18:8). But in order to give full and complete protection to His bride, Jesus would have to go to the Tree of Knowledge and die.

Such, then, was the process of education before Adam. We cannot know explicitly what steps might have been involved. Perhaps after protecting his wife, Adam would instantly have known that he needed the kingly and glorifying gift of the Tree of Knowledge. Perhaps he would have asked Yahweh for that gift, and died and been glorified on that same day.

It seems more likely, however, that a time of maturation in awareness would be involved. Satan would continue to attack Eve, and Adam would continue to have to defend her. The attacks might become physical, for Satan's attacks are certainly physical in the rest of the Bible. Adam would fight as a warrior prince, and become more and more aware that he needed full kingly powers. He would need not only the power of the Word, to rebuke Satan, but the power of the Spirit, to overcome and crush him.

At some point, perhaps, Satan would try to kill Eve, and Adam would have to sacrifice himself to save her. He would go to God and say, "I now know what death means. I am willing to die to save Eve. Not my will, but Yours be done." I think we can say that at that point, God would give Adam permission to eat of the Tree of Knowledge. Not Satan but God would put Adam to death, and then raise him glorified and empowered to cast Satan from the garden forever.

Or perhaps better, the hypothetical conversation would have gone like this:

Adam: I must destroy this serpent, or at least drive him from the garden. I fear for Eve. I feel weak and naked. I'm desperate. I love Eve, and will do anything to protect her.

Yahweh: Yes, and I can provide you what you need. You need a royal garment, and then you can exercise judgment and exile the serpent from the garden.

Adam: How will You do this for me?

Yahweh: I now hereby give you permission to eat from the Tree of the Knowledge of Good and Evil. It will make you into a judge and ruler, and I will invest you with robes of authority.

Adam: But You have said that I will surely die when I eat from it?

Yahweh: Yes, you will.

Adam: Will I rise again? Is that what You have in mind?

Yahweh: Think about it, my son. What has happened to you already?

Adam: Well, I did go into a deep-sleep when I became aware that I needed a helper fit for me. But if I go into deep-sleep again, or down even deeper into this "death" state, I'll be unconscious. How can I protect Eve if the serpent attacks her again while I'm in this "death" state?

Yahweh: Do you trust Me? Do you trust Me fully, my son? Are you ready and willing to commit your spirit into My care, and also commend Eve into My care?

Adam: Yes.

Yahweh: Then eat, and do not doubt.

Adam must mature in faith to the point where he is ready to die for Eve. We see a perfect example of this in Romans 9:3, where Paul writes, "For I could pray that I myself were accursed away from Christ for the sake of my brethren, my kinsmen according to the flesh." In order to defeat Satan, who had Israel in his grip, Paul is ready to die and be separated from God, confident we may be sure of eventual resurrection, since he had the example of what happened to Jesus before him. Moses had prayed the same way in Exodus 32:32. When Adam was ready to die for Eve, God would bring him to the Tree of Death and Glory.

Let us return to the garments given to Adam. We now know that Adam must deal with the serpent, but he does not have the full ability to do so. Specifically, Adam must exile the serpent to protect Eve and guard the garden. He needs the empowerment of the Tree of Knowledge in order to do this. After prematurely eating of that Tree, Adam still does not have the power to deal with the serpent, so God does it for him. God kills an animal and uses its skins to cover Adam and Eve. If this was not the serpent itself, it is symbolically equivalent.

The Holy War and the Messiah

We are now in a position to reflect fully on the nature of Adam's projected sojourn in the garden. It was a time of childhood, during which he would grow in wisdom. He needed a wife to develop his strength in the area of the "cultural mandate," and from naming the animals he learned of his need. Putting Adam into a death-like coma, God freely gave him what he had learned that he needed. Thereafter, Adam would mature in strength and wisdom in the area of the cultural mandate.

But Adam must also mature in the area of the religious mandate, guarding the garden. Proper guarding means siding with God against God's enemies, and protecting the bride. As Adam fights the serpent day after day, he does not move from strength to strength so much as he becomes more and more aware of his weakness. This is not a process of merit and works, but precisely the opposite! It is a process of pro-gressively experienced impotence. Adam comes to see that he needs the power to deal with the serpent once and for all, and that in order to have that power he must be glorified above the angelic world. Another death, a more serious one, awaits him.

These are not two separate developments. The more Adam devel-ops in his knowledge of the world and of the garden—the more he grows in strength in the cultural mandate area, the more aware he becomes of his need for empowerment to deal with the serpent. The more he loves the garden, and especially the more he matures in love for Eve, the more concerned he becomes to exile the serpent and deliver Eve and the garden from his baleful influences. Hence, maturing from strength to strength in the area of cultivating the garden is accompa-nied in growing from "weakness to weakness" in the area of guarding the garden.

Another way to put the matter is this: In the area of the cultural mandate, of Adam's work with the world, his activity is in the fore-ground and his faith-trust in God is in the background. He is still trusting God, but not as a conscious act. His faith is a "subconscious presupposition" behind what he is putting his mind and hands to performing In the area of the religious mandate, the emphasis is reversed. Adam has to think about his trust and faith in God, and perform acts of faith. Activity (works) are present, but the activity is that of reminding himself to trust God, and the activity of worshipping God.

Adam's religious maturation is a growth in faith. He sees more and more that he must depend wholly on God for the victory over Satan. He becomes more and more aware of his own powerlessness, and of God's power and promise. While he develops in strength in his interaction with the world "below" him, he develops in faith, in awareness of need, in his interaction with the God "above" him.

Hence, faith and works must be distinguished, but cannot be separated. Faith is the attitude that accompanies work, either true faith in the true God, or false faith in a false god. At certain "sabbath" times, however, faith comes into the foreground, and specific acts (works) of faith are engaged in. Such sabbath times are not only the weekly sabbath, but also crises in our lives and in history ("days of the Lord," to use biblical language). In such times, we have to concentrate on our trust in God, renewing and developing our faith. There can be no doubt but that the serpent's attack, requiring Adam to concentrate on his faith in God or reject Him, came on the first sabbath day. Man was made on the sixth day, and received his wife on that day. The next day, God came to the garden for special fellowship with Adam and Eve.[39] This was the sabbath day, the time when Adam would need to set aside his cultural labors and focus his attention on worship.

When God saw that Adam was ready, God would allow him to eat of the Tree of Knowledge. Adam would eat of the Tree, fall into death, and be raised empowered to deal with the serpent. He would kill the serpent, and the skin of the serpent would become part of his glorious clothing. He would then be ready to move into the outer world as a king.

I believe that at this point, Eve would also be given the fruit of the Tree of Knowledge, and would join her husband as world-ruler. Jesus said, "Greater love has no one than this, that he lay down his life for his friends." Adam would come the point of laying down his life in order to protect and guard Eve. We see from the New Testament that first

Jesus and afterward His Bride are glorified. This is the true order that Adam allowed to be reversed in the fall, when he allowed Eve to eat first.

I hesitate to bring this up, but for a full discussion of Adamic maturation I must do so. I believe that what follows is important, even essential. I ask you, courteous and kind reader, graciously to allow me to set it forth; and I plead with you not to reject it out of hand, but to consider it thoughtfully.

It is often thought that the only reason the Son of God became incarnate was to deal with Adam's sin. Most people do not think this through. If they did, they would realize that it is a problematic idea, for it means that the only reason humanity becomes the Bride of Christ is because of the fall of Adam. And this means that the fall was a good thing. The notion that the fall was a good thing is called the doctrine or heresy of the felicitous fall.[40]

This is a thorny question, and theologians have been divided on the question for centuries. Louis Berkhof summarizes:

> Rupert of Deutz was the first to assert clearly and positively that He would have become incarnate irrespective of sin. His view was shared by Alexander of Hales and Duns Scotus, but Thomas Aquinas took the position that the reason for the incarnation lay in the entrance of sin into the world. The Reformers shared this view, and the churches of the Reformation teach that the incarnation was necessitated by the fall of man. Some Lutheran and Reformed scholars, however, such as Osiander, Rothe, Dorner, Lange, Van Oosterzee, Martesen, Ebrard, and Westcott, were of the contrary opinion.[41]

Berkhof himself struggles with this view, but ultimately rejects it because he thinks it moves in a pantheistic direction.[42] But he summarizes it well when he writes, "He is Mediator, but also Head; He is not only the *arche*, but also the *telos* of creation, 1 Corinthians 15:45–47; Ephesians 1:10, 21–23; 5:31, 32; Colossians 1:15–17."[43]

I can perceive nothing that is pantheistic about the notion that God's design, even if man had not fallen, was to bring His Son into the world to bring about the final transfiguration of humanity and to be a Husband to the human Bride. After all, there is nothing humiliating about the incarnation itself. If a man makes a beautiful garment, it is not humiliating but glorifying for him to put it on and wear it. The creation was and is good, indeed "very good." It is entirely fitting for the Creator to put on the creation as a garment, to be incarnate into the world. And after all, the Holy Spirit was present in the creation from the beginning (Gen. 1:2). Was it a humiliation for the Spirit to be housed in God's good creation?

Of course, because of Adam's sin, the Son came into the world in a body that was under the debilitating effects of judgment. The actual event of the incarnation included humiliating aspects. And of course, because of Adam's sin, the Son had to go to the cross and take the sting of death for humanity.

I am persuaded that the incarnation of the Son of God, who would also be a son of Adam, was planned all along, apart from sin. As far as I can see, the only alternative to this idea is that of a felicitous fall, and I do not believe this doctrine can be entertained. Orthodox Christian theologians, like Berkhof, distinguish between the predestinating will of God and the moral will of God. This is an inescapable distinction, and should be acknowledged by all thinking people. God predestinated the fall of Adam, but did not wish for Adam to sin. We as human beings cannot fully comprehend how this could be, but it must be so. It is impossible that anything should happen that God does not wish to happen in some sense (predestinating will), but on the other hand, the holy God cannot wish for man to rebel against Him (moral will). These are two negative (apophatic) statements that defend two things that must be true.

But there is a conflict of categories when we say that God absolutely predestinated the fall of man in order to bring about the "morally" good result of the incarnation. If God "wanted," in the moral sense, for His Son to come into the world and be the Husband of humanity, and the only way this could happen was for man to rebel, then God "wanted," in the moral sense, for man to fall. To put it another way, this position says that the *only* way God could bring about the wonderful Divine-Human marriage of His only-begotten Son and His created daughter was by means of predestinating the rebellion of that daughter.

This, I submit, is intolerable.

Hence, the only alternative is to say that even if Adam had not sinned, the Son would have come into the world to bring humanity to final glory and to be Husband to humanity.

For this reason, I doubt that Adam would have received a glorified body at the Tree of Knowledge. Rather, he would have received power to kill the serpent and exile Satan from the garden, and he would have received animal garments of glory as a sign of his new kingly position. But the conflict would continue in the new outer world into which Adam would now be sent. Satan would continue to attack, perhaps not through animal (serpent) agents, but directly through his host of fallen angels. The conflict would be intensified. As the generations went by, humanity would become more and more aware of the need for a full and final disposition of the problem of evil. The ultimate Holy Warrior would need to come in order to bring about full transfiguration into glory. That coming one would be the son of Adam, the seed of Eve. It would be His passage through the good-death of the Tree of Knowledge that would bring "many sons to glory" and complete the victory in the holy war.

At this point we need to reintroduce a consideration of the garments—the coverings—of the priests of Israel. The regular priests were clothed in linen with a multicolored woolen sash, with vegetables and animals. The High Priest was clothed with these but also with gold and gemstones, minerals. Now bear in mind that Adam and Eve were covered not with all three elements, but only with animal skins (and perhaps by implication, vegetable matter also). They became like the priests, but not like the High Priest.

An examination of the data in Exodus 28 and 39 reveals that the High Priest was covered first in linen undergarments, and then with woolen robe and a multicolored sash consisting of wool and linen. Over this as a third layer included gold thread woven into the fabric, along with golden chains and gemstones. I submit that these layers, moving outward from the High Priest, correspond to holiness, initial glory, and final glory.

If we look back at Genesis 2, we find that the garden of Eden consisted of trees, but that animals were also present in it. The outer world, however, is characterized as a place of glorious minerals: gold, onyx, and bdellium (2:11–12). The other datum that we must take into consideration is that when the glorified Jesus appears in Revelation 1:14–15, His glory includes wool and bronze.

I submit that reflection on this data leads us to a three-phase understanding of history. First, Adam is in the garden, clothed as it were in vegetables, but present with animals. After eating of the Tree of Knowledge, he is given initial glory consisting of animal clothing, and is sent out into the mineral world. He is clothed with animals, but present with minerals. The data before us suggests that full glorification will come when the outer mineral world is also transformed into glory clothing.

What this sequence implies, I submit, fits with what has been discussed above. Coming to the Tree of Knowledge, Adam would experience a first kind of death and glorification, but not the final kind of death and glorification. He would be glorified with the plant and animal realms, but not with the mineral realm. Full glorification with all the elements of the world would await the coming of the son of Adam, who would also be the Son of God the Father, after which the Bride would also be glorified with all the elements of the world (Rev. 21–22).

The history in the Bible is often called "redemptive history," but it is more than that. It is "covenant history," and involves maturation toward glory as well as salvation from sin. Redemptive history is laid under the original covenant history, and after Adam's fall it makes that covenant history possible, but both aspects are always present in biblical history. Biblical history is not only a history of repeated salvations from sin, but also a history of progressive maturation in glory and responsibility.

What that overarching covenant history implies is this: While fighting Satan in the garden, Adam would learn that he needs glorification, that he needs to be made higher than the angels. Coming to the Tree of Knowledge, he would be given that higher status, and be enabled to drive the (small) serpent from the garden and also to battle the (great) dragon successfully in the outer world. A full and complete victory in the holy war, however, entails driving the serpent not only from the garden but also the dragon from the whole world, and that final victory would be accomplished by the incarnate Son of God.

We are at present in the second phase of that historical progression. We have been made higher than the angels, in union with the man Christ Jesus. Satan has been bound from deceiving the nations, but not driven from the world wholly. We are able to crush Satan under our feet, but he is able to come back again and again. The ascension of Jesus has resulted in Satan's banishment from the heavenly sanctuary (Rev. 12), but not from the world.

If we continue to allow covenant history to inform us, we see that Jesus by Himself came to the Tree of Knowledge and ascended to rule. The result was the driving of Satan from the heavenly sanctuary and the ushering of the Bride into the outer world (the book of Acts). In order for the victory to become complete, to be worked out in history so that Satan is driven from the world, Jesus must be joined by His Bride. The Bride must also undergo death and resurrection at the Tree of Knowledge, which is what the Book of Revelation is about. It is the meaning of the "first resurrection" in Revelation 20.[44] The Bride must battle Satan in the world until she comes to the second resurrection and is fully glorified, with "mineral" as well as "vegetable" and "animal."

We have seen that the biblical logic of Genesis 2–3, apart from the fall, was for Adam to eat of the Tree of Knowledge first, and then be joined by Eve. Together they would move into the outer mineral world to battle the dragon there. Eventually the seed of the woman, the Son of God, would come into the world and crush the dragon, and remove Satan from the world altogether, bringing final and full glorification to humanity.

Because of Adam's sin, a history of redemption had to be added to this covenant history, interlaced with it and undergirding it. The covenant history is not possible apart from a foundation of redemptive history. Sin must be dealt with in order for the covenant history to mature to its fullness, for the holy war to be completed. Sinners are on Satan's side in the holy war. Some sinners must be converted over to God's side in order for the holy war to be prosecuted. The covenant history of holy war (and of cultural mandate) cannot happen apart from the redemption of some sinners from Satan's grasp.

Nothing that I have written here subtracts one iota from the history of redemption, from the salvation of sinners through the work of

Jesus Christ. But if salvation from sin were all that the Bible is about, the Son could have been born into the world from the womb of Eve herself, and dealt with the matter right then and there. The Bible is about more. It is about the history and development of humanity as the image of God, in the twin areas of holy war and cultural mandate, with a primary emphasis on the holy war. Understanding that history helps us understand what God initially set up in the Adamic Covenant, and what that history might have been had Adam not rebelled.

The Bible history shows the maturation of humanity in the area of the cultural mandate, from strength to strength, but also the maturation of humanity in the area of the religious mandate, from weakness to weakness. It took 4000 years, biblically speaking, for the central representatives of humanity (Israel) to become fully aware of the need for a Messiah, so that when the Son of God finally came into the world, the Jews were filled with messianic fervor and expectation. But Jesus came not only to pay the price for Adam's sin, replacing with His own body the fruit Adam and Eve stole from the Tree of Knowledge by being crucified on that Tree of Death, but also to defeat and destroy the dragon once and for all. Jesus not only forgave sins, but also expelled demons.

Had Adam not sinned, he would have come to the Tree of Knowledge and been enabled to perform an initial defeat of the serpent. But the full and final victory in the holy war would be accomplished by a descendant of Adam who would be the incarnate Son of God the Father.

Objections

I have argued that the gift promised in the Adamic Covenant was not "life" as such, but glorified and kingly life on the other side of some kind of death and resurrection. I have argued that Adam was called to maintain a daily life of faith-filled obedience to God until God saw fit to grant him this transfiguration. I have argued that it was not Adam's growth in strength, but his increasing awareness of need and weakness, his growth in faith, that would have made him fit to receive a transfigured life.

It can be objected, however, that later passages of the Bible state that God gives rewards in response to faithful obedience, as in Leviticus

26 and Deuteronomy 28. This seems quite true, and for the moment let us assume that it is true. Let us notice, however, precisely what is promised in these passages, and what is not promised. God does not promise that if they faith-fully keep His statutes and commandments they will be rewarded with a glorified life. Rather, in both Leviticus 26:3–13 and Deuteronomy 28:1–14, God promises that they will mature *in the land* He has given them. They will grow and develop, moving from strength to strength. God will confirm (i.e., maintain afresh) His covenant with them. He does not promise that by doing these things they will earn a new and better covenant. They will mature in cultural strength, but also mature in awareness of religious weakness. It is out that awareness of weakness that a new covenant would arise.

This is, in fact, implied in Genesis 2:15, where we read: "And Yahweh God took the man and put him into the garden of Eden, to serve it and to guard it." Adam began by naming animals. This was the beginning of his maturation *in the garden*. Adam would go on to do other good things, growing and developing in strength *in the garden*. Within the garden Adam might, so to speak, earn or merit further blessings. But there is no thought that he would earn or merit the transfigured life. The transfigured life would come as a new free gift from God - a new *creation!* - when God was ready to give it, and when Adam was mature enough to receive it.

Similarly, Israel's life in the land, had they been faithful, would not have earned a new covenant. Rather, as they moved from strength to strength, and increased in power and wisdom, they would see the need to extend God's kingdom throughout the world, to all the gentile nations.[45] At the same time, they would more and more see that they did not have the ability to deal with sin and evil. Their maturation in cultural strength would by its very nature force a maturation in their awareness of religious (holy war) weakness. They would see the need for the Messiah to come and bring in a new world-wide covenant. And this is precisely what the faithful in Israel did learn, as they suffered at the hands of faithless Israelites and pagan gentiles.

Even here, however, Adam's (and Israel's) new blessings would arrive not simply as a result of merit and work, but also as he matured so as to be able to handle the new blessings. Adam would grow in strength and weakness, in works and faith, and as he matured would be given more and more blessings and new responsibilities. The climax of this development would come when he became fully aware of his weakness and need, and thus was ready for the new glorified life.

The earning of rewards by merits, then, operates only *within* a given covenant, and has nothing to do with bringing in a new covenant. Better, the earning of rewards by merits operates only in the area of the cultural mandate. It is a part of growth and maturation within a covenant, but a new covenant only comes through death and resurrection as a free and unmerited gift of God. Doing faith-full works and growing in rewards does not even bring a man up to the point where he is ready for the new covenant to come. What makes men ready for the new covenant is their sense of what they lack.

At the same time, however, it is not really all that clear that new rewards for faithful obedience are promised in Leviticus 26 or in Deuteronomy 28. Rather, what seems to be promised is continuance in the gifts already given. The "rewards" set forth in these passages have already been promised in Exodus and Leviticus, and were freely given in the book of Joshua: rain in its season, plenteous crops, huge crops in the years preceding sabbath years, the removal of harmful beasts from the land, total victory in warfare, fruitfulness and multiplication, the presence of God in His Tabernacle in their midst, and influence over the nations.

Along these lines, a few comments on Leviticus 18:5 are relevant: "So you shall guard My statutes and My ordinances, by which a man may live if he does them." Imported to the passage by many theologians is the notion that God is holding out the theoretical possibility of eternal and glorified life if the people are faithful. Such is not in the horizon of the passage at all. Once again, it is life *in* the covenant that God has made, not transformation into a new covenant, that is in view. The passage begins by reminding them that God had delivered them from Egypt and telling them not to behave like Egyptians (v. 3). It ends by threatening to expel them from the land, and thus back into "Egypt," if they sin (vv. 24–30).

In other words, Israel is to fight the holy war, against their own sinful inclinations as well as against the draconic nations, in order to *maintain what they have already been given.* But nothing they could do would move them beyond what they had already been given into something better. Moving beyond into something better would come only when God was ready to give it, and when they were ready to receive it by faith alone, trusting Him to raise them after death.

In summary, the notion of earning blessings through "merit" is questionable even within a given covenant. The whole emphasis is that faithfulness results in *continuance*, not in the reward of something new and better. The arrival of new and better things is *always* a free gift from God, not something earned.

The Merits of Jesus Christ

I submit that the confusion over merit and works came into the Protestant tradition as a hangover of Medieval theology. Medieval theologians wrestled mightily with merit, distinguishing it into "condign" and "congruent" and making other distinctions. Traditional hymns praised the merits of Christ, and traditional prayers were prayed "through the merit(s) of Christ Thy Son." The language of merit was thus woven into the warp and woof of Christian thinking and experience. It is still with us, and still affects us.

If the "merits of Christ" means only the "accomplishments of Christ," as it often does,[46] the phrase is vague and innocuous enough. The language, however, has the subtle effect of creating the idea that Jesus in His life on earth somehow earned or merited by works His translation into glory.

We have seen, however, that such a notion is quite foreign both to the Adamic Covenant and to the rest of the Old Testament. Hence, we should be surprised to find it in the New. And we don't find it there. Nowhere is Jesus' accomplishment spoken of as earning salvation.

Rather the notion, consistent with what we have seen, is that Jesus in His life did only what He was told to do by the Father and prompted to do by the Spirit who baptized Him (John 5:19, 30; 8:28; 12:49; 14:10). The notion that Jesus earned or merited a reward, the reward of glorification, is settled by His own statements in Luke 17:7–10:

> But which of you, having a slave plowing or tending sheep, will say to him when he has come in from the field, "Come immediately and recline to eat"? But will he not say to him, "Prepare something for me to eat, and gird yourself and serve me until I have eaten and drunk, and after these

things you will eat and drink"? He does not thank the slave because he
did the things that were commanded, does he? So you, too, when you do
all the things that are commanded you, say, "We are unworthy slaves; we
have done only that which we ought to have done."

The fact that Jesus, who took upon Himself the form of a bond-
slave (Phil. 2:7), claimed to be doing only what He had been ordered
to do by the Father makes it clear that this saying applies to Him. In
fact, Jesus alone could say that He had done "all the things that are
commanded."

Jesus' saying sets us up to understand that glorification is a free
gift from God, and not something earned. Even Jesus' own glorification, when the Father surely did say, "Come immediately and recline
and eat," is pure gift. Having done all that was required of Him, Jesus
simply said, "Father, into Your hands I commend My spirit" (Luke
23:46). Jesus' glorification is a gift that was indeed *promised*, but not a
gift that was *earned*. It was given to Him because the Father loves the
Son, not because the Son had earned the right to demand it in payment for His works.

Notice how Paul puts it in Philippians 2:9, "Therefore also God
highly exalted Him, and bestowed on Him the name that is above
every name." The Greek word for "bestow" (*kharidzomai*) is related to
the noun for "grace" (*kharis*, from which we get "charity") and means
"to give freely." Far from earning His exaltation, Jesus received it as a
free grace or gift from the Father.

Jesus came under the Old Covenant, which is ultimately the Adamic
Covenant. He properly "cultivated and guarded" His garden. He grew
from strength to strength within the Old Covenant, so to speak, but
also from weakness to weakness. Becoming fully convinced, as a man,
that there was no other way to accomplish God's work save through
total weakness and the death of the cross, after asking that "if it be
possible, let this cup pass from Me" (Matt. 26:39), He willingly went
to the cross. He became the first mature man, perfect in faith toward
the Father and in obedience to the Father's will. He thus became eligible for transformation into glory through death, not because He had
earned the right to it, but because He had matured to the point of

being fit for it. He became fit for glory not by earning merits or by growing in strength, but precisely by coming to an awareness of need.

By Himself, Jesus was eligible for transformation. This, however, was not the Father's sole purpose. God intended to save His people from their sins, and for this to happen, Jesus had to take upon Himself the liability for their sins. He had to die not in some peaceful way, but under the sting of death, which is sin. "He made Him who knew no sin, sin on our behalf, that we might become the righteousness of God in Him" (2 Cor. 5:21). He had to pay back what Adam stole by making Himself the replacement fruit on the Tree of Death.

Hence, Jesus took his people, their liabilities, with Him on the cross, and in His resurrection they also are raised so that He might bring many sons to glory, and that even now they might mature from glory to glory (Heb. 2:9–10; 2 Cor. 3:18).

This brings up the matter of Jesus' "active and passive obedience." The merit theology sometimes assumes that Jesus actively earned a reward, and passively went to the cross. This notion cannot stand inspection. We have seen that everything Jesus did was passive under the command of the Father and the prompting of the Spirit. Moreover, of course, everything He did was active on His part, as He agreed to do it, including His active refusal to come down from the cross until the Father's will had been perfected. Even when this view is refined to say that Jesus' active and passive obedience are inseparable, like two sides of one coin, the notion remains that the active side of His obedience was meritorious. We have seen that this cannot be the case.

It also brings up the matter of double imputation. That there is a double imputation of our sins to Jesus and His glory to us is certainly beyond question, and I am *not* disagreeing with the general doctrine of imputation, or of double imputation. But merit theology often assumes that Jesus' *earthly* works and merits are somehow given to us, and there is no foundation for this notion. It is, in fact, hard to comprehend what is meant by it. What does it have to do with my life that Jesus raised Lazarus from the dead and this good deed is given to me? The miracles that Jesus did were not required of *me* to satisfy God's justice. Salvation does not return us to the Old Adamic Covenant, even in a good and perfect way. Salvation gives us the glory of Jesus Christ, so that we do greater things than He did during His Adamic earthly life (Matt. 11:11;

John 14:12). The New Testament is clear throughout that what is given to the saints is the Spirit, who comes from the glorified Jesus. It is not Jesus' earthly life and "works and merits" that are transferred to us, but His glorified and resurrected life in the Spirit that is transferred to us.

There seems to be nothing in the Bible to imply that we receive Jesus' earthly life and then also His death. His earthly life was "for us" in the sense that it was the precondition for His death, but it is not given "to us." What we receive is not His earthly life and His death, but His death and His glorified life. What we receive is not Jesus' merits, but His maturity, His glorification.

Conclusion

There is no "merit" theology in the Bible. There is no "covenant of works." Good works, "merits," only have meaning within a given covenant, as part of the process of maturation. They have nothing to do with transitions to new covenants, which are free gifts from the Gifting God, new free creations from the Creator. If the term "covenant of works" has any meaning, it applies only to the cultural mandate side of life. It is not good works but maturation in awareness of weakness that fits us for a new covenant.

God is the Gift-giver, the Creator. He has little interest in paying people what they have earned. Adam was not supposed to merit anything, but to prepare himself through faithfulness to receive God's new gift, His new creation and patiently to wait for it. That is what Jesus did. That is what we, in union with Him by the Spirit, are called to do.

In this essay there has been much that is "new" and doubtless controversial. In my defense I can only say that in Reformed theology the nature of the Adamic administration, or "covenant of works," is an open question—anyone who thinks is it not is simply ignorant of the Reformed faith—and that after more than 25 years of personal reflection and labor in this area, I believe that what I have propounded in this essay can help to advance the ongoing discussion. I have not sought here to say the last word on the subject, but only a helpful word.

Notes - Chapter 5

[1] Thanks to Peter Leithart and Jeffrey Meyers for reading the first draft of this paper and making valuable criticisms and suggestions. I hasten to add that they are in no way responsible for such infelicities as remain herein.

[2] I shall argue at the end of this paper that in another sense there were to be three stages: childhood, initial glory, and final glory, corresponding to what actually happened: childhood under the Old Creation covenants, initial glory in the Gospel age, and final glory after the final judgment. As a way of leading to that thesis, however, I shall limit myself to two phases: childhood and maturity.

[3] For a full discussion, see Richard B. Gaffin, Jr., *Resurrection and Redemption: A Study of Paul's Soteriology* (Phillipsburg, NJ: Presbyterian and Reformed Pub. Co., [1978] 1987). Previously published as *The Centrality of the Resurrection* (Grand Rapids: Baker, 1978).

[4] Murray was concerned to approach the Bible afresh and to bring the language of dogmatic theology into more careful conformity with the language of the Bible; hence, since the Bible does not use the word "covenant" in connection with God's arrangement with Adam, Murray sought to avoid it. While I applaud Murray's quest, I believe that all the elements of a covenant are present in Genesis 1–2, and hence the term can and should be used for the Adamic administration.

[5] Vol. III; ed. by Philip E. Hughes (Marshalton, DW: The National Foundation for Christian Education, 1972), pp. 199–216. Reprinted in *The Collected Writings of John Murray*, vol. 4 (Carlisle, PA: The Banner of Truth Trust, 1982), pp. 216–240. Murray's pamphlet, *The Covenant of Grace* (Phillipsburg, NJ: Presbyterian and Reformed, 1953) was also in circulation.

[6] Trans. by H. Evan Runner and Elizabeth W. Runner; vol. 1 (St. Catherines, ON: Paideia Press, 1977).

[7] Ibid., p. 37.

[8] Herman Hoeksema's *Reformed Dogmatics* (Grand Rapids: Reformed Free Pub. Assoc., 1966) includes an attack on the covenant of works idea; pp. 214ff. See also the attack on the notion in Cornelis van der Waal, *The Covenantal Gospel*, trans. by Dr. & Mrs. G. L. Bertram (Neerlandia, AB: Inheritance Pub., 1990), pp. 47–56. The position for which I argue in this paper is different from those advocated by both Hoeksema and van der Waal. I reference them to show that the matter is not a settled part of Reformed theology, and is certainly open for reassessment at the present time. Both authors seem to assume that the prohibition on the fruit of the Tree of the Knowledge of Good and Evil was permanent, which I shall show was not the case. Also, Hoeksema seems to assume that if Adam had not sinned he would have continued in what I am calling his first phase of life forever. At the same time, both men issue devastating criticisms of the traditional covenant of works construction. Where I differ is more in the area of what they do not say than in the areas of what they do say.

[9] Murray, "Covenant Theology," *Collected Writings* 4:220.

[10] Ibid., p. 222.

[11] Yet today one encounters men who deny that Adam was to live by faith, and denying even that Jesus lived by faith in His Father. These notions seem to arise particularly in circles influenced by the thought of Meredith G. Kline, though I hesitate to ascribe such bizarre notions to him personally. Both of these extreme positions arise from a fanatical devotion to the notion of a covenant of meritorious works.

[12] For an example from the conservative Southern Presbyterian milieu, see the criticism of the "nonbiblical covenant of works" by Wilson Benton, "Federal Theology: Review for Revision," in W. Robert Godfrey and Jesse L. Boyd III, eds., *Through God's Word: A Festschrift for Dr. Philip E. Hughes* (Phillipsburg, NJ: Presbyterian and Reformed, 1985), pp. 180–204. For an example from recent Scottish theology, though of a somewhat neo-orthodox bent, see James Torrance, "The Concept of Federal Theology—Was Calvin a Federal Theologian?" in Wilhelm H. Neuser, ed., *Calvinus Sacrae Scripturae Professor* (Grand Rapids: Eerdmans, 1995). Torrance argues persuasively that the covenant of works model presupposes a nature/grace dualism of sorts and is not thoroughly grounded in the Trinity.

[13] *Op. cit.*, p. 5.

[14] Rich Lusk, private communication, 27 May 2003.

[15] I have discussed this, in less philosophical language, in James B. Jordan, *From Bread to Wine: Toward a More Biblical Liturgical Theology* (Draft ed., 1.1; Niceville, FL: Biblical Horizons, 2001).

[16] While Murray had reservations about the term "Adamic Covenant," I believe that the majority of Biblical theologians are quite correct in noting that all the aspects of a covenant are present in the original Adamic arrangement, and so I shall use the term "Adamic Covenant" here without arguing the point.

[17] James B. Jordan, *Trees and Thorns: An Exposition of Genesis 2–4*, published as an ongoing series of papers from Biblical Horizons, Box 1096, Niceville, FL 32588.

[18] De Graaf puts it this way: "When man ate the fruit of this tree and thereby affirmed the covenant, his faith that God would bring him to eternal life, that is, to full, eternal dominion in His Kingdom, was [would have been — JBJ] confirmed." *Loc. cit.* Speaking of the choice before Adam, De Graaf writes: ". . . God had provided man with something to strengthen his faith that he would possess God's favor forever if he remained obedient. In the middle of the garden there was another important tree, namely, the tree of life. . . . The two trees standing in the middle of the garden represented opposing directions. If man ate from the tree of life, he would be choosing God's everlasting favor and rejecting the fruit of the other tree." *Op. cit.*, p. 40f.

[19] Thanks to Joel Garver for alerting me to the full implications of Adam's first "death" as anticipating what would happen to him at the Tree of Knowledge.

[20] In Revelation 14, the 144,000 are on the earth; in chapter 15 they are in heaven on the sea of glass. In between is a harvest of grain and grapes, bread and wine, representing not a destruction of the wicked but the harvest of the Apostolic Church. For a fuller discussion, see James B. Jordan, *A Brief Reader's Guide to Revelation* (Niceville, FL: Transfiguration Press, 1999).

[21] Consider Adam's personal experience. Arguably he has never fallen asleep before. He begins to lose consciousness. "What is happening to me", he wonders. But Adam at this point trusts God. Surely God knows what is happening to him. He is able to fall asleep, confident that God knows what He is doing in bringing this strange event upon him.

[22] Once again, consult 1 Corinthians 15:44 and Gaffin's study *op. cit.* Since Adam was supposed to expect a transfigured Spiritual body, and since he had been told that someday he would eat of the death-dealing Tree of Knowledge, then he was supposed to expect some kind of "death and resurrection" experience that would lead to that glorification.

[23] Given that the Tree of Life is also found in the eschatological New Jerusalem, we may suppose that eating from the Tree of Life initially would have confirmed Adam in initial life, while eating of the Tree of Life a second time after passing through the death-resurrection of the Tree of Knowledge would confirm him in glorified life. God's prohibition of the Tree of Life after Adam ate of the Tree of Knowledge seems to bear this out. Had Adam eaten from the Tree of Life in a state of sin, he would have been confirmed in that state of sin, and been irredeemable.

[24] Additional passages that support this interpretation are found in van der Waal, *op. cit.*, pp. 49–51.

[25] On the royal robe of authority, see discussion below.

[26] A married couple are naked to each other under the larger garment of their bedsheets, or within the larger covering of their bedroom. They clothe themselves in the company of others, when such larger coverings are not around them. Notice along these lines Genesis 9:21. Noah uncovered himself within his tent. He was still covered by the tent. Ham invaded the tent, without Noah's kingly permission, and saw Noah naked.

[27] p. 7.

[28] Virtually every apostate Calvinist I have ever known who has gone into Rome or Orthodoxy immediately became involved in apologetical labors designed to win others to his newfound heresy. This is an act of self-justification designed to cover up the shame of abandoning the truth.

[29] Note that the priests of Israel were dressed in holy linen garments under their outer garments of glory.

[30] "Those whom He justified, them He also glorified." (Romans 8:30). "Glorified" is in the same past tense as "justified." "Sanctified" is absent. The thought is that God

justifies and also gives glory, and that we are to develop in integrity (sanctification) as people already housed in glory. We are to grow up, as it were, into the large clothing that has been given to us. As we shall see, this is precisely what God did, by anticipation of Jesus' future work, for Adam and Eve. He forgave them and He glorified them. Then they needed to develop in inner integrity within the new glory garments He gave them. What God did not do is somehow miraculously give them full inner integrity.

[31] The woman's statement, by way of contrast, is quite correct and need imply no refusal to accept her position: "The serpent deceived me, and I ate." This is not "blaming the serpent." Paul twice affirms that the woman was in fact deceived (2 Cor. 11:3; 1 Tim. 2:14). We must again bear in mind the specific statements of the text. Eve was not yet created when God told Adam not to eat of the Tree of Knowledge. She heard God say that every tree would be for them to eat from. Her knowledge about the prohibition came, therefore, from her husband and pastor, Adam. Moreover, the text is clear that Adam was standing by silently during Eve's conversation with the serpent. (I shall discuss this later in this essay.) By failing to interrupt and protect Eve, Adam sided with the serpent in leading her into transgression. Rather obviously, he wanted her to eat so he could see what would happen! The distinction between Adam's self-conscious sin and Eve's deception is reiterated in Leviticus in the difference between "sins of inadvertency, or of wandering" and "high-handed sin."

[32] Notice in the history of Israel that Yahweh had ordered the Israelites to be His witnesses to the nations. When they failed to do what He had sent them to do, He drove them out into the nations, or brought the nations in over them, so that they would have to bear witness to the nations.

[33] Recall that wisdom is a kingly attribute, especially associated with Solomon, who prayed for wisdom and for the knowledge of good and evil.

[34] The analogy between mankind and animals has also been established by Adam's naming the animals in Genesis 2, for Adam did not deduce from this that he was different from the animals in this respect, but that he needed a companion just as each of them had one. Adam's deduction was only possible on the basis of the analogy.

[35] The glory garments of the High Priest also included gold and gemstones. He was clothed in vegetable, animal, and mineral materials. He was clothed in the whole world. On the nature of colored yarn as wool, see Jacob Milgrom, "Of Hems and Tassels," *Biblical Archaeology Review* 9:3 (May/June, 1983), pp. 61–65.

[36] The Ark consisted of two separate items: the Ark or chest proper, and the Cover with cherubim attached to it over it. The Cover represents the firmament, with humanity-Ark below and angelic heaven above. God's people, the Ark, are to have the Law inside themselves as the tablets of the Law were inside the Ark. The Cover is analogous to the Sea of Glass, on which stand the angels, and over which God presides on His throne, as His glory also hovered over the angels on the Ark.

[37]The infelicitous chapter break between Genesis 2 and 3 obscures the unity of this paragraph.

[38]Arguably the fall of Satan came right at the point when he contradicted God's Word. At the end of creation week, God had pronounced everything "very good." The first part of the serpent's conversation with Eve is unobjectionable: Arguably he is no more than seeking to help her understand God's command. Satan, however, understands that the meaning of the Tree of Knowledge is that mankind will go from being a little lower than the angels to being over the angels, as we shall see. Evidently this is what he was trying to prevent. It may be that his decision to undermine God's plan for humanity happened precisely between Genesis 3:3 and 3:4.

[39] "It is not good for he man to be alone." "And God saw all that He had made, and behold, it was very good" (Gen. 2:18; 1:31).

[40]"Happy Fall," "Fortunate Fall," or in Latin, *Felix Culpa.*

[41]Louis Berkhof, *Systematic Theology,* 4th ed. (Grand Rapids: Eerdmans, 1941), p. 333.

[42]Ibid., p. 334.

[43]Ibid., pp. 333f.

[44]On this, see Jordan, *Brief Reader's Guide to Revelation,* cited above.

[45]Notice that during the period of the judges, when God had not yet given them the king promised in Deuteronomy 17, they became more and more aware of a need for a king. Like Adam, they did not wait. They made Abimelech king. Then they offered a crown to Jephthah, but God took Jephthah's only child to serve in His palace. Then in 1 Samuel they demanded a king, and got Saul. In Saul, God gave them what they demanded, just as He honored Adam's seizure of the Tree of Rule. It was only with David, who was willing to die for the people, humbly waiting for God to elevate him, that God provided the promised king at the time He knew was right.

[46] "MERITS OF CHRIST, a term used to denote the influence of moral consideration resulting from the obedience of Christ—all that he wrought and all that he suffered for the salvation of mankind." John McClintock and James Strong, *Cyclopedia of Biblical, Theological, and Ecclesiastical Literature* (Grand Rapids: Baker, [1867–1887], 1981) 6:102.

Chapter Six

"Judge Me, O God":

Biblical Perspectives on Justification[1]

Peter J. Leithart

Contrary to modern rationalistic accounts, metaphor is not an adornment to thought and speech, but a primary medium of both. It is not the case that we think and speak literally, and subsequently cast about for appropriate metaphors and symbols to express those literal ideas. Rather, our thinking and speech is metaphorical from the ground up. As George Lakoff and Mark Johnson have written, "conceptual metaphors are mappings across conceptual domains that *structure* our reasoning, our experience, and our everyday language" (emphasis added). Lakoff and Johnson give numerous examples of what they call "primary metaphors" that shape experience: the metaphorical association of intimacy with physical proximity ("we used to be close"), the link between quantity and height ("stock prices are sharply higher"), the notion that organization is similar to physical structure ("he pieced together the theory of quantum gravity"), the metaphorical link of purposes and destinations ("I'm working on it, but I'm not there yet"), and so on.[2] These metaphors are so much a part of our basic mental and linguistic equipment that we rarely recognize them as metaphors.

"Foundation" is one of the primary metaphors of philosophy, particularly of modern philosophy. Descartes is the supreme example of what today's philosophers call a "foundationalist," who attempted to "clear the ground" of earlier philosophy through the systematic use of doubt, so he could come to a "foundation" that no one could question, an uncorrupted foundation on which he could "rebuild" an entire edifice of philosophy. Dooyeweerd employed a similar metaphor in talking about the "ground motives" of Christian and unbelieving thought. Or, think of the key role that notions of "purity" have played in modern philosophy, or the centrality that visual metaphors like "mirrors" have played in Western conceptions of knowledge.

Root or primary metaphors also play a formative role in theology and Christian piety. Paul H. Jones has argued that for centuries eucharistic theology has gotten sidetracked because it has been pursued under the metaphor of "tomb" rather than "table," and eucharistic piety has often worked from the metaphor of the Supper as "fast" rather than "feast." My objection to these metaphors is not that they exist; they are all but unavoidable. My objection is that the particular metaphors of "tomb" and "fast" are inappropriate to the Supper, and that they therefore lead theology and piety into side-roads and blind alleys. Metaphors, especially unrecognized ones, take on a life of their own, determining the questions we ask and putting their particular stamp on our answers. To change the terminology slightly, the "picture" of communion that a theologian assumes goes a long way to determining his theology of the Supper. If we begin by picturing the Supper as a miramorphocle, then we will ask questions like, "How does the bread change into body?" and "Why does it still look and taste like bread?" If, similarly, we begin thinking about baptism by picturing baptism as a "sign," then our main question will be, "What does it signify?" and we may neglect to notice that baptism *accomplishes* something. If we begin with the root picture of "ritual," our questions will be more about what baptism *does*. Theologians, of course, are called to submit to the root metaphors that Scripture provides, and to teach in accord with what the Scriptural metaphors dictate. And if theologians adopt metaphors or basic pictures that are not directly derived from Scripture, then we should recognize that, and pay attention to the limitations of our metaphors.

The purpose of this essay is to explore the "picture" (more accurately, the pictures) surrounding the Bible's use of "justification" and related terms. In what kind of "scene" or scenes does justification come into play? By examining the variety of Scriptural "scenes" where justification is at work, I hope to show a glimpse of the fullness of the biblical doctrine of justification and to draw some conclusions about what "justify" means in Scripture. There are a host of other related issues currently in debate concerning the doctrine of justification: the nature of faith, the relation of faith and works, the basis for justification, the relationship between corporate and individual justification, the relationship of sacraments and justification, the biblical basis for the Protestant doctrine of imputation, and so on. Though this essay holds implications for those issues, my focus here is narrowly on the question of the meaning of "justification" itself. And I propose to explore that issue by examining the "root metaphors" in the context of which the terminology of justification emerges.

A brief review of the historical options will set the context for my discussion. From Augustine and through most of the Middle Ages, *iustificare* was understood etymologically as "making just" (*iustum facere*). God justifies when He transforms a sinner into a sainnter, and thus the doctrine of justification is worked out as part of the picture of an unjust man made just. Alister McGrath summarizes Augustine's position:

> Although Augustine is occasionally represented, on the basis of isolated passages, as understanding justification to comprise merely the remission of sins, it is clear that he also understands it to include the ethical and spiritual renewal of the sinner through the internal operation of the Holy Spirit. Justification, according to Augustine, is fundamentally concerned with "being made righteous."[3]

According to McGrath, Augustine's concept of justification as "universally accepted during the medieval period,"[4] and a more detailed summary of how this worked out in Thomas's doctrine of justification will clarify both the medieval doctrine and its flaws. Thomas thinks of justification primarily under the metaphor of "motion," and for him justification describes the motion of the soul in a four-step progression toward God: a) infusion of grace; b) the motion of the will toward God in faith; c) the motion of the will against sin; d) the remission of sins. The sequence must be in that order: For the soul to be moved toward God, it must first *be* moved, so the infusion of grace must take place prior to the soul's turn toward God. Since Thomas commonly defines a thing or process in terms of its final end, he sometimes defines justification as if it were nothing more than the remission of sins. Technically, however, for Thomas justification is the whole process; it *is* the motion: Justification is "a certain motion by which the human mind is moved by God from the state of sin into the state of justice."[5]

There is more to both Augustine's and Thomas's understanding of justification, but enough has been said to indicate some of the major flaws of their teaching. First, even as a piece of Latin philology, Augustine's understanding of *iustificare* is very doubtful, and even if it were correct at that level it simply does not match the biblical usage (see below). Though justification terminology has a number of different nuances in Scripture, it does not refer to an act of "making just." Second, Thomas's doctrine in particular describes the inward movements of the sinner's soul, so that justification is fundamentally a *motus animi*. To be sure, Thomas believed that the Divine Mover graciously initiated the motion of the soul, but still justification is *not* conceived primarily as an act of God; rather, it is a motion of the soul moved by God. Biblically, this gets things upside down: Paul insists, "It is *God* who justifies" (Rom. 8:33). The subject of "justify" is not *animus* but *Deus*. The Protestant confessions reflect the biblical teaching when they claim that justification is an "act of God's free grace" by which *God* pardons and forgives and counts us as righteous. Finally, both Augustine's and Thomas's doctrine is led astray in part because they attempt to expound justification under the wrong metaphors, as part of the wrong story-line or scene or picture. For Augustine, justification is understood under the heading of moral transformation, while for Thomas justification is shorthand for the story of the soul's return to God, understood by means of a teleology shaped by Aristotelian theories of motion. As we shall see below, neither of these contexts matches the biblical "scenery" of justification.

The Reformers did not merely adjust the medieval *ordo salutis* here and there, but instead changed the basic picture or root metaphor of justification; they did not merely move around the props, but changed the backdrops, the costuming, and the entire scene. Instead of expounding justification under the heading of moral transformation (Augustine) or through the metaphor of motion (Aquinas), the Reformation discerned that justification language belonged in the courtroom. Instead of being the End of a journey of return, God in the Protestant doctrine assumed the role of Judge; instead of playing out the story of the soul's moral renewal, justification became the story of the guilty soul's acquittal; instead of being the soul's movement, justification became God's pronouncement.

This shift in root metaphor did not occur all at once. In one of Luther's early treatises, he employed a marital image to describe the transfer of righteousness from Christ to the believer:

> . . . if Christ is a bridegroom, he must take upon himself the things which are his bride's and bestow upon her the things that are his. If he gives her his body and very self, how shall he not give her all that is his? And if he takes the body of the bride, how shall he not take all that is hers? . . .
>
> Christ is God and man in one person. He has neither sinned nor died, and is not condemned, and he cannot sin, die, or be condemned; his righteousness, life, and salvation are unconquerable, eternal, omnipotent. By the wedding ring of faith he shares in the sins, death, and pains of hell which are his bride's. . . .
>
> Who then can fully appreciate what this royal marriage means? Who can understand the riches of the glory of this grace? Here this rich and divine bridegroom Christ marries this poor, wicked harlot, redeems her from all her evil, and adorns her with all his goodness. Her sins cannot now destroy her, since they are laid upon Christ and swallowed up by him. And she has that righteousness in Christ, her husband, of which she may boast as of her own and which she can confidently display alongside her sins in the face of death and hell.[6]

For Luther, the Bride possesses the righteousness of her Husband because He lovingly shares all that is His with her. Though this is clearly not a medieval theory of justification, neither is it the standard Protestant "forensic" theory.

Luther did speak of an imputation of righteousness, and following his successor, Melanchthon, Protestants came to understand justification in a strictly forensic sense, as a legal declaration regarding the standing of the justified, which does not itself change the character or habits or condition of the justified.[7] To be sure, it has often been recognized that sanctification also has a definitive starting point that is simultaneous with justification, an event that John Murray called "definitive sanctification."[8] Protestant commentators have also commonly recognized that Scripture uses the language of justification more loosely than systematic theologians have. Yet, even when these factors have been noted, Protestant theologians and Confessions have stressed that justification and sanctification are distinct acts—a legal declaration and a distinct act of deliverance from the power of sin—and the other dimensions of justification language have played almost no role in the Protestant formulation of the dogma of justification.

Turretin's discussion can be taken as representative of the mature doctrine of Reformed Orthodoxy.[9] Turretin recognizes that Scripture uses "justification" and related terminology in various ways, which he describes as "proper" and "improper." In the proper sense, the word group has a judicial or forensic sense: "Properly the verb is forensic, 'to absolve' anyone in a trial or 'to hold' and to declare 'just'; as opposed to the verb 'to condemn' and 'to accuse' (Ex. 23:7; Deut. 25:1; Prov. 17:15; Luke 18:14; Rom. 3–5)." He claims that the key passages on the doctrine of justification use the term "properly," since they are set in a judicial context. In these texts, "a judicial process is set forth and mention is made of an accusing 'law,' of 'accused persons,' who are guilty . . . , of a 'hand-writing' contrary to us . . . , of divine 'justice' demanding punishment . . . , of an 'advocate' pleading the cause" and so on. Further, in a number of key passages, "justify" is set in opposition to "condemn" (e.g., Rom. 8:33–34) or is used interchangeably with such phrases as "reckon righteous" or "remit sins." Though there are indeed passages where "justification" is to be "taken in another than a forensic sense," Turretin argues that these do no damage to the Protestant teaching, since "the proper sense is to be looked to in those passages in which the foundation of the doctrine is formed." And, even if "justify" does not always mean "to pronounce just," it *never* carries the "physical sense" of infusion.[10]

At one level, Turretin's evidence can hardly be disputed. In many of the texts he cites, "justify" (Heb. *zadaq*) indeed has a strictly forensic sense, referring to a legal sentence of absolution. For instance:

> "Keep far from a false charge, and do not kill the innocent or the righteous, for I will not acquit (*zadaq*) the guilty" (Ex. 23:7).

> "If there is a dispute between men and they go to the judgment and they judge them and they justify (*zadaq*) the righteous and condemn the wicked, then it shall be if the wicked man is a son of beating, the judge shall then make him lie down and be beaten in his presence with the number of stripes according to his wickedness" (Deut. 25:1–2).

"He who justifies (*zadaq*) the wicked, and he who condemns the righteous, both of them alike are an abomination to Yahweh" (Prov. 17:15).

As is often pointed out, these passages make no sense on an Augustinian understanding of "justification," for why would it be an abomination to "make just" the wicked? Nor do they make sense on the full Thomistic understanding of justification; how is a judge qualified to "move the soul" toward God? "Justify" clearly has a forensic or legal sense in these passages.

Nevertheless, I find it difficult to ignore those passages that use "justification" in what Turretin calls an "improper sense," or to treat them as irrelevancies in our formulation of the doctrine of justification.[11] My argument in this paper is that by ignoring the "improper uses" of justification and by failing to take into account the larger biblical theology of justification that these uses imply, the Reformation doctrine of justification has illegitimately narrowed and to some extent distorted the biblical doctrine. As far as it goes, the Protestant doctrine is correct; if the scene of a sinner in the dock before the Judge is put before us, and we are asked, "What does justification mean?" or "On what grounds is a person justified?" then the proper answer is the Reformation answer: Justification is an act of God's free grace whereby He pardons all our sins and accepts us as righteous in His sight, only for the righteousness of Christ reckoned to us and received by faith alone.

The problem is, this is *not* the only setting for justification in Scripture. Many recent studies have concluded that "righteousness" (Heb. *zedeq* or *zedaqah*; Gr. *dikaiosune*)[12] is a covenant term, describing loyalty within a covenanted relationship.[13] If this view can be sustained, then "righteousness" and "justification" have a much wider scope of application than the strictly judicial, but pertain to a whole range of covenant-relational settings. Mark A. Seifrid has recently mounted a vigorous critique of the covenantal view of righteousness,[14] arguing that "righteousness" language has to do with God's rule over creation and His determination to establish His rights by establishing right throughout the creation. Though He is covenantally faithful to Israel, this "is only one manifestation of the saving righteousness which he exercises as ruler of all."[15] Seifrid recognizes, however, that "righteousness" language finds a place in a number of different contexts in Scripture, citing

Franz Reiterer's study that grouped instances of *zadaq*-language into three main categories: "juridical, ethical-social and conflictual-military."[16]

Several examples may help to illustrate the broader "covenantal" or "ethical-social" usage of "righteousness":

> "So my righteousness (*zedaqah*) will answer for me later, when you come concerning my wages which are before you" (Jacob speaking to Laban regarding his wages [Gen. 30:33]).

> And [Saul] said to David, "You are more righteous (*zedeq*) than I; for you have dealt well with me, while I have dealt wickedly with you. . . . For if a man finds his enemy, will he let him go away safely? (1 Sam. 24:17, 19).

> "If a man sins against his neighbor and is made to take an oath, and he comes and takes an oath before Thine altar in this house, then hear Thou in heaven and act and judge Thy servants, condemning the wicked by bringing his way on his own head and justifying (*zadaq*) the righteous (*zedeq*) by giving him according to his righteousness (*zedaqah*)" (Solomon's dedicatory prayer [1 Kings 8:31–32]).

In the first example, Jacob defended his actions as a servant in Laban's house ("you yourself know my service which I have served you," v. 26), and described this faithful service as "righteousness." As von Rad points out, Jacob's later, fuller defense of his faithfulness emphasizes that he consistently went beyond the strict demands of duty (31:38–42). Jacob bore the costs of his business, costs that he could have passed on to Laban, and this was testimony to his righteousness. Saul's recognition that David was "more righteous" arises in a similar interpersonal context. David had been brought into Saul's servant and been faithful in that service; as Saul suddenly recognized, David did not count him as an enemy, but as a friend, and that witnessed to David's undiminished loyalty to the king. Neither passage takes place in a formal courtroom setting. Jacob is in a sense asking Laban to "judge" him (explicitly so in Gen. 31:37), but Laban is, strictly speaking, acting as employer rather than judge; he's giving a performance review more than he is trying a case. David's appeal to Saul is likewise a quasi-judicial scene, but the "quasi" is as evident as the "judicial." One might argue that these passages represent a transfer of courtroom language to a more personal sphere, but even if that is so, these passages prove that *zedeq* finds a perfectly suitable home within that personal setting and that "justification" terminology is not limited to "strictly forensic" concerns. "Justification" in these passages is flexible enough to include not only "counting someone as legally innocent" but also "counting someone as a loyal friend/servant."

In the final example, several uses of words related to *zedeq* are found in a more explicitly forensic context, and the verbal form (the *hif'il*) is rightly translated as "declare or pronounce righteous." Yet, even here "justify" is not limited to the mere declaration of a sentence; Solomon asked Yahweh to "justify the righteous *by giving him according to his righteousness.*" Solomon is not only asking for a verdict; he is asking that God reward those whom he declares righteous; indeed, he is asking Yahweh to declare the righteous by giving rewards. More on this below.[17]

Again, what this discussion illustrates is that "justification" language has a wider and more flexible usage in Scripture than in Protestant systematics. We have narrowed our attention to one "picture" or "setting" for justification among several, and the result has been a narrowing of our doctrine of justification, a narrowing evident in several ways. First, the Protestant doctrine of justification has mainly been concerned with the question of applying the redemption of Christ to individual believers. While that is certainly a central part of the gospel and the apostolic doctrine of justification, in a number of places in Scripture justification language is used in an explicitly corporate context. Though I do not address the corporate and redemptive-historical dimensions of justification in great detail below, this paper is part of a larger effort to integrate ecclesiological factors into an account of justification.

Second, the Protestant doctrine has been too rigid in separating justification and sanctification, more rigid certainly than Scripture itself (see below). I argue below that, when examined under a military-conflictual metaphor rather than solely under the imagery of the "courtroom," justification and definitive sanctification are not merely simultaneous, nor merely twin effects of the single event of union with Christ (though I believe that is the case). Rather, they are the same act. God's declaration that we are justified *takes the form of* deliverance from sin, death, and Satan. God declares us righteous by delivering us from all our enemies, or, to use the language of 1 Kings 8, God "justifies by giving to the righteous according to his righteousness," by keeping His covenant promises with those counted righteous.

It is true that God "reckons" or "considers" us righteous prior to His taking action on our behalf, and that "reckoning" is an act of sheer grace for the sake of Jesus. But that secret decision is not justification, any more than the decree to save the elect *is* the salvation of the elect. A judge may conclude that the accused is innocent, but his private conclusion does not constitute a legal decision. A legal decision must be promulgated as a decision of the court, and in many passages of Scripture, God's public declaration of righteousness occurs when He "gives to the righteous according to His righteousness." God's forensic declaration does not ring through the heavens while leaving earth in silence; rather, God's declaration "He is righteous" affects the righteous in real time and real history. In many passages, history is imagined as a legal battle carried on before the Judge of all the earth, and "justification," the language of the law-court, is used to describe God's interventions in history, His deliverance of the people He graciously reckons as righteous. This is still a "forensic" notion of justification, but within the military setting "forensic" has split open the wineskins of the traditional understanding. We might call this either a "militorensic" or a "forilitary" view of justification, though I think the former is far preferable.

Third, whether or not "righteousness" can be defined as "covenant loyalty," it is still important to fit the doctrine of justification more fully in the overall covenantal setting of biblical faith. God delivers His righteous people from their enemies in fulfillment of His covenant promises and threats. In delivering His people (demonstrating that He considers them righteous), He is simultaneously demonstrating His own covenant faithfulness (justifying Himself). Thus, God "justifies" not only when He intervenes to deliver (as He promised), but whenever He makes or keeps promises to His people. Making or keeping promises is "justifying the righteous by giving him according to his righteousness." When God makes a promise, He is implicitly treating the promisee as a covenant partner, and thereby publicly declares him righteous; that is, He justifies him. Whenever He keeps a promise, He is treating the recipient as a covenant partner, as "righteous," and thereby justifies him. If, by contrast, God considered a man righteous, but *never* kept any promises to him, then we would have every right to wonder if the man had ever really been justified.

In this paper, I cannot address all of these limitations of the traditional Protestant doctrine of justification. Instead, this is a narrowly-tailored first thrust against narrowness. In what follows, I offer three lines of argument. First, I sketch an important element of the biblical doctrine of judgment, namely, that a judge not only passes sentences but enforces sentences. According to this theology, "justifying" is never *merely* declaring a verdict; biblically, the scope of "forensic" is bigger than systematicians have normally suggested. Second, I examine a number of Psalms and prophetic passages to indicate that Yahweh's favorable judgment to believers and to Israel manifests itself as "deliverance from enemies" and "restoration of good fortune." These are not merely *results* of a favorable judgment; they constitute the public declaration of the favorable judgment. They constitute an act of "justification" or "vindication." Finally, I briefly examine Paul's use of Scripture to show that his use of "righteousness" and "justify" is informed by the usage of the Old Testament, and therefore suggest that the "improper" uses of justification have an important role in the formulation of Paul's doctrine.

I. "Judge" in the Old Testament

Decades ago, Leon Morris wrote in his little book on *The Biblical Doctrine of Judgment* (1960) about the difference between modern and Hebraic conceptions of judgment. For moderns, to pass judgment means to weigh evidence and declare a sentence. Once the sentence has been passed, the judge's job is finished, and someone other than the judge ensures that the sentence is carried out and that justice is actually done. In Scripture, however, judgment includes establishing justice as well as deciding what is just. Two passages using some form of the Hebrew *shaphat* ("to judge") are sufficient to make this point:[18]

> [Yahweh] executes justice [*shaphat*] for the orphan and the widow, and shows His love for the alien by giving him food and clothing (Deut. 10:18).

Give the king Thy judgments, O God, and Thy righteousness to the
king's son. May he judge [*shaphat*] Thy people with righteousness, and
Thine afflicted with justice . . . May he vindicate the afflicted of the
people, save the children of the needy, and crush the oppressor (Ps.
72:1–2, 4).

The NASB translation of *shaphat* in Deuteronomy 10:18 captures
the sense of the passage—Yahweh is doing justice for the orphan and
widow and alien, not merely passing sentences in their favor. To "judge,"
to *shaphat*, includes acting to see justice done. Similarly, the king in
Psalm 72, as the image of God, judges by delivering the afflicted, saving those in need, crushing the oppressor. For the biblical writers, if a
king decided in favor of the afflicted, but did nothing to deliver him
from his oppressor, he would be a failure as a judge. Until justice is
done, the innocent delivered, and right established, the work of judging is unfinished.

Further support for this conception comes from the book of Judges.
Though the heroes of that book are called "judges" (*shophetim*), their
work was not limited to passing sentences. In fact, we rarely see them
doing that (but cf. Judg. 4:5). Instead, we see them acting as "saviors,"
delivering Israel from their enemies, as did Moses before them: "When
Yahweh raised up judges for them, Yahweh was with the judge and
delivered them from the hand of their enemies all the days of the judge;
for Yahweh was moved to pity by their groaning because of those who
oppressed and afflicted them" (Judg. 2:18). For Scripture, however,
this *is* the work of judgment. Citing Judges 3:9, 15, W. Schneider points
out that the judges "obtain justice for the tribes of Israel in the face of
their enemies, annihilate or drive out their oppressors, and so bring
salvation, rest and peace." Given these uses, it is not surprising that
shaphat sometimes means "rule," and encompasses all the duties of ruling and protecting a people. Absalom said that he wished that he could
be appointed "judge" in the land, but what he was really aiming for
was David's throne (2 Sam. 15:4–6).

It is in this sense that Isaiah confesses that his hope is in Yahweh
as judge, lawgiver, and king—the one who will save Israel (Isa. 11:22).
This same conception is in view in many passages where God is said to
"judge" nations or Israel. To be sure, in some passages, Yahweh "judges"

nations merely by passing verdicts; Yahweh sets up His throne of judgment and deals out sentences (cf. Joel 3:12; Mic. 4:3). In other passages, however, it becomes clear that Yahweh's "judging" includes the execution of the sentence, whether a sentence of condemnation or exoneration. Several judgment oracles from Ezekiel will make the point:

> "Now the end is upon you, and I shall send My anger against you; I shall judge (*shaphat*) you according to your ways, and I shall bring all your abominations upon you. For My eye will have no pity on you, nor shall I spare you, but I shall bring your ways upon you, and your abominations will be among you; then you will know that I am the Yahweh!" Thus says Lord Yahweh, "A disaster, unique disaster, behold it is coming!" (Ezek. 7:3–5).

> "Now I will shortly pour out My wrath on you, and spend My anger against you, judge (*shaphat*) you according to your ways, and bring on you all your abominations. And My eye will show no pity, nor will I spare. I will repay you according to your ways, while your abominations are in your midst; then you will know that I, Yahweh, do the smiting" (Ezek. 7:8–9).

> The king will mourn, the prince will be clothed with horror, and the hands of the people of the land will tremble. According to their conduct I shall deal with them, and by their judgments I will judge (*shaphat*) them. And they will know that I am Yahweh (Ezek. 7:27).

In each of these passages, Yahweh is acting as the judge of His people, but His *judicial* action is pouring out His wrath, showing no pity, smiting Israel. Popular usage that describes disasters as "judgments from God" is consistent with biblical language.

Mark Seifrid has summarized the point well, in a brief critique of the work of John Ziesler. According to Seifrid, Ziesler defines "forensic" uses of the *zadaq* word-group as those that have to do with "'status' and not with activity or behavior." Seifrid points out that this does not match the biblical categories: "especially from the start of the monarchical period, legislative and executive decisions appear to have been effected primarily in the judicial setting. In such instances one cannot legitimately separate 'status' from the vindicating act of the king, nor should one, as Zeisler does, treat 'legal activity' and 'governing, ruling activity' as separate categories." More succinctly, Seifrid later adds that "administration of justice in the biblical contexts, as in the ancient world generally, is simultaneously judicial, legislative and executive."[19]

Much more could be said along these lines, but there is enough here to lead to this conclusion: defined biblically, judging is never simply a declaration that changes one's legal standing without changing one's condition or situation. When God condemns, He acts to enforce that sentence; in fact, a calamity *is* a sentence of condemnation, publicly announced.[20] When God judges favorably, He also acts to see that justice is done, and to ensure that the righteous are delivered and the wicked punished. That punishment and deliverance *is* the judicial verdict. As absolute Judge, Yahweh promulgates deliverdicts.

II. Psalms and Prophets

In the Psalms and prophets, it becomes particularly evident that "justification" or "God's favorable judgment" includes deliverance from enemies. These passages will confirm the conclusion developed in Part I: God's "forensic" actions consist not merely of declaring sentences, but executing them. Here especially the militorensic picture of justification becomes clear.

1. Psalm 7:6–11

Arise, Yahweh, in Thine anger;
Lift up Thyself against the rage of my adversaries,
And arouse Thyself for me; Thou hast appointed judgment.
And let the assembly of the peoples encompass Thee;
And over them return Thou on high.
Yahweh judges the peoples;
Vindicate me, Yahweh, according to my righteousness and my integrity
that is in me.
O let the evil of the wicked come to an end, but establish the righteous.
For the righteous God tries the hearts and minds.
My shield is with God
Who saves the upright in heart.
God is a righteous judge,
And a God who has indignation every day.

According to the setting in verses 1–2, David is beset by an enemy who threatens, like a raging lion, to tear him and drag him away. He cries out to Yahweh, pleading for help, and the language of the plea is thoroughly forensic. He raises the possibility that he deserves the treatment he receives from his enemy, and is willing to accept God's verdict against him (vv. 3–5). David thinks of and prays about the enemy as if he were an accused man pleading for the Judge to judge him innocent. "Vindicate" in verse 8 is *shaphat*; David is calling on Yahweh to "judge me," and clearly he is asking for a favorable verdict, a verdict that recognizes and responds to David's own righteousness (v. 8). He is asking Yahweh to pass a sentence of "not guilty." He is pleading for Yahweh to "justify" him. Despite the forensic-judicial language, however, the actual setting for the Psalm is one of military or personal rather than judicial conflict.[21] Here is a non-judicial setting conceived in judicial terms.

An unfavorable verdict would mean shame and defeat, with the enemy overtaking him, trampling him to the ground, and laying his glory in dust. If that happened, then David would conclude that Yahweh had condemned him; his defeat would *be* Yahweh's condemnation, or at least the public evidence of Yahweh's condemnation. By the same token, David's prayer is not merely a prayer for Yahweh to *pronounce* Him innocent. Suppose Yahweh appeared to David and told him, "I'm justifying you," but left David in the midst of his enemies, still threatened on every side by slander or death. Would David think that an answer to his prayer? Hardly. His prayer will be answered only if Yahweh passes a favorable verdict *by delivering him.* Yahweh's verdict must take empirical form and become an episode in the history of David's life. David will know that Yahweh judged in his favor when "the evil of the wicked comes to an end" and when the righteous man (i.e., David) is "established" (v. 9). David's public deliverance will be Yahweh's public declaration; to meet David's hopes, it must be a deliverdict.

Another important feature of this Psalm may also be noted. By asking Yahweh to judge him according to "my righteousness that is in me," David is asking Yahweh to pass a just sentence. When Yahweh does intervene to judge and to save, then it will be evident to all that "God is a righteous judge, and a God who has indignation every day" (v. 11). By delivering David, in short, Yahweh will not only be vindicating His righteous servant, demonstrating publicly that David is under Yahweh's protection and love, but He will also be vindicating His own righteousness. By intervening to save David, Yahweh will be showing that He is a God who keeps His promises, a God who can be trusted, a heavenly Creator-King who can be counted on to set things in order. That is to say, in this Psalm David is anticipating Paul's gospel, in which the righteousness of God is revealed in Yahweh's "justification" of those who believe in Jesus.

2. Psalm 35:22–28

> Thou hast seen it, Yahweh, do not keep silent;
> Yahweh, do not be far from me.
> Stir up Thyself, and awake to my right,
> And to my cause, my God and my Lord.
> Judge me, Yahweh my God, according to Thy righteousness;
> And do not let them rejoice over me.
> Do not let them say in their heart, "Aha, our desire!"
> Do not let them say, "We have swallowed him up!"
> Let those be ashamed and humiliated altogether who rejoice at my distress;
> Let those be clothed with shame and dishonor who magnify themselves over me.
> Let them shout for joy and rejoice, who favor my vindication;
> And let them say continually, "Yahweh be magnified,
> Who delights in the prosperity of His servant."
> And my tongue shall declare Thy righteousness
> And Thy praise all day long.

The picture in this Psalm is similar to that of Psalm 7 above. David is again being attacked (vv. 1, 4) and betrayed by former friends (vv. 13–16). He initially describes his situation in judicial terms: His adversaries are engaged in a legal wrangle with him (*rib*, v. 1). Courtroom language emerges now and then throughout the Psalm: David is beset with "malicious witnesses" (v. 11) who "slander" him (v. 15) and conspire with "deceitful words" against the people of the land (v. 20). Given this courtroom scenery, it is not surprising that David appeals to Yahweh to "judge me" (v. 24). Through the early verses of the Psalm, however, the picture changes from the courtroom to the battlefield. Instead of immediately calling on Yahweh as the "Judge" who will pronounce and enforce a favorable verdict, He calls on Yahweh as the Divine Warrior who will arm Himself with "buckler and shield" as well as "spear and battle-axe" to rescue David (vv. 2–3). Whether the actual situation was one of slander, legal attack, or military engagement, David describes the situation with a combination of forensic and military imagery. The very fact that the imagery is so mixed that we cannot determine the exact nature of the threat to David is evidence that the "forensic" language is not always strictly tied to "forensic" situations.

As in Psalm 7, David's appeal is partly a passionate demand that Yahweh vindicate Himself. Yahweh has promised all manner of blessing to David, and yet David is oppressed, betrayed, in danger. Can the Yahweh keep silent and maintain His reputation as a righteous God? Can He leave His faithful worshiper, His anointed king, to be devoured by enemies, and still be considered a just Judge? This is the theology behind David's plaintive cry, "Thou hast seen it, Yahweh, do not keep silent" (v. 22) and behind his exultant conclusion: When Yahweh delivers him, His righteousness will be magnified, because David promises that "my tongue shall declare Thy righteousness and Thy praise all day long" (v. 28).

Of course, David wants Yahweh to justify Himself *by justifying David*, as he states explicitly in verse 27. Clearly what David hopes for is victory over his enemies, a victory so complete that all who favor him in the conflict will rejoice with shouting. He describes this hope for victory, however, using the language of righteousness: The noun "vindication" in verse 27 is *zedeq*, one of the righteousness-group of Hebrew words. If, as he has prayed, Yahweh did "judge according to my righteousness" and did "vindicate" him, David would take that as God's favorable verdict. If Yahweh declared him righteous, but left him to be swallowed by his enemies, left him shamed and dishonored, would the prayer for vindication be answered? If Yahweh had proclaimed to the hosts of angels that He did in fact judge David innocent in this conflict, would those "who favor my vindication" be able to "shout for joy and rejoice"? Of course not. Victory would mean vindication, and it is not going too far to say that for David victory would be "justification."

3. Psalm 94:1–7

> O Yahweh, God of vengeance;
> God of vengeance, shine forth.
> Rise up, O Judge (*shophet*) of the earth;
> Render recompense to the proud.
> How long shall the wicked, O Yahweh,
> How long shall the wicked exult?
> They pour forth, they speak arrogantly;
> All who do wickedness vaunt themselves.
> They crush Thy people, O Yahweh,
> And afflict Thy heritage.
> They slay the widow and the stranger,
> And murder the orphans.
> And they have said, "Yahweh does not see,
> Nor does the God of Jacob pay need."

Here, the Psalmist's vision is broader. His concern is not merely for his individual deliverance, though this remains an element of the situation (vv. 17–22). Rather, he is appealing to Yahweh to judge on behalf of those who are oppressed by the wicked, and he is hoping that Yahweh will not only pass a sentence against the wicked but also intervene to defend and save them. Yahweh preserves His people in the midst of adversity (v. 12–13), and eventually He will come to their aid and deliver them (vv. 14–16). Verse 15 describes this in judicial terms: "judgment will again be righteous," and the courtroom language continues into the following verse: Yahweh is the one who "will stand up for me against evildoers" and "will take his stand for me against those who do wickedness" (v. 16). In short, the Psalmist hopes that Yahweh, acting as the "judging One of the earth" will bring "their wickedness upon them, and will destroy them in their evil" (v. 23). An appeal for God to judge the wicked is an appeal for Him to *do* something about the wicked, and an appeal to God to establish "righteous judgment" is an appeal for Him to *do* something to save His people. Mouthing verdicts without action on behalf of the oppressed will not satisfy the Psalmist's passion for just vengeance.[22]

4. Isaiah 54:11–17

David is the representative Israelite, and so his vindication is at the same time the vindication of Israel. This corporate aspect of justification comes out explicitly in the prophecy of restoration in Isaiah 54:11–17:

> O afflicted one, storm-tossed, and not comforted,
> Behold, I will set your stones in antinomy,
> And your foundations I will lay in sapphires.
> Moreover, I will make your battlements of rubies,
> And your gates of crystal,
> And your entire wall of precious stones.
> And all your sons will be taught of Yahweh;
> And the well-being of your sons will be great.
> In righteousness you will be established;
> You will be far from oppression, for you will not fear;
> And from terror, for it will not come near you.
> If anyone fiercely assails you it will not be from Me.
> Whoever assails you will fall because of you.
> Behold, I myself have created the smith who blows the fire of coals,
> And brings out a weapon for its work;
> And I have created the destroyer to ruin.
> No weapon that is formed against you shall prosper;
> And every tongue that accuses you in judgment you will condemn.
> This is the heritage of the servants of Yahweh,
> And their vindication is from Me, declares Yahweh.

The larger context of this passage is Isaiah's famous "second exodus," the promised deliverance from Babylonian captivity and the accompanying restoration and glorification of Israel. More specifically, chapter 54 follows on the prophecy of the suffering servant of chapter 53, whose vicarious sufferings remove the transgressions of Israel and secure the nation's renewal. Because the servant has borne away the sins of the people, the "barren woman," Jerusalem, will give birth. Like Sarah, Jerusalem will rejoice in children, once the Servant has undergone his circumcision by being "cut off from the land of the living" (cf. Gen. 17–20). Jerusalem's children will be so numerous that the tent will have to be extended and spread abroad to make room for them all (vv. 1–3). In verse 4, Yahweh addresses Israel not as Mother but as bride. Israel has been "like a wife forsaken and grieved in spirit," but this was not a permanent divorce: "For a brief moment I forsook you, but with great compassion I will gather you" (vv. 6–7). In verses 11–17, the imagery is civic-architectural; the city that has been devastated by enemies will be rebuilt with precious stones; the city assailed by enemies will be secure. Thus, the sequence of the passage is from the opening of the womb, through the restored marital covenant, to the rebirth and glorification of the city.

All this is in the background when we get to the climactic verse 17, which adds a whisper of forensic imagery to the mix. Jerusalem will be protected from the weapons of the destroyer, and even from the slander and accusations of an enemy-at-law. Yahweh will stop the mouths of Israel's enemies, and since it is God who justifies no one dare condemn. This, the chapter concludes, is "their vindication." "Vindication" is again *zedeq*, and could be translated as "justification." "This" is Israel's "justification."

But what exactly is Yahweh referring to as "their justification"? What is "this"? Is it the fact that no one will be able to condemn or accuse? Yes. Yet, though stopping the mouths of the accusers is certainly one aspect of Israel's justification, the climactic placement of this sentence within the chapter suggests that it summarizes the whole passage. Further, what is the source of the slanders against Jerusalem? And what will be done to silence the slanderers? No doubt, the slander is the hissing of the nations against Israel's claims about being the elect of Yahweh, the chosen nation of the Creator. So long as Israel is in ruins, the nations can say, "If Israel be the son of Yahweh, let him come up from the grave" and "Israel trusted in Yahweh; let Yahweh now save him." And the *only* thing dramatic enough to silence the slanderers will be Israel's resurrection.

That is to say, Israel's "justification" takes the form of Israel's restoration and rebirth; Israel's justification looks like Abram's, like death being swallowed up by life. As in the Psalm passages discussed above, justification does not refer merely to a declaration that changes the legal status of Israel but leaves them in ruin and defeat. Their justification is their deliverance from ruin, exile, and the curse. Israel's restoration *is* Yahweh's declaration that they are the righteous ones. "This" *is* "their vindication." What does the "vindication/justification of Israel" look like? It looks like a barren woman giving birth to many children; like a forsaken bride being restored to her husband, her grief melted into joy; like a ruined city rebuilt and reinhabited, boiling with energy and hope. "Justification" here is not militorensic; it is forenstorational, a forensurrection.

Again like David, Isaiah sees that the justification of Israel is simultaneously the justification of Yahweh. Yahweh had promised that Israel would be redeemed, and if she is not, Yahweh's fidelity is put into question. By redeeming Israel, therefore, Yahweh proves Himself a righteous God, a God who establishes right by delivering His people. This is why "righteousness" and "salvation" are so often parallel in Isaiah:

> My righteousness is near, My salvation has gone forth (51:4).

> But my salvation shall be forever,
> And My righteousness shall not wane (51:6).

> But My righteousness shall be forever,
> And My salvation to all generations (51:8).

In this context, the "salvation" referred to is redemption from exile:

> Awake, awake, put on strength, O arm of Yahweh;
> Awake as in the days of old, the generations of long ago.
> Was it not Thou who cut Rahab in pieces,
> Who pierced the dragon?
> Was it not Thou who dried up the sea,
> The waters of the great deep;
> Who made the depths of the sea a pathway
> For the redeemed to cross over?
> So the ransomed of Yahweh will return,
> And come with joyful shouting to Zion;
> And everlasting joy will be on their heads.
> And they will obtain gladness and joy.
> And sorrow and sighing will flee away (51:9–11).

When Yahweh keeps His promise to deliver Israel from captivity, that will be both their salvation/justification and a public demonstration of His righteousness.

5. Jeremiah 51:5–10

According to Isaiah, the justification of Israel is an act of Yahweh. What the law could not do, and what Israel could not do by keeping the law, God did: He restored Israel and thereby demonstrated to the satanic accusers among the nations that He counted them His righteous people. Justification is thus wholly by grace, not by the works of the law. Jeremiah agreed, and took things a step further by talking about the justification of *ungodly* Israel:

> For neither Israel nor Judah has been forsaken
> By his God, Yahweh of hosts,
> Although their land is full of guilt
> Before the Holy one of Israel.
> Flee from the midst of Babylon,
> And each of you save his life!
> Do not be destroyed in her punishment,
> For this is Yahweh's time of vengeance;
> He is going to render recompense to her.
> Babylon has been a golden cup in the hand of Yahweh,
> Intoxicating all the earth.
> The nations have drunk her wine;
> Therefore the nations are going mad.
> Suddenly Babylon has fallen and been broken;
> Wail over her!
> Bring balm for her pain;
> Perhaps she may be healed.
> We applied healing to Babylon, but she was not healed;
> Forsake her and let us each go to his own country,
> For her judgment has reached to heaven
> And towers up to the very skies.
> Yahweh has brought about our vindication;
> Come and let us recount in Zion
> The work of Yahweh our God!

Again, "justification" is a way of describing the deliverance of Israel from her enemies. In particular, in this passage, Jeremiah is describing the judgment on Babylon, the conquest of Babylon by the Medes (vv. 11–14), and the consequent restoration of Israel to her land.

While condemning the nations that judged Israel, Yahweh is at the same time vindicating/justifying Israel herself. But Jeremiah makes it clear that Israel's deliverance from Babylonian captivity is not based on the "reformation" of Israel. On the contrary, the Lord will restore Israel and condemn and shame her enemies in spite of her wickedness, "although their land is full of guilt before the Holy One of Israel" (v. 5). Jeremiah, in short, sees the restoration of Israel as a corporate form of "justification of the ungodly."

III. Paul: "Militorensic" and "Forenstorational" Justification

Paul's teaching concerning justification is worked out against the background of these Old Testament texts. Paul's use of the example of Abram is obvious, but, though less obvious, Paul also appeals to Psalms and prophets to develop his theology of justification. Richard Hays has highlighted Paul's practice of echoing Psalms and prophetic texts throughout his initial discussion of justification in Romans 1–4.[23] In Romans 3:20, Paul concludes his litany of condemnation with "by the words of the law no flesh shall be justified in His sight," an allusion to Psalm 143:2 ("And do not enter into judgment with Thy servant, for in Thy sight no man living is righteous"). Paul's use of the Psalm, however, is not limited to this brief quotation. David's appeal to Yahweh's "truth" (or faithfulness) and righteousness (Ps. 143:1–2, 10–11) forms the background to the whole of Romans 3. As Hays summarizes:

> The psalm provides Paul not only with the language for a blanket indictment of humankind but also with the expectant language of prayer that looks to God's righteousness as the source of salvation. When Paul writes in Rom. 3:21 that "Now, apart from Law, the righteousness of God has been manifested, *witnessed by the Law and the Prophets*," he is making a claim that anyone who had ever prayed Psalm 143 from the heart would instantly recognize: God's saving righteousness, for which the psalmist had hoped, has at last appeared.

Psalm 143, in short, provides a bridge from Paul's condemnation of sinful humanity to his declaration that the righteousness of God has now been manifested in the gospel. Hays writes, "If Psalm 143 implicitly spans verses 20 and 21 of Romans 3, then the righteousness of God proclaimed by Paul is the same righteousness invoked in

David's prayer . . . the righteousness in question must be God's own
righteousness, that is, God's own moral integrity."[24]

A glance at Psalm 143 will indicate that this Psalm employs "righteousness" language in much the same way as the Psalms and prophetic
passages examined above. Again, David appeals to Yahweh because of
persecution and attack from his enemies: "the enemy has persecuted
my soul; he has crushed my life to the ground; he has made me dwell
in dark places, like those who have long been dead" (v. 3). His prayer is
that Yahweh would "deliver me from my enemies" and "cut off my
enemies, and destroy all those who afflict my soul" (v. 12). It is in this
context that David recognizes that he has no meritorious claims on
God, since "in Thy sight no man living is righteous" (v. 2). Yet, he
appeals to God's lovingkindness, with the reminder that he is Yahweh's
servant (v. 12). Though David does not here use the language of justification or vindication, the situation is the same as found in other Psalms
where David does employ this language, and Paul, remarkably, brings
David's prayer for deliverance explicitly into a discussion of justification. Psalm 143 provides an insight into the "justification of the
unrighteous," for David cries out for deliverance and vindication despite his acknowledgment that "no man is righteous." Like Paul, he
knows he has nothing to stand on but the overwhelming lovingkindness
of Yahweh (v. 12).

Several things emerge from this examination of the interplay between Psalm 143 and Romans 3. First, as Hays points out, in both
passages, the "righteousness of God" refers to God's own righteousness,
manifested in the Psalm in Yahweh's action to "bring my soul out of
trouble" (v. 11) and in Paul in the redemption achieved by Christ (Rom.
3:21–24). Psalm 143, in short, is one of those places where "the Law
and the Prophets" witness to the righteousness of God that comes apart
from the law (Rom. 3:21). Second, in the Psalm, David's plea for Yahweh
to display His righteousness is simultaneously a plea for Yahweh to
deliver David. If Paul is working from Psalm 143 (among other texts)
in Romans 3, it seems reasonable to assume that he has the same conception of the manifestation of God's righteousness. Finally, and this is
the crucial point, Paul expresses the manifestation of "the righteousness
of God apart from law" in terms of "being justified as a gift by His
grace" (Rom. 3:21, 24). With the Psalm texts in the background, it

seems plausible to conclude that Paul understood "justification" here in the same way that David did, that is, as a favorable judgment of God rendered through deliverance from enemies. Paul's citation of David suggests that he is assuming the same "militorensic" picture for justification. In short, passages using "justification" in an "improper" sense echo in the background of Paul's discussion.

Paul's treatment of Jesus' resurrection shows, similarly, that he is operating with the same conception of "justification" as the Psalms and prophets. For Paul as well as for David, to "justify" is not merely to issue a statement that so-and-so is righteous; God declares His verdict of "not guilty" by delivering *the* "righteous one" from oppression and from enemies. As Richard Gaffin has argued, the resurrection of Jesus is the ground of our justification (Rom. 4:25) because it is first of all the vindication (justification) of Jesus (1 Tim. 3:16).[25] The resurrection is not the *result* of a prior verdict from the Father; the resurrection is instead the public declaration of the verdict (as it is the public declaration of His sonship, Rom. 1:4). By raising Jesus, the Father proclaimed that His Son, condemned by Roman and Jew alike, was in fact the Righteous One, and was righteous precisely in His obedience to death on a cross. Obviously, the resurrection did more than change Jesus' "legal" status. Deliverance from death *was* the verdict.

Jesus' resurrection is the paradigmatic case of justification. We are justified because we are joined to the One who has been justified by being raised from the dead. Since Jesus' justification is the pattern of our justification, our justification must likewise involve deliverance from the power of death and from the threat of enemies, including the enemies of sin and Satan. In this sense, justification and definitive sanctification are two ways of describing the same act: God renders a verdict in our favor by cutting off our enemies—our chief enemies being death and sin and Satan—and by delivering us from their power. This is still a "forensic" act, but it is "forensic" in the full biblical sense; God in Christ justifies and vindicates as Divine Warrior as well as Judge. As in Isaiah's second exodus, Jesus' resurrection is a forensurrection.

Paul, indeed, occasionally uses "justification" language explicitly in this militorensic or forenstorational sense. Romans 6, for instance, describes the sinner's deliverance from sin and death through baptismal union with Christ's death and burial, and in this context Paul

writes that through our union with Christ's death we have been "justified from sin" (v. 7). John Piper has recently argued that even here Paul
is using "justification" in its strictly forensic sense, meaning "to declare
righteous." Instead of describing liberation from sin, Paul is speaking
of "God's imputed righteousness, and our right standing with God,
over against our sin," which is "the clear and distinct and necessary
ground for sanctification" but not sanctification itself.[26] Piper's interpretation, however, does not take into account the specific force of Paul's
use of "sin" in Romans 6. In many passages, Paul does indeed emphasize the guilt or stain of sin in view, but in Romans 6, "sin" is virtually
personified as a dominating power and a tyrannical ruler: it enslaves
(vv. 7, 17, 20), reigns in the mortal body (v. 12), accepts the tribute of
the members of the body (v. 13), is a master (v 14) who pays out the
wages of death (v. 23). In short, Paul is not dealing with the guilt of
sin; the "picture" here is not the courtroom; Paul presents a scene of
battle, or, better, he pictures the sinner an oppressed slave under the
thumb of a harsh master. To be "justified" from "master sin" is to be
delivered from his hand, from his lordship and mastery; in this context, to be justified from sin is to be liberated. When we were joined to
the Risen One by baptism, because we were joined with the vindicated
Son, the Father judged us favorably and passed (and executed) a sentence of condemnation against sin. Like David, we looked for vindication;
as with David, our vindication takes the form of deliverance from accusing and attacking enemies. If I may be pardoned yet another
neologism, Paul is using "justify" here in a "liberorensic" sense.

Piper appeals to Acts 13:36–39 to support his interpretation of
Romans 6:7, but it seems rather that Paul uses "justify" in Acts 13 in
the "liberorensic" sense that I described above. To be sure, Paul does
say that "forgiveness of sins is proclaimed to you" (v. 38) through the
death and resurrection of Jesus, and that this is immediately followed
by Paul's claim that believers are "justified from all things, from which
you could not be justified through the Law of Moses" (v. 39). Yet,
despite the close proximity of "forgiveness" and "justified," that does
not mean that they are synonymous, or that "justify" is being used in a
narrowly forensic sense. Note the oddity of the prepositional phrases
that follow "justify" in verse 39, which, apart from Romans 6:7 have no
clear parallels in Paul's letters. The fact that this phrasing ("justified

from") appears only here suggests that Paul is using "justify" in the same sense in both passages. Since "justify" in Romans 6:7 means "liberate" or "deliver," it is *prima facie* plausible that it has the same nuance in Acts 13 as well. Many translators have noted the unusual usage of Acts 13, and have translated *dikaioo* as "freed" (e.g., NASB).

Further, several larger contextual features suggest that "justify" here has a broader than forensic sense. The gospel that Paul announces is the fulfillment of "the promise made to the fathers" (v. 32), which is specifically fulfilled in the exaltation of Jesus as Son at the Father's right hand (vv. 33–37). According to Psalm 2, quoted in verse 33, the Son of Yahweh is exalted on Zion to rule the nations and to bring the earth into trembling submission. From many other passages of Scripture, it is clear that the exaltation of the Davidic king means the establishment of peace and righteousness on earth (cf. Ps. 72). The promise fulfilled in Jesus, then, is not merely one of individual redemption; Paul would have no doubt agreed with Zacharias that "the oath which [Yahweh] swore to Abraham" included the promise "that we, being delivered from the fear of our enemies, might serve Him without fear, in holiness and righteousness before Him all our days" through the "horn of salvation" raised up in the house of David (Luke 1:67–79).

Paul's statement about justification comes into the midst of this larger covenantal gospel, this gospel of fulfilled promise. This promise includes (miraculously!) the forgiveness of sins (v. 38), but it includes much else beside. And the chiastic structure of 13:39 indicates how this promise has now come to be fulfilled:

> through Him
> everyone who believes is justified
> from all things
> from which
> you could not be justified
> through the Law of Moses.

That is, two alternative instruments of "justification" are suggested: Jesus the Risen One, and the Law of Moses. But only one actually "justifies," the Resurrected Jesus: What the Law could not do, weak as it was through sin, God did in Christ by condemning sin in the flesh (cf. Rom. 8:3).

In the larger context of Paul's sermon, "all things" includes every-thing that threatened the fulfillment of the promise, whether death or life or principalities or powers or things present or things to come or any other creature. The whole promise fulfilled in Jesus the Risen and Exalted King is included under the phrase "justified from all things." The Law could not save Israel from the calumny of the nations, since Israel broke the law and ended in exile. The Law could not bring final forgiveness, because the blood of bulls and goats did not take away sin. The Law could not raise the dead. Through faith in Christ, and in Him alone, we are "justified from all things."

Conclusion

The discussion of justification in this paper is hardly definitive, complete, or flawless. Yet, a number of conclusions may be advanced that I hope will help to perfect the Church's teaching on justification:

1. "Justification" and "righteousness" are used in a number of contexts in Scripture, and our doctrine of justification must take account of the rich variety of those contexts. In some cases, the context is strictly judicial—the scene is a courtroom. In other passages, the root metaphor is not judicial but military or personal conflict, or oppression by an overlord. Justification fits into the latter contexts as well as the former. It has a "forensic" cast to it, but bibli-cally speaking "forensic" covers what I have called "covenantal," "militorensic," "forenstorational," and "liberorensic" situations.

2. Justification is God's judgment that a man or a people is righteous, but God's judgments are never simply verbal sentences. When God passes judgment in someone's fa-vor, that judgment includes His "righteous deeds" by which He ensures that the one judged righteous receives justice. God's Word is active and effective.

3. One of the important implications of this study is that "justification" language can be applied in a variety of situ-ations and contexts within the life of the Christian and the Church:

a. Prayer in the Psalms is often framed in terms of accusation (or attack of some other kind) and vindication. God has promised that His people will shine like the sun, and be a light on a hill; when that does not happen, we have every right to pray with the same importunity as David did that the Triune God would intervene to set things right, to vindicate us, and to vindicate Himself in vindicating us. This should lend considerable power and confidence to our prayers, for if there is one thing we can be sure of it is that God will vindicate Himself before the world.

b. Individually, any deliverance from persecutors, dangers, sickness and death can be seen as God's public "vindications" of His faithful people. A close friend of my family's has for several years been the target of a legal attack orchestrated by powerful political enemies, including some of his former political allies. This battle is not over, but when the case was taken to court in an earlier phase, this friend's opponents blundered and stumbled so badly that the case was thrown out of court. *That* was a divine act of vindication, a justification.

c. Corporately, the deliverance of the Church from the threat of Jewish and Roman persecution is the "justification" of the Church. When the walls of Jerusalem were breached and the temple burned in A.D. 70, God was declaring His verdict against apostate Judaism, and likewise declaring His verdict with regard to Jesus and His disciples. In the centuries that followed, God declared His verdict against the Roman Empire, whose assaults against the Church ended in conversion. God has been "justifying" the Church, publicly declaring them His righteous people, ever since.

4. In all of this, it is crucial to remember continually that justification, however defined, is by faith. And in part that means that our justification/vindication is not completely and fully revealed before the Last Judgment. We are justi-

fied in the present, but in another sense we await final public vindication. Many believers have been faithful to death, and their bones now lie in forgotten graves or scattered on the earth. God our Father, for His own infinitely wise reasons, did not intervene to rescue and justify them. But they are not forgotten, and someday they will rise to public vindication, while their enemies and accusers are silenced in darkness. Vindication may not be now; it may not be soon; but it will come. Or God is not God.

Notes - Chapter 6

[1] This is the second draft of the first stage of what I hope will eventually be a more rigorous and thorough treatment of justification, and should therefore not be taken as a definitive statement. I have benefitted enormously from comments on an earlier draft by Douglas Wilson, Joel Garver, Mark Horne, and other participants in the Biblical Horizons discussion group, as well as more critical comments and challenges from Stephen Lewis and Grover Gunn. I am grateful too for editorial corrections from Mark Horne.

[2] George Lakoff and Mark Johnson, *Philosophy in the Flesh: The Embodied Mind and Its Challenge to Western Thought* (New York: Basic Books, 1999), ch. 4. For more, see Lakoff and Johnson, *Metaphors We Live By* (Chicago: University of Chicago Press, 1980).

[3] Alister McGrath, *Iustitia Dei: A history of the Christian Doctrine of Justification* (2 vols.; Cambridge: Cambridge University Press, 1986), vol. 1, p. 32.

[4] Ibid., vol. 1, p. 41.

[5] In this paragraph, I am closely following McGrath in *ibid.*, vol. 1, pp. 44–45. The definition of justification at the end is my translation of "*quidam motus quo humana mens movetur a Deo a statu peccati in statum justitiae.*"

[6] Luther, "The Freedom of a Christian," in *Three Treatises* (Minneapolis: Fortress, 1978), pp. 286–287.

[7] For the early development of the Protestant doctrine, see McGrath, *Iustitia Dei*, vol. 2, pp. 1–53.

[8] "Definitive Sanctification" in *Collected Writings of John Murray* (4 vols.; Carlisle, PA: Banner of Truth, 1977), vol. 2, pp. 277–284.

[9] Further illustrations of this doctrine may be found in Heinrich Heppe, *Reformed Dogmatics* (trans. G. T. Thomson; London: Wakeman Great Reprints, 1950), ch. 21.

[10] Turretin, *Institutes of Elenctic Theology* (trans. George Musgrave Giger; ed. James T. Dennison; 3 vols.; Phillipsburg, NJ: P&R, 1994), vol. 2, pp. 634–635.

[11] Several issues are at stake here: First, while "justify" is found in courtroom passages, this is not the *only* setting in which it is found. Indeed, second, I will argue below that Paul actually makes use of passages that use "justification" in an "improper sense" when he is formulating his teaching on justification, and Paul indeed uses "justify" in an "improper" sense in some passages. These texts therefore are relevant to our understanding of justification. Third, by what standard does one decide that some passages that treat justification or use the terminology of justification are more fundamental to the doctrine than others? How does Turretin *know* that the passages that use justification in a forensic sense are the ones on which the doctrine should be built, unless he has already determined that the doctrine should have a forensic cast to it? Shouldn't our "doctrine of justification" be an effort to summarize *everything* Scripture says about the subject?

[12] I don't mean to insult anyone's intelligence, but perhaps a word needs to be said to explain why a discussion of "righteousness" is relevant to the doctrine of justification. In both Hebrew and Greek, "justification" and "justify" are based on the same root words as "righteous" and "righteousness," and thus these terms form a single family of words and ideas. Because of the peculiarities of English, this connection is more difficult to see, but I have not found the suggested neologisms ("right-wise" instead of "justify," for example) very useful.

[13] In an earlier draft of this essay, I employed this concept of righteousness throughout. I am not convinced that it is wrong, but in the light of Seifrid's work, it has become clear that I need to study the question more thoroughly.

[14] "Righteousness Language in the Hebrew Scriptures and Early Judaism," in D. A. Carson, et. al., eds., *Justification and Variegated Nomism: Volume 1: The Complexities of Second-Temple Judaism* (Grand Rapids: Baker, 2001), esp. pp. 415–430; and "The 'New Perspective on Paul' and Its Problems," *Themelios* 25:2, pp. 12-18. For defenses of the covenantal view of "righteousness," see Gerhard von Rad, *Old Testament Theology* (2 vols.; New York: Harper & Row, 1962), vol. 1, pp. 370–383; H. Seebass, "Righteousness," in *Dictionary of New Testament Theology* (ed. Colin Brown; 3 vols.; Grand Rapids: Zondervan, 1978), vol. 3, pp. 354–356.

[15] Seifrid, "'New Perspective,'" p. 14.

[16] Seifrid, "Righteousness Language," p. 421.

[17] Of course, since God is always and everywhere the Judge, any righteousness language used in the context of God's relation to man by definition has a forensic cast. God is never simply "partner," but always King and Lord. But it still seems fairly evident that God does not always *explicitly* play the role of Judge. Though Yahweh was Abram's Judge as much as Ahab's, His dealings with Abram seem on the face of things to be less overtly "judicial" than His dealings with Ahab (1 Kings 22).

[18] These passages are cited by W. Schneider, "*krima,*" in *The New International Dictionary of New Testament Theology* (3 vols.; ed. Colin Brown; Grand Rapids: Zondervan, 1976), 2.363.

[19] Seifrid, "Righteousness Language," pp. 422, 426–427.

[20] I don't mean that every calamity is ultimately a sentence of condemnation. Christian suffer for their faithfulness, and the calamities that befall them are actually a sign of God's favor rather than his condemnation. Yet, God's judgments are not arbitrary. When fire and brimstone fall from heaven—or when trade towers collapse in horrific clouds of dust and smoke—we should tremble, because the Judge of all the earth has just passed sentence in dramatic fashion.

[21] At least, so it seems from the way David describes the threat ("lest he tear my soul like a lion" [v. 1] and "let the enemy pursue my soul and overtake it . . . and lay my glory in the dust" [v. 5]). David also issues a warning to His enemies that God, the Divine Judge, is also Divine Warrior, who "will sharpen His sword; He has bent His bow and made it ready. He has also prepared for Himself deadly weapons; He makes

His arrows fiery shafts" (vv. 12–13). If David was actually facing *legal* opposition, the point of my argument stands, for in that case too David would be expecting Yahweh to publicly exonerate Him in some manner, hoping that Yahweh would frustrate the legal plots and conspiracies and machinations of his enemies.

[22] Of course, Yahweh cannot "mouth verdicts" without effect. But that is precisely the point: God's Word is active, like a sword, and the judicial verdicts that come from His mouth slay and make alive.

[23] The following paragraphs summarize Hays's argument in *Echoes of Scripture in the Letters of Paul* (New Haven: Yale, 1989), pp. 51–53.

[24] My point here is not to defend Hays's conception of "righteousness" as "moral integrity," a definition I find unconvincing. I do, however, agree with Hays's point that throughout this section, Paul is talking about the "righteousness that belongs to God," which is demonstrated in the gospel.

[25] *Resurrection and Redemption: A Study in Paul's Soteriology* (Phillipsburg, NJ: P&R, 1987), pp. 122–124.

[26] *Counted Righteous in Christ: Should We Abandon the Imputation of Christ's Righteousness?* (Wheaton, IL: Crossway, 2002), p. 77.

Chapter Seven
Justification and the Gentiles
Steve Schlissel

We must settle theological differences by appeal to the Bible. That's what the Reformed standards demand. The Westminster Confession, for example, insists that "The Supreme Judge, by which all controversies of religion are to be determined, and all decrees of councils, opinions . . . (and) doctrines of men . . . are to be examined, and in whose sentence we are to rest, can be no other but the Holy Spirit speaking in Scripture" (1.10).

Further, it is evident throughout our Confessions that we recognize the necessity of covenantal *obedience* (not works-righteousness) for salvation. Consider, for example, a statement made in the Westminster Confession of Faith at 1.7. Dealing with the perspicuity of Scripture, the Confession teaches that:

> Those things which are necessary to be known, believed, and *observed* for salvation, are so clearly propounded, and opened in some place of Scripture or other, that not only the learned, but the unlearned, in a due use of the ordinary means, may attain unto a sufficient understanding of them.

Note carefully: salvation, according to this, requires knowledge, belief *and observance*; all, it says, are *necessary.*

Again, the Confession at 14.2 expounds saving faith as that which "yield(s) obedience to the commands" of God. While faith is extolled as the alone *instrument* of justification, it is freely and plainly admitted in the Westminster Confession (11.2) that such faith never appears on Planet Earth by itself. If you want life, you don't choose between heart and lungs: you need both. Faith is never "alone in the person justified,

Steve Schlissel

but is *ever* accompanied with all other saving graces, and is no dead faith, but worketh by love." Well, there ya go.

We ask you to remember John Owen's explicit statement on this very point. He said, "We absolutely deny that we can be justified by that faith which *can be alone*; that is, without a principle of spiritual life and *universal obedience*, operative in all the works of it, as duty doth require" (*Justification By Faith*, p. 73; italics his). Owen categorically rejects the idea that justifying faith can be separated from "holy obedience": "We allow no faith to be of the same kind or nature with that whereby we are justified, but what virtually and radically contains in it universal obedience." Note what Owen is asserting: Obedience is not merely a test or evidence of saving faith; it is inseparably bound up in its character. There is no disobedient yet saving faith. It is not faith+obedience, but the obedience of faith.

Further still, Westminster Shorter Catechism (85) asks, "What doth God require of us, that we may escape his wrath and curse due to us for sin?" The answer? "To escape the wrath and curse of God due to us for sin, God requireth of us faith in Jesus Christ, repentance unto life, with the diligent use of all the outward means whereby Christ communicateth to us the benefits of redemption." Repentance unto life is defined in answer 87 as a saving grace whereby a sinner turns from sin to God "with full purpose of, and endeavour after, new obedience." This, the Westminster Standards affirm, is *required* for salvation, for "it is of such necessity to all sinners, that none may expect pardon without it." There is no such thing as an alone faith. Period.

If any doubt remains, Heidelberger 87 tries to remove it: "Can they be saved who do not turn to God from their unthankful, impenitent life?" Answer? "By no means, for, as Scripture says, no unchaste person, idolater, adulterer, thief, covetous man, drunkard, slanderer, robber, or the like shall inherit the kingdom of God." Methinks this is plain enough.

Yet the value of the Reformation's rediscovery of Scripture's authority is mitigated by the insistence that the Bible be read through the lens of downstream systematics. We must learn to read Scripture according to its own categories rather than sifting it through ours. A curse be on abstractions!

I'm afraid that what God has actually written cannot be clearly read in Luther's shadow. The cure? Our post-Reformational obsession with the question "What must I do to be saved?" must be replaced by "What does God require?" (as the Shorter Catechism does at #85). The latter includes the former. By reading the Bible with the larger question we have better opportunity to hear its comprehensive answer. Thus, profitable reading begins with a heart disposed to hear the *whole* message. Too, too often the Bible is read as a mere set of texts, a collection of 31,173 propositions (verses), dropped from heaven as a "personal promise toolkit," or as a convenient sourcebook for human systematics.

It is vital to remember that God has given us His Word to *reveal* Himself, not to hide Himself. Some systematicians seem to expect— without warrant—that simple readers of the Bible would or could read it through Hellenic, slice-and-dice presuppositions. The Book of Hosea, by itself, shatters the demands of these systematicians. God is Israel's passionate and jealous Husband. Jealousy seeks the flesh-and-blood return of the object of its desire; it is not satisfied with a flowery description of abstractions and conceptions. Just so, God demands that all sinners present *themselves*—not merely their ideas—to Him through Jesus Christ. That is not done by mental assent to neat propositions, but by a life lived in and with God. "He hath shewed thee, O man, what is good; and what doth the LORD require of thee, but to do justly, and to love mercy, and to walk humbly with thy God." This is unchangeable truth.

Firm Foundations

In discussing his conversion from agnostic rationalism to Christ, Phillip E. Johnson said in a recent interview that he rejected rationalism when he realized it couldn't rationally account for itself. "There is an instinct, or revelation, or whatever you want to call it, that underlies your thinking, and the only interesting thing in philosophy is how you get *that*." That is to say, since presuppositions govern all subsequent interpretation, a man had better make sure his presuppositions are firm and in order.

What we are trying to accomplish in these essays is difficult: a reassessing of the mindset—the presuppositions—we bring to the Scripture-reading enterprise. But though it be difficult, it is do-able. We must continually seek from God (through His Word and prayer) an exchange of our concerns for His. We need to reorient ourselves so that we learn to see Him and ourselves from *His* revealed perspective. And we need to repent of our insistence that the Lord conform to ours.

A problem with some modern Reformers is that they have no abiding interest in reforming. They have come to equate "continuing reformation" with liberalism, a petrifying error. Such brothers are more tightly wrapped up in their traditions than any arch-Romanist opponent of their ancestors, yet they deny it. Chanting *sola scriptura* rings hollow when what is really meant is "*sola*-those-parts-of-*scriptura* that serve the system I bring to the Bible." Johnson saw how premises (and, we must add, methods) determine conclusions. The difficulties we've been addressing involve that same dynamic. What is the "*that*" which we are bringing to our Bible reading? More to our point, are we allowing Scripture to refine our "that"? Or do we simply go again and again to the Word with the demand that it confirm our grids? The Reformers at their best urged continual, wholesale exchange of man's premises for God's. But no single generation can complete that work.

It would be good if our generation at least resolved to learn from Scripture to ask the right questions. That would be progress, for we have spent 400 years breaking the Scripture down into propositions. It's past time for us to see all the Word's words as comprising *one* perfect story. It is unfair to criticize Dispensationalism while refusing to recognize the distorted view some of us share with them. The *unity* of the Bible is an indispensable starting point. The New Testament Church read the Old Testament Scriptures as their Bible. That is significant. It did not view any of its doctrines as departures from that which had previously come from the mouth of God.

Just because we're good at spotting specks in the eyes of others doesn't mean we've purged all the logs from our own. We tend to think that doctrinally, at least, we have arrived. Yet too much of our thinking about doctrine is predicated on the very wrong notion that the New Testament repudiates the Old. Deep down (though sometimes not so far from the surface) we suspect that the Old Testament offered a different way of salvation from the New. Wrong. Big-time wrong.

It is also wrong to expect the Word of God to be yielding and still under the systematician's scalpel. It is here to carve and re-piece *us*. The

Word of God is a living and active sword, not a cadaver awaiting dissection.

Bavinck has beautifully said that the

> declaration of faith on the part of the church is not a scientific doctrine, nor a form of unity that is being repeated, but is rather a confession of a deeply felt reality, and of a conviction of reality that has come up out of experience in life. The prophets and apostles, and the saints generally who appear before us in the Old and New Testament and later in the Church of Christ, did not sit and philosophize about God in abstracted concepts, but rather confessed what God meant to them and what they owed to Him in all the circumstances of life. God was for them not at all a cold concept, which they then proceeded rationally to analyze, but He was a living, personal force, a reality infinitely more real than the world around them. Indeed, He was to them *the* one, eternal, worshipful Being. They reckoned with Him in their lives, they lived in His tent, walked as if always before His face, served Him in His courts, and worshipped Him in His sanctuary (*Our Reasonable Faith*, p. 25).

We have descended from this grand height to the point where the right to be called Reformed is equated by some with a commitment "to philosophize about God in abstracted concepts." The same arrogant method employed in stripping God of His self-disclosed character is too often used in doctrinal formulation. I do not mean that systematics is evil, only that it can be too eager, too ambitious. To be fruitful, systematics must be ever humble before the Word. This is the irresistible attraction of Calvinism at its best—myriads are won to our creed because it starts by confessing God as *God*. Nevertheless, we Reformed do tend to expect doctrinal truth to be neater and tidier than it is actually found in Scripture. Even Ezekiel, when asked if the dry bones might live, could only answer: "O Sovereign LORD, you alone know." The best theologians cultivate Ezekiel's spirit. We need not dread rough edges! Not every tile has a straight edge, yet even scalloped tiles can be used to make a symmetrical and beautiful wall. Our demand that every aspect of every truth fit in a neat compartment will find a Bible that resists the claim. That is a problem for the Greek mind, but not the Jewish, covenantal mind. The covenantal mind is practiced at repeating Paul: "I do not know—God knows."

What's the Big Idea? (Hint: It isn't Justification)

But what we can know requires context. The Bible cannot be properly interpreted if context is ignored. And, as Gordon Fee notes, "the first step toward valid interpretation of Scripture is . . . historical investigation," that is, ascertaining the "original setting(s) of the biblical texts." This means that when we read Paul's letters we must ask why he wrote what he wrote. God inspired him to write *into certain situations.* Paul's letters generally contain *arguments* which require contexts for true understanding. They are not strings of aphorisms.

When we 1) fail to consider the polemical contexts of Paul's letters, 2) add our demand for system, and 3) read Paul's letters backwards through Luther's sad experience, one result is an emphasis on "justification" that simply does not exist in the Bible. One writer, with whom we have no shortage of disagreements, has nevertheless very properly written, "Justification is a Pauline concept in Romans and Galatians, but it plays a smaller role" in his epistles than in many systems. "Luther's rediscovery of justification was important for himself and for sixteenth-century reforms, but it is not as central for . . . an astute interpretation of Paul's theology."

This agrees with the important observations of W. D. Davies (in *Paul and Rabbinic Judaism*) that:

> [I]n those contexts where the idea of Justification by Faith is central, we
> find that this is so only because of certain polemical necessities. It is only
> in those Epistles, namely, Galatians and Romans, where Paul is con-
> sciously presenting the claims of his Gospel over against those of Judaism
> that Justification by Faith is emphasized (p. 220).

As noted by another, "For Paul, justification tells us how God accepts Gentiles." Exactly. "Justification for him [Paul] had less to do with a guilty conscience than with the new age inaugurated by the resurrection of Jesus."

This is vital, for it represents an effort to see the Romans and Galatians treatment of justification in its actual, historical context. Justification by faith is *true*, but it was not *new*. It was not, for Paul, a doctrine to beat people with or to display in a museum. Why did Paul emphasize it when and where he did? There was nothing abstract about it for him. His treatment of it in the epistles is concerned with setting forth the relationship of Jews and Gentiles in light of Christ's work. For 2,000 years "the story" of God's activity was peculiarly Jewish. Christ's accomplishments in history, however, meant that "those who once were far away have been brought near through the blood of the Messiah." God now *fully* accepts Gentiles in the same way He accepts Jews—by grace through faith.

Paul is explicit about what is "new" in the New Administration: "that through the gospel the Gentiles are heirs together with Israel, members together of one body, and sharers together in the promise in Christ Jesus" (Eph 3:6). Galatians was not written to tell us about a new way of salvation: salvation has *always been by grace through faith*. It was written to guard the new way of *inclusion*, of being reckoned among the people of God. Full membership is indicated by Christian baptism, which is universal, not by Jewish circumcision, which is provincial.

It is not grace that is new in the New Testament. It is not faith that is new in the New Testament. It is not justification that is new in the New Testament. What is new is that Gentiles are fully incorporated into Israel by faith alone, i.e., apart from circumcision, apart from an earthly priesthood or Temple, and certainly apart from any rabbinic conception of merit. When we say that Gentiles are incorporated into Israel by faith "alone," the word "alone" is not used to set faith against covenantal obedience. It is rather used to distinguish the true means of covenantal inclusion from three erroneous ones:

1) That one must become a Jew to have access to God in Christ.
2) That one must approach God through the Levitical priesthood, offerings, and Temple.
3) That one is made right with God by one's own merit.

Davies:

> How little . . . Paul intended that Faith should be opposed to obedience (is) clear when we recall his work as ethical *didaskalos* (instructor, master, teacher). A doctrine such as Justification by Faith . . . cannot have been the dominant factor in the thought of one who could never have separated religion and life.

This is why we affirm justification by faith but insist (as good Calvinists do) that true faith *never* appears alone. Tearing faith away from its Scriptural setting, and resetting it in opposition to covenant obedience, is more than an abstraction: it is rebellion against God.

The problem we are discussing arises from this three-step mis-step: 1) the reduction of Scripture to a collection of propositions, 2) the extraction of texts from contexts, and 3) reorganizing, resetting texts into systems which replace Scripture, rather than serve it. Let us see how this triple boo-boo operates in two cases.

It's 3:28. Do You Know Where Your Verses are?

Galatians 3:28, "There is neither Jew nor Greek, slave nor free, male nor female, for you are all one in Christ Jesus" and Romans 3:28, "Therefore we conclude that a man is justified by faith apart from the deeds of the law" are verses which have oft been extorted from their contexts, stripped of their author's intent, dressed in the style of their captors, and reduced to servitude in contrived systems. If anyone should speak of restoring the verses to their original settings, the taskmasters scurry to their battlements and snipe. That's understandable, I suppose. After all, it's hard to find good servants; their lords are loathe to let them go.

But God's Word doesn't take well to chains (2 Tim 2:9). We are thus confident that, sooner or later, these 3:28's will be manumitted. In fact, while Romans 3:28 has a history of being hauled into service by the seigniors of systematics, the struggle for Galatians 3:28 is pretty modern, and has not quite been concluded. Perhaps the freshness of the tussle for the Galatians verse will help us look at the Romans passage with *re*freshed appreciation.

Imagine for a moment that you are a feminist who wishes to claim biblical support for your views. I know, I know: that's a tall order. Honest Christians and frank feminists have both recognized the fundamental incompatibility of the two worldviews. Ted Letis once surveyed in an essay several prominent intellectual feminists who had tried to persuade their sisters and brother-ettes that feminism and the Bible don't mix. Elizabeth Cady Stanton produced *The Women's Bible* because, she asserted, Judaism and orthodox Christianity had to be eliminated if feminist ideals were to triumph. It was not her intention to make the Bible less sexist. In her view that was impossible. Rather, she set out to undermine canonical biblical authority altogether, focusing on what she regarded as absurdities and contradictions. More recently, Naomi Goldenberg lamented that "Many of today's feminists are not yet willing to reject Jewish and Christian tradition at such a basic level. Instead they turn to exegesis to preserve Jewish and Christian religious systems." She warned that this is a self-deceptive enterprise. "Jesus Christ cannot symbolize the liberation of women. A culture that maintains a masculine image for its highest divinity cannot allow its women to experience themselves as the equals of its men." And philosophical feminist Mary Daley, using more violent language, called for the castration of God. "I have already suggested that if God is male then male is God. The divine patriarch castrates women as long as he is allowed to live on in the collective imagination." She would do away with Holy Scripture and the God revealed therein, period.

Still, imagine yourself an "evangelical feminist." Just how would you seek "to preserve (the) Christian system" while promoting your revolutionary agenda? You would craft approaches and select verses to harmonize with the non-negotiable premise you brought to the Bible. You would equate power over others with evil. You would argue that uxorial submission was not expected at creation but was a temporary result of the fall. You would equate the traditional wifely role with slavery. You would argue that Jesus intended to usher in *the* Jubilee in which all "power-over" situations are to be eliminated through power redistribution, voluntary or coerced (ahem). You would detect a general *drift* in the Bible toward ever-increasing emancipation of all people in subservient roles (including, ultimately, children). Above all, you would hang your hat (and your scarf and your coat and yourself) on Galatians 3:28. "There is neither Jew nor Greek, slave nor free, male nor female, for you are all one in Christ Jesus."

Yes, you would. Try to find an "evangelical feminist" who hasn't made this her life verse. Richard and Joyce Boldrey fantasize that "Galatians 3:28 does not say 'God loves each of you, but stay in your places'; it says that there are no longer places, no longer categories, no longer differences in rights and privileges, codes and values." Rebecca Merrill Groothuis maintains that "Biblical equality is . . . a consequence of salvation through Christ, as indicated in Galatians 3:26–28."

Letha Scanzoni and Nancy Hardesty have been cited as saying that in view of Galatians 3:28, "all social distinctions between men and women should [be] erased in the church." Websites abound which feature this as an anchor verse (e.g., *Christians for Biblical Equality, Evangelical and Ecumenical Women's Caucus, WomanPriest.org,* etc.).

Per-verse

While no Christian feminist relies solely on Galatians 3:28, the value of the verse in their system is enormous, for it offers a convenient summary of what they wish Paul to say and want the Bible to teach. How many think that the mere citation of the verse is the end of argument! But the feminist use of this verse is *per*verse. The proper understanding becomes plain when the light of context is admitted.

The problem at Galatia was simple: Someone was insisting that full covenantal inclusion for Gentiles could only be had by submitting to circumcision. In short, they were saying that you could only be a Christian if you were Jewish. They were trying to *compel* Gentiles to become Jewish. *This is the crisis Paul is addressing in the letter.* The crisis forms the context of the letter and provides the key to proper interpretation. That this was Paul's concern is clear from several statements.

In 2:3 he addresses the problem by inference, noting that "not even Titus, who was with me, was compelled [by the Jerusalem church] to be circumcised, even though he was a Greek." Toward the end of his letter he expresses his contempt for those who wanted to confine the Gospel to the Jews. "Those who want to make a good impression outwardly are trying to compel you to be circumcised. The only reason they do this is to avoid being persecuted for the cross of Christ. Not even those who are circumcised obey the law, yet they want you to be circumcised that they may boast about your flesh."

Here it becomes clearer that the issue of keeping the Law is a subset of becoming Jewish. Paul refutes his opponents by various polemical and rhetorical means, including adopting their position "for argument's sake" and showing its absurdity. The arguments about justification arise because of the crisis: Gentiles are being told they must become Jewish to become Christian. Paul makes it pretty clear that this ain't so: "Indeed I, Paul, say to you that if you become circumcised, Christ will profit you nothing. And I testify again to every man who becomes circumcised that he is a debtor to keep the whole law. You have become estranged from Christ, you who attempt to be justified by law; you have fallen from grace."

The distinction which must always be kept in mind is between the Law as God gave it and the Law as it had come to be used by the Jews. Robert Lewis Dabney properly scorned the idea that the Law *as given by God* was futile. When Peter says in Acts 15 that "the ritual was a yoke which neither the Jews nor their fathers were able to bear," Dabney responds that "well disposed Jews" certainly *did* bear the Law as given by God, and God Himself says they did (e.g., Luke 1:6). Dabney then asks, "Did God signalize His favour to His chosen people by imposing an intolerable ritual?" That is an important question. Law-Gospel dichotomists ask us to believe that God showed His love for Israel by placing them under an un-bearable burden which He then commanded them to love! The thought comes close to blasphemy; it is certainly an insult to our God. "No: Peter has in view the ritual used in that self-righteous sense, in which the Judaizing Christians regarded it while desiring to impose it on Gentiles" (*Systematic Theology*, p. 458).

Dabney's dictum is critically important: "We must always remember that the Apostles are using, to a certain extent, an *argumentum ad hominem*: they are speaking of the Mosaic institutions under the [mistaken] Jewish view of them. They are treating of that side or aspect, which alone the perverse Jew retained of them. Here is the key." Bingo.

In other words, Paul is arguing against Jewish abstractionism, the separation of Law and grace: the "perverse Jew"—as opposed to the faithful Jewish Christian—sought from the Law only that which could be credited to his account in the bank of righteousness. G. Dix calls Paul's argument in Galatians "a brilliant and vigorous attack on the whole Pharisaic conception of *Zekuth* (lit. 'satisfaction'), i.e., the notion that it is only by 'satisfying' the demands of the Law upon him that a man can attain to . . . righteousness" (*Jew and Greek*, p. 45). It is only against a *wrong* view of the Law the Apostles argued.

This wrong view of the Law has, not surprisingly, prevailed in Jewish history after Christ. The Encyclopaedia Judaica defines *Righteousness* as "the fulfillment of all legal and moral obligations." It is regarded as "a learned trait resulting from sustained performance of obligations." Today, serious discussion is had among orthodox Jews concerning the following: May one tie his shoelaces on the Sabbath, or squeeze a sponge, or open the refrigerator, or turn on his hearing aid, or play with nuts on the ground? (It depends, no, it depends, it depends, no.) This attitude was confronted by Jesus over and again. The famous hand washing encounter of Mark 7:1–23 lives on in spirit among my people. They debate whether hands are efficaciously washed—i.e., according to ceremonial requirements—if they were not perfectly dry when the washing commenced. These and *thousands* of other regulations are rooted in the notion of acquired merit.

Though Sabbath and ceremonial issues continued to be refined by the Jews hundreds of years after Christ, the New Testament makes it plain that codification had already enjoyed a long history when Jesus ministered on earth. The Sermon on the Mount is tough to explain without that very background ("You have heard that it was said . . . "). One tradition with obvious roots reaching back to Second Temple Judaism is that portion of the Daily Prayer which thanks God for certain privileges. In the Jewish liturgy, a series of *b'ruchas* (blessings) is recited every morning. Three blessings are of special interest to those hoping to understand Galatians 3:28. Here's the relevant section from the *siddur*:

> Blessed are You, Lord our God, King of the universe,
> who has not made me a Gentile.
> Blessed are You, Lord our God, King of the universe,
> who has not made me a slave.
> Blessed are You, Lord our God, King of the universe,
> who has not made me a woman.

Hmmm. The very same order used by Paul in 3:28. Isn't *that* interesting! Yes, but not half as interesting as the *reasoning* behind these *b'ruchas*. Keep in mind that the threat in Galatia was posed by those who held the view that "the Law and its fulfillment offer the *sole* divinely-given means and opportunity for righteousness before God" (Dix).

This is the key point in understanding Paul's argument. *If* righteousness is, as Jewish thought held (and still holds) a "result . . . (of) sustained performance of obligations," then the one with the most obligations can attain the most righteousness. On this supposition it is easy to see why the Jew gives thanks for being a Jew. It is to the Jews that the Law was given. At the time of Paul, with the Temple standing and the priesthood operative, this was an especially important point. If Gentiles were not obligated to keep the whole Mosaic code, erroneous Jewish reasoning could argue that there would consequently always be a two-tiered membership in the Church. Thus Paul emphasizes that in Christ there is neither Jew nor Gentile. Thus far, the meaning of Galatians 3:28 is obvious.

Obvious, too, is the fact that a slave has less opportunities than a free man to fulfill the Law's commands, and thus, according to some Jews, attain unto righteousness.

The third condition (that of being a man, not a woman) suggests no obvious advantage—until the Jewish thinking behind it is introduced. Then it makes perfect sense. Remember that Paul is telling the Galatians that the Jews are wrong: you don't become more Christian by coming under more commands. But according to Jewish practice, men have more obligations than women. Women are not required to fulfill all the commandments! For example, it is only the *males* who were obligated to attend the three great festivals in Jerusalem (Deut. 16:16; women and children were permitted but not *required* to attend: cf. 1 Sam 1; Luke 2).

Rabbi Dr. Louis Jacobs writes, "The wording of the benediction recited each day in which a man praises God for not having made him a woman (Men. 43b) should not be overinterpreted since from the context it is clear that *the thanks are for greater opportunities a man has for carrying out the precepts,* women being exempt from those positive precepts which for their performance depend on a given time of the day or year (Kid. 1:7)" (*Jewish Values,* p. 151. Keter Books, Jerusalem). In *The Jewish Book of Why,* A. J. Kolatch notes, "Over the centuries, this prayer has been viewed by most Jews as an expression of thanks on the part of man for the good fortune of having been born male *and thus being privileged to perform so many more commandments (mitzvot) than a woman* . . . Women are considered on a par with slaves and minors because, unlike men, *none of the three classes is obligated to fulfill all of the 613 commandments (mitzvot)* [the Jews count 613 commands in the Five Books of Moses] . . . Women are obligated to observe all the negative commandments in the torah (*mitzvot lo taaseh*). These are commandments that begin with the words, 'Thou shalt not . . . "

However, women are exempt from some of the positive commandments in the torah (*mitzvot asay*). The Talmud ruled that women are not obligated to observe 'positive commandments dependent upon time,' commandments that must be observed at a specific time of year" (I've added emphases in this paragraph).

Compare this last observation with Galatians 4:10–11—"You are observing special days and months and seasons and years! I fear for you, that somehow I have wasted my efforts on you"—and the naturalness of the correct interpretation of Galatians 3:28 will grip your heart. Is God saying in 3:28 that "all social distinctions between men and women should [be] erased in the church"? Not at all. Is He saying that "there are no longer places, no longer categories, no longer differences in rights and privileges, codes and values"? The thought is repugnant and contradicted by a thousand Scriptures. He is saying that the Jewish way of reckoning rightness before God—viz., that "the Law and its fulfillment offer the *sole* divinely-given means and opportunity for righteousness before God"—is patently false. You do not need to become Jewish to be a Christian. The commands which separated Jews from Gentiles are obviated in Christ. We have fellowship at the same Table, access into the same Presence in heaven, *by faith*, not by race. And the false notions of climbing a ladder of merit are washed away by the very sight of His blood.

Now let's take what we learned in Galatians and go to Romans 3:28.

Stephen and Paul

Pick a book, any book. If you would have it get into you, you must get into it. Feel its rhythm, hear its rhyme, grasp its theme, identify its purpose—get its *movement*. This is especially important in absorbing the Bible and its constituent books, for these form God's Word to us. God gave them as a history and an interpretation of history. We are not to approach the Bible as if it were thousands of splinters compressed into a plywood block, just waiting to be carved into our image. God has not given us His oracles so we can cast a totem; He has given us His Word to recast *us* into the image of His Son. His is a living Word, a life-giving Word. Only the living move; only the moving live. And it's when we are moved by the Word that we live. This is what we've been aiming to convey. We are, in this recent series, warring against covenant stasis. The Word of God is not stagnant, but reading it as though it were creates a Church that is. The Greek mind wants a static book that submits to dissection. The Hebrew mind wants the active book from the active God. Which shall it be? Well, how does the Book characterize itself? "Living and active." And it says that—how aptly!—in the Book of *Hebrews*.

So what's the story? The One Book tells how the Jewish promises have been fulfilled for the world in Jesus Christ. The 66 books give the details. You can often get a good sense of the purpose—or at least the drift—of a Bible book by mulling over its beginning and its end. Genesis, for example, begins with life in Paradise and ends in a coffin in Egypt. Hmm...what happened? Creation, the fall, the flood, the judgment on the nations, then the singling out of one man through whose seed a promise would be realized.

Catch the movement, see the grace. Adam and Eve had been barred from the Tree of Life, yes, but not before they were promised a Savior, not before they were clothed with tokens of assurance: "I will cover you." The tokens are important. God loved them. Shem and Japheth imitated God—they covered their daddy's sin. "Be imitators of God, therefore, as dearly loved children." Concern yourself less with a "doctrine of covering" than with being a coverer.

Grace apace: The nations cursed, dispersed at Babel, but a promise of regathering follows close on its heels: "Abram, come with Me. I have a plan. Through you all peoples will have the curse reversed." The call of Abraham is the spine of the book. The promise to him had in view the future blessing of *all* nations (12:1–3). Genesis is the story of God, Abraham, and a promise. It tells us what preceded their union (1–11), and what flowed from it (12–50). It's about God and Abe. It's about a place called "The LORD-Will-Provide" (22:14).

God loved the nations. On the Day of Pentecost, He provided for them. "Devout men, from every nation under heaven" declare—in many languages but one voice—"the wonderful works of God." Acts 2 stands on Genesis 11 and 12. Speaking of tokens, this "speaking in other languages" miracle was once for all. God hadn't forgotten His promise to unravel Babel. Speaking of speaking, God mused (16:18),

Shall I hide from Abraham what I am doing, since Abraham shall surely
become a great and mighty nation, and all the nations of the earth shall
be blessed in him? For I have known him, in order that he may command his children and his household after him, that they keep the way
of the LORD, to do righteousness and justice, that the LORD may bring to
Abraham what He has promised to him.

Look how tightly woven God's thoughts are! He called Abram *in
order to* bless the nations. (Do we think of our election in this way? We
should: "For we are His workmanship, created in Christ Jesus for good
works, which God prepared in advance for us to walk in and do.")
Further, the One who appointed the end appointed the means. Abe
was called *so that* he could teach his house God's ways. And his house
must walk in God's ways if they would inherit the promises. There is
no separating *being known* from *knowing* from *doing* from *transmitting*
from *inheriting*. God has bound them up like matter, time, and space;
like height, width, and depth. Give up one, you give up all.

"Through your seed, Abram." But first, "your descendants will be
enslaved and mistreated four hundred years." The Book of Exodus:
what's the story? It begins with God's people seemingly abandoned by
Him and forgotten, but ends with them being overwhelmed by His
presence. "The glory of the LORD filled the Tabernacle." It stopped
Moses in his tracks. Eden revisited: God dwells with man. Something
big occurred between getting pushed around by Pharaoh and getting
pushed out by God's glory. What was it? In the center of that Book,
Jehovah married Israel. From/to. From bondage to marriage. This is the
core event of the Old Administration. God takes His name from it: "I
am the Lord your God who brought you out of Egypt," brought you
out to marry Me. For this cause Israel will leave Egypt, to be united to
her Husband. God reminisces in Ezekiel: "When I looked at you and
saw that you were old enough for love, I spread the corner of my garment over you and covered your nakedness. I gave you my solemn oath
and entered into a covenant with you," declares the Sovereign LORD,
"and you became mine." This is not a record of propositions, but of a
proposal, an acceptance (19:1–8; 24:1–7), and a marriage contract
signed and sealed in blood.

Pick a book, any book. See it open. See it close. How did it get
from here to there? Matthew begins by introducing us to the King of

the Jews and closes with a command from the King of the Universe. The Passion was the path leading to Christ's dominion; one-fourth of the book is devoted to one week in Christ's life. God had provided Himself a sacrifice. See the fire, see the wood, behold the Lamb. Isaac is saved, and so are we.

Luke begins: John's priestly parents in the earthly temple. Luke concludes: John's cousin, the Priest-King, pronouncing the benediction en route to the heavenly Temple. In His ascension He has "raised our human nature on the clouds to God's right hand . . . Man with God is on the throne." The Second Adam, the Son of God, eats from, is, the Tree of Life. "Tell all the nations about this," He says. "Begin at Jerusalem." Naturally.

Acts begins its great account by focusing on the ministry of Peter (the apostle to the circumcision) in Jerusalem, the Jewish center, and ends with Paul (the apostle to the uncircumcision) in Rome, the Gentile center. How the message got from one place to the other is the Story. The Bible moves. *There are no verses.*

But there are sermons. A few, anyway. Stephen's is unforgettable. It should be memorized. Though it sounds like an excerpt from a *People Magazine* cover, it is fair to say that Stephen should be classed among "the most underrated saints of history." Alexander Whyte couldn't praise him enough: "a young man of original genius and of special grace," he "far outstripped even such pillar apostles as Peter and James and John." The world was not worthy of him. He knew the story, and got killed for telling it. It is not the story of the *ordo salutis,* but nevertheless is a story we must know if we would know the Bible. Stephen was the linchpin joining Peter to Paul. Peter laid hands on Stephen's head; Stephen took hold of Saul's heart. The killers laid down their clothes at Saul's feet while Stephen laid down his Christ in Saul's soul. If any human instrumentality was involved in delivering Paul to the Lord, it was surely the man whose speech is recorded in Acts 7. He placed the goads which Jesus removed on the Damascus road.

Stephen is accused in Acts 6: "This man does not cease to speak blasphemous words against this holy place and the law." He is called before the Sanhedrin and makes his defense. The response? They gnash their teeth at him, cry out, stop their ears, cast him out and kill him, with Saul's full consent. Saul makes havoc of the Church. Then Christ makes havoc of Saul: He converts him. About twenty years later, when Saul has long been known as Paul, a very new man, he returns to the scene of the crime (Acts 21–22). But on this trip *Paul* is accused of defiling the holy place. The response to his defense? "They raised their voices and said, 'Rid the earth of him, for he is not fit to live!'" Same dance, different partner. The next day Paul stood in the very spot where he had seen and heard Stephen—on trial before the same council, in the same city, on the same charge. The accuser had become the accused! The baton had been passed. Stephen's murderer now pleads Stephen's cause.

A careful reading of Stephen's sermon in Acts 7 and Paul's letter to the Romans will reveal a similar message. Yes, Paul takes it to the next level, yet it is obvious they were building on the same foundation. What was their message? Justification by faith apart from obedience? No. Stephen's address surveys Jewish history to establish two indisputable points: 1) From God's side: The one true God is not, and never has been, inextricably bound to the Temple in Jerusalem. Implication: He is not inextricably bound to other Jewish distinctives: the land, the priesthood, the offerings, the calendar, and so on. 2) From the Jews' side: Despite their privileges, the Jews have not, in their history, generally shown themselves to be faithful to their covenant God.

These are *exactly* Paul's points in Romans, to which he adds a third: God's purposes, far from being thwarted by Jewish unbelief, are (surprisingly) advanced. For all that was happening was fulfilling God's covenant with Abraham. The nations are swarming into Israel through faith in her Messiah.

Stephen's first point was established by noting that God spoke to Abraham *in Mesopotamia* (v. 2), was with Joseph *in Egypt* (v. 9), and called Moses *in the wilderness* (v. 30). In fact, the very oracles which distinguished Israel from the nations were delivered *outside* of the land of Israel. And even Solomon's edifice—the epitome of Israel's religious distinctiveness—could not contain the living God. God is bigger than Israel, and He had told them so repeatedly (1 Kings 8:27, Isa. 66:1, 2).

Stephen's second point resounds throughout his sermon. Joseph, who would become Israel's savior, had been rejected by the patriarchs out of envy. Moses, their lawgiver and shepherd, had also been rejected: "Who made you a ruler and a judge?" The answer, of course, was God, but they didn't get it. Israel had been delivered not because of her righteousness but *despite her unrighteousness.* "Now," Stephen says, "the One Moses spoke about has come. And what do you do? Just what you've always done: you disbelieve." As they had rejected the Angel of the Lord at Sinai, preferring the works of their own hands *and attributing their deliverance to that* (Ex. 32:4; cf. 1 Kings 12:28), so they now rejected the Just One. They are recipients of the Law, indeed, but not keepers of it. This is Paul's message *exactly.*

Earlier in this chapter we sought to deliver Galatians 3:28 from the versifiers. We showed that the issue addressed in the epistle was *not* justification by faith as opposed to covenantal obedience, but justification for the Gentiles apart from becoming Jewish. The Gospel Paul was defending was *not* assent to a proposition, but was rather the good news that Gentiles need not become Jewish to be Christian. God's Law is mediated for the world through Messiah, not Moses (1 Cor. 9:21).

Remember what we said earlier about detecting the flow by looking at the beginning and the end of a book? Well, it isn't just the narrative portions of Scripture which can reveal their sense in starts and conclusions: it is often the case with epistles, too. Anyone not thoroughly infected with Luther's malady can see that Galatians is not about the Law as God gave it, but the law as misappropriated by and misapplied in Jewish traditions, and especially about Sinai distinctives being foisted upon Gentiles. Paul is not defending faith apart from obedience. He is defending *the Gospel he has preached among the Gentiles.* See 1:16; 2:2, 8, 9—oh, forget it. Just read the whole letter. See how the issue is the status of the Gentiles in Christ—beginning, middle and end. Must Gentiles be circumcised? If so, then the promise to Abraham is not yet fulfilled. And Christianity is nothing more than aggressive Judaism. Must Gentiles gain full access to an earthly temple, avail themselves of a human priesthood, abide by the Jewish calendar, make annual pilgrimages, and so on? Then Christ died for nothing!

Paul didn't care if Jews, even Jewish Christians, did these things. *He did these things himself, after his conversion, and after Acts 15!* James and the other elders at Jerusalem knew that the rumors about Paul were *false:* The Jews of Jerusalem who had believed in Jesus had "been informed that you teach all the Jews who live among the Gentiles to turn away from Moses, telling them not to circumcise their children or live according to our customs." They asked Paul to prove that this was nonsense, and he was only too glad to do so. The issue is not the Law as given by God. It is not even the ceremonial Law as given to Israel. It is always and only, "Must Gentiles become Jewish?" If Christ is the Christ, the answer must be no.

Look at the conclusion of Galatians to see where Paul was aiming. It's not faith opposed to works, but faith opposed to compulsory Judaism:

> As many as desire to make a good showing in the flesh, these would compel you to be circumcised, only that they may not suffer persecution for the cross of Christ. For not even those who are circumcised keep the law [remember Stephen's conclusion? He spoke to those who "have received the law that was put into effect through angels but have not obeyed it"], but they desire to have you circumcised that they may boast in your flesh. But God forbid that I should boast except in the cross of our Lord Jesus Christ, by whom the world has been crucified to me, and I to the world. For in Christ Jesus neither circumcision nor uncircumcision avails anything, but a new creation. And as many as walk according to this rule, peace and mercy be upon them, and upon the Israel of God. (Gal. 2:11)

Could it be any clearer? If focus is still needed, does not Ephesians 2:11–22 provide it?

> Therefore, remember that formerly you who are Gentiles by birth and called "uncircumcised" by those who call themselves "the circumcision" (that done in the body by the hands of men)—remember that at that time you were separate from Christ, excluded from citizenship in Israel and foreigners to the covenants of the promise, without hope and without God in the world. But now in Christ Jesus you who once were far away have been brought near through the blood of Christ. For he himself is our peace, who has made the two one and has destroyed the barrier, the dividing wall of hostility, by abolishing in his flesh the law with its commandments and regulations [not the moral Law, obviously, but those ordinances which incubated Israel]. His purpose was to create in himself one new man out of the two, thus making peace, and in this one body to reconcile both of them to God through the cross, by which he put to death their hostility. He came and preached peace to you who were far away and peace to those who were near. For through him we both have

access to the Father by one Spirit. Consequently, you are no longer foreigners and aliens, but fellow citizens with God's people and members of God's household, built on the foundation of the apostles and prophets, with Christ Jesus himself as the chief cornerstone. In him the whole building is joined together and rises to become a holy temple in the Lord. And in him you too are being built together to become a dwelling in which God lives by his Spirit.

This is what Paul's all about. People who try to interpret his letters apart from this key end up looking for lint in their navels the rest of their lives. Missing the real point, they (ironically) turn faith into a new work. But the New Administration is not about faith divorced from obedience, not about abstractions, not about propositions, not about mental assent, not about introspection: it is about the efficacy of Christ's work demonstrated in the inclusion of the nations in fulfillment of God's promise to Abraham. *That* is Paul's Gospel.

> For this reason I, Paul, the prisoner of Christ Jesus for the sake of you Gentiles—Surely you have heard about the administration of God's grace that was given to me for you, that is, the mystery made known to me by revelation, as I have already written briefly. (Eph. 3:1–3)

No, Paul. Pretend I don't know. Tell me.

> In reading this, then, you will be able to understand my insight into the mystery of Christ, which was not made known to men in other generations as it has now been revealed by the Spirit to God's holy apostles and prophets. (Eph. 3:4–5)

Can you be more specific, Paul? What is your gospel?

> This mystery is that through the gospel the Gentiles are heirs together with Israel, members together of one body, and sharers together in the promise in Christ Jesus. (Eph. 3:6)

Okay, now I've gotcha! Thanks, Rabbi Paul, son of Stephen.

And so it goes in Romans. "But," you will ask, "doesn't it say in Romans, 'Therefore we conclude that a man is justified by faith without the deeds of the law'?" It sure does. Just remember: *there are no verses.* There's a story. What story is Paul telling in Romans? The story of the fulfillment of the promise to Abraham: the story of how, in Christ, the nations are being gathered to God. It certainly is *not* a story of faith opposed to obedience.

Let me say plainly that I do not know what all of Romans is meant to convey in all its particulars. I feel as though its depths have yet to be searched; its order is yet to be perfectly framed. Still, there are clearly things Paul is *not* saying which have somehow been mistaken for gospel by some. It would be as though someone asked us to believe Stephen to have despised the Temple. He did not! He, like all the prophets, despised *the way* the Temple had been misunderstood and misused, but he would never speak against the Temple itself, *properly* understood. How could he? And how could Paul speak *against* God's Law, as God intended it? Impossible!

But law/gospel-dichotomist confusion abounds. A professor from a Reformed seminary in the Midwest recently preached on Romans 3. His struggle is evident throughout his sermon. I excerpt the following:

> When the law is doing its job we realize, *it's* not the Savior. But it points us to the Savior. Because it points us to our heart. "But *now* a righteousness from God apart from law has been made known." A mighty, new epoch within redemptive history, a new regime, has arrived . . . *Now* a righteousness from God *apart* from the law has been made known.

This good brother is assuming what he's seeking to prove without realizing the pitfalls. Does he mean to suggest that in the Old Administration someone *was* made righteous by meritorious Law keeping? Then what happens to the grace this man is seeking to uphold? Was it absent from the Old Testament? That's where his reasoning leads, you know. He's making Romans 3:28 into an absolute, epochal comparison. It seems to me that the only way to be extricated from this dilemma is to recognize that when Paul speaks of righteousness apart from the Law he must be referring to the "deeds of the law" as something uniquely *Jewish*—however you understand it—and not as something uniquely *convicting.* The administrative difference is that Gentiles are now included apart from the Law understood in *that* sense. But Paul *never* sets faith against obedience.

Remember: get the movement, the flow. Look at how Paul begins: "Through Him and for His name's sake, we received grace and apostleship to call people from among all the Gentiles *to the obedience that comes from faith.*" Look at how he ends:

> Now to him that is of power to establish you according to my gospel, and the preaching of Jesus Christ, according to the revelation of the mystery, which was kept secret since the world began, but now is made manifest, and by the scriptures of the prophets, according to the commandment of the everlasting God, made known to all nations *for the obedience of faith*: to God only wise, be glory through Jesus Christ for ever. Amen. (Rom. 16:25–27)

How can a book that opens and closes with talk of the obedience of faith be imagined to teach that obedience stands *against* faith? Where is Perry Como when you need him? *It's impossible!*

It has oft been noted that the theme of Romans is found in 1:16–17. But the emphasis has been misplaced. It is not that "the just will live by faith," but that the gospel "is the power of God to salvation for everyone who believes, for the Jew first and also for the Greek." That is the good *news*. For the fact that the just will live by faith is hardly new. There is no antithesis between faith and obedience in either Paul (as just noted) or Habakkuk. One commentator (R. D. Patterson of Liberty University in Lynchburg, VA) has summed up Habakkuk's idea of faith as "persevering and obedient trust in God." Well, yeah! C. E. Armerding of Regent College in Vancouver, BC, had it right: "To the Hebrew mind no dichotomy existed between faith and faithfulness." So also Gordon Wenham in his commentary on Numbers:

> Whereas Christian theologians, following Paul's supposed distinction, often contrast faith with obedience, this dichotomy is unknown to the Old Testament. Faith is the correct response to God's word, whether it is a word of promise or a word of command. Psalm 119:66 can say, 'I believe in thy commandments.' The opposite of faith is rebellion or disobedience.

People have plastered this "supposed distinction" to their noses so as to be unable to read Paul's letters without it. But give it a try. Have faith. It works. Paul begins the body of Romans with an indictment of the Gentile world. But when he turns to the Jews, he concludes that they are (in a manner of speaking) worse. To whom much is given, much is required. The Gentile world had violated God's general revelation; the Jewish world had violated His special disclosure. Following Stephen, Paul labors to show that: 1) God is not inextricably bound to Jewish distinctives, and 2) the Jewish possession of the Law does not equal *compliance* with the Law. Presumptuous-ness is the killer sin in the covenant.

Now just as Stephen proved this second point by a recitation of Israel's long history of rejecting God's deliverers along with His Word, so does Paul provide a list of stinging condemnations from the Old Testament (Rom. 3:10–18). Contrary to the common understanding that Paul is indicting all of humanity here, the text makes it clear that he is using the Jewish Scriptures to indict the Jews. Verses 10–18 are intended to prove that Jews are no better than Greeks (verse 9). That this was in Paul's mind is certain, for after his list he adds this comment: "Now we know that whatever the law says, it says to those who are under the law." That is to say, the sinners described in 10–18 *were Jewish sinners.*

Shades of Stephen! 1) God is bigger than Israel, bigger than their distinctives. 2) The possession of these distinctives, though real (Rom. 3:1–2), did not mean automatic heaven. Outsiders who loved God and responded in faith to His Word were better than insiders who disdained both. "For not the hearers of the Law [unbelieving Jews] are just in the sight of God, but the doers of the Law [believing Gentiles and Jews] will be justified." This statement is not a theoretical proposition concerning some meritorious method of being righteous before God. The presuppositions undergirding Paul's statement include the facts that the Law is "obeyable," that truly responding to the Law (the Word) in faith does justify, and that such justification *is not an exclusively Jewish possession.* Thus when Paul says in 3:28, "Therefore we conclude that a man is justified by faith without the deeds of the law," he is not speaking of faith versus obedience. Such a thought is nonsense in every sense. He means one is reckoned among the righteous—not by merit, not by presumption, not by being a Jew, but—by faith. Whatever specific Paul might have in mind when speaking of the "deeds of the law" in Romans 3:28, it clearly has reference to a *Jewish thing*, and not to a Lutheran conception of the Law. *Follow the flow*. What does Paul say *after* verse 28? "Is he the God of the Jews only? Is he not also of the Gentiles? Yes, of the Gentiles also: Seeing it is one God, which shall justify the circumcision by faith, and uncircumcision through faith." It is Jewish exclusivism that is being rejected here; Christ's resurrection made it anachronistic. Throughout the book the issue is Jews and Gentiles. It permeates the whole. He begins by talking about Jews and Gentiles. He concludes the same way. Look at 15:7ff.!

> For I tell you that Christ has become a servant of the Jews on behalf of God's truth, to confirm the promises made to the patriarchs so that the Gentiles may glorify God for his mercy, as it is written: 'Therefore I will praise you among the Gentiles; I will sing hymns to your name.' Again, it says, 'Rejoice, O Gentiles, with his people.' And again, 'Praise the Lord, all you Gentiles, and sing praises to him, all you peoples.' And again, Isaiah says, 'The Root of Jesse will spring up, one who will arise to rule over the nations; the Gentiles will hope in him'. . . . I have written you quite boldly on some points, as if to remind you of them again, because of the grace God gave me to be a minister of Christ Jesus to the Gentiles with the priestly duty of proclaiming the gospel of God, so that the Gentiles might become an offering acceptable to God, sanctified by the Holy Spirit. Therefore I glory in Christ Jesus in my service to God. I will not venture to speak of anything except what Christ has accomplished through me *in leading the Gentiles to obey God* by what I have said and done.

It's at the beginning, it's at the end, and it is the issue at the heart of the book, chapters 9–11. There Paul goes beyond Stephen, explaining with pains how Israel's rejection of the truth has served God's expansive redemptive purposes.

Chapter Eight

The Church:
Visible or Invisible

Douglas Wilson

Since a great deal of attention is likely to be paid to what is said here, I want to begin by simply stipulating a few things for the record. In no way have I altered my views of decretal theology; I remain a high Calvinist. If the Synod of Dordt had come up with seven points of Calvinism, I would gladly affirm the extra two as well. As an historic evangelical, in no way have I altered my conviction that a man must be converted to God in order to see the kingdom of heaven. In no way have I changed my conviction that the sole instrument by which an individual may appropriate the righteousness of Christ is a living faith, which also is a gift from God, lest any think to boast. Has *nothing* changed then? No, there have been changes in my thinking—but these changes amount to me saying more than all this—not less than this.

Why the hubbub then? Since the controversy broke, I have found that when I affirm what I believe in confessional language, I am not believed. When I try to clarify in my own words, I am asked why I don't think the confessions are good enough. When I get out the fiddle there are those who will not dance, and when I play the violin, they do not mourn—and one would think that *everyone* would mourn when I play the violin.

We are all eager to maintain a *biblical* peace, and I would urge us all to heed the words of Isaiah—come, let us *reason* together. We're not here to shout about how great Diana of the Ephesians is. We all intend to do this remembering the context of Isaiah's great invitation. Nothing is more important than keeping the gospel straight—so that our sins, like scarlet, may be white as snow.

Introducing Our Mother

We are accustomed to talk about the visible and invisible Church, but this is strange. The issue is important because the Church is our *mother*, and the law of God requires us to honor our mothers.

> But Jerusalem which is above is free, *which is the mother of us all.* For it is written, Rejoice, thou barren that bearest not; break forth and cry, thou that travailest not: for the desolate hath many more children than she which hath an husband (Gal. 4:26–27).

Calvin notes this in his *Institutes,* referring to the famous statement of Cyprian. But who talks about the distinction between a visible and invisible *mother?* Put this way, the expression makes you think of two mothers, not one, and then the natural question arises. Which is the true mother?

Background

Christians know that God is our Father (Eph. 3:14–15) and that Christ is the Bridegroom (Eph. 5:25). But few modern Christians know that we have a spiritual mother. The Christian Church is called the New Jerusalem and is the bride of Christ. "And I John saw the holy city, new Jerusalem, coming down from God out of heaven, prepared as a bride adorned for her husband" (Rev. 21:2). In the same chapter the Church, again, the new Jerusalem, is called "the bride, the Lamb's wife" (v. 9). And in Hebrews 12:22–24, the Church is called "the city of the living God, the heavenly Jerusalem." Putting this all together, we see that our mother is a holy city, a lovely bride. In the passage quoted already from Galatians, this Jerusalem above is plainly identified as the mother of us all.

So we are not talking about an abstraction, but rather about *her,* our glorious Mother Kirk. However detailed and theological the discussion gets, we should still stand up in respect when she—one woman—comes into the room.

Visible and Invisible *Somehow*

Since the time of the Reformation, evangelical Christians have struggled with the problems caused by the concepts of the *invisible* Church and *visible* Church. However, the distinction (terms aside) is a necessary one, as can be seen from a moment's reflection on the problem of hypocrisy in the Church.

I used to believe that this distinction between visible and invisible Church was a Reformed distinction over against Rome, but have since discovered (much to my astonishment and delight) that the Reformers were simply continuing a medieval scholastic distinction, one which appears to have originated with Augustine.

The general historic terms were *ecclesia militans* (the Church militant) and *ecclesia triumphans* (the Church triumphant). But the scholastics, with their genius for division and subdivision, said that the *ecclesia militans* needed to be divided further. There was the *ecclesia militans* defined *proprie et praecise* (properly and precisely), and then defined *improprie et per synecdochen* (improperly and by synecdoche).

With the Reformation, the Lutheran and Reformed began to speak of *ecclesia visibilis* (the visible Church), which is to say, all those who belong outwardly to the Church (*ecclesia militans improprie dicta*), with the elect and non-elect together—a mixed multitude. The *ecclesia invisibilis* (the invisible Church) refers simply to the elect—*coetus electorum*, or community of the elect. The shift was really one of terminology only. In using the terms of visible and invisible Church, the Reformers were in no way operating outside established theological categories. There were, of course, differences on what constituted the boundaries of the visible Church, but the concept itself was not introduced by the Reformers.

In the early thought of Augustine, his distinctions were of course thoughtful and subtle—not at all simplistic.

> The most important distinctions are: the terrestrial church and the celestial church; the church in time and space and the church as city of God, reign of God, or kingdom of heaven; *the pilgrim church and its eschatological fulfillment*; the church as institution and as body of Christ; the church as sociological entity and as lived relationship with Christ and the Holy Spirit; the holy church and the sinful church. (*Augustine Through the Ages*, p. 169. Emphasis mine.)

Nevertheless . . .

At the same time, the historic Reformed terminology can be applied in such a way as to cause some problems of its own. While it was a valuable distinction, it was still not an inspired distinction. I say this *while embracing the distinction,* as far as it goes. Analogical distinctions, like analogies, can break down at some point, particularly when we are dealing with a subject as complex as this one.

For example, the Protestant terminology can make us think there are really *two* churches, one invisible in heaven and the other visible here on earth. The assumption then can easily be made, and has been made among American Protestants *ad nauseam,* that the invisible church is the true church. How many times have we heard someone claim his membership in the invisible church as his grounds for disparaging the church he ought to be joining?

But the medieval terminology (expressing the same distinction) can almost make us think in baptistic categories (i.e., that a baptized hypocrite is not truly a Christian in *any* sense).

Now I am not dealing here with any creedal statements—rather I am addressing how this terminology (and creedal terminology) can be mishandled at the popular level. What is our corporate common consciousness of these things? I want to suggest that the difficulty is not that we have made a distinction, but rather that by misunderstanding our terminology, we have tended to make an *ontological* distinction instead of an *historical* distinction.

If, like John Murray, we expressly guard against that kind of ontological division, I have no problem with it. It was John Murray incidentally who drove me most of the way down this particular road. Certainly the Church has invisible aspects. But to *define* the Church this way is, according to Murray, "invalid." "There are liabilities that can be avoided if other terms are employed." As he put it, the Church "in the New Testament never appears as an invisible entity and therefore may never be *defined* in terms of invisibility." As he continues, invisibility is a "term that is liable to be loaded with the misconceptions inherent in the concept 'invisible church', and tends to support the abuses incident thereto." And I agree with him that this is no matter of theological gnat-strangling. This matter is of "deep practical significance."

All that said, this is why I prefer the language of the Heidelberg Catechism, Lord's Day 21.

Q. What do you believe concerning the holy catholic Church?

A. That the Son of God, out of the whole human race, from the beginning to the end of the world, gathers, defends, and preserves for Himself, by His Spirit and Word, in the unity of the true faith, a Church chosen to everlasting life; and that I am, and forever shall remain, a living member thereof.

There it is. The Church is an entity *in* history, and *throughout* history. We can understand this as the *gathering* Church and the *gathered* Church. Also see the Belgic Confession (27). The gathering Church is what I have called the historical Church and Augustine, the pilgrim Church. The gathered Church is what I have called the eschatological Church.

Historical and Eschatological

Our problem is that we have tended to think in the Platonic categories of the Greeks instead of the historical and eschatological categories of the Jews. (This is *not* a charge of Hellenism against the Westminster Confession of Faith.) That which is heavenly (and hence invisible) is true, we assume, and that which is earthly can at best be only a dim shadow of that which is true. Thus, because we think of the heavenly and earthly as two separate and distinct ontological realms, existing at the same time, and because we *tend* to think of a Church in each realm, we find ourselves stuck with two separate and distinct churches. But Christ is the Head of only *one* Church.

The biblical teaching is that earthly history is eternally significant. Just as our individual sanctification occurs over the course of our earthly lives, so the sanctification of the Church occurs throughout the process of earthly history. Consider the feeble strength of the Church when it was first visibly organized in the household of Abraham—an old man and woman, childless. Consider it today, as countless thousands are calling upon the God of Abraham in truth. And for those who have the faith of Abraham, consider it in the centuries to come, when all the ends of the world shall remember and turn to the Lord, and all the families of the nations shall worship before our God (Ps. 22:27).

Instead of thinking of the elect as composing an invisible church in hyper-space (a category which neglects the importance of history), we should think of the full number of the elect as composing the eschatological church—the church as it will be visibly on the last glorious day of *history—ecclesia triumphans.* At the last day, all the fruitless branches will finally be detached from His tree, and all the permanent branches will be there, bearing abundant fruit. (But I want to be careful here because the phrase *ecclesia triumphans* was also understood as a partial church, consisting of those saints who are in heaven now.)

So, in our discussion of this point, rather than using the categories *visible* and *invisible,* or *heavenly* and *earthly,* I want to use the categories of *earthly historical* and *earthly eschatological.* I want to do this to protect against particular misunderstandings and abuses, not to introduce a new concept.

Therefore, rather than thinking of a visible Church, we should think of the historical Church. Obviously, not all of this historical Church is visible to us now. *Yesterday is invisible and so is tomorrow.* And yet the saints of seven hundred years ago, or the saints five hundred years from now, are all part of the historical Church, the Church as it grows, develops, and matures throughout all history.

An emphasis on an eschatological Church like this does not neglect the importance of history; this Church is the culmination of the entire process of redemptive history. Those who are in the historical Church should not see that church as defiled because it is earthly, but rather as immature because it is *early.*

The Unconverted Among Us

This distinction helps us to understand the relationship of unconverted professing Christians to the Church as well. The Bible teaches clearly that in the historical Church there are fruitless branches (but real branches nonetheless) which will not be there in the eschatological Church. Jesus sternly warns that, "If a man abide not in me, he is cast forth as a branch, and is withered; and men gather them, and cast them into the fire, and they are burned" (John 15:6). And Paul says the same. "For if God spared not the natural branches, take heed lest he also spare not thee" (Rom. 11:21).

This does not mean that the elect can lose their salvation. But it *does* mean that branches can lose their position on the tree. The elect always bear fruit, and their fruit remains. And yet some false professors, with a genuine historical connection to the tree, never bear lasting fruit, and consequently fall under the judgment of God

Conclusion

So what is the true Church? The true Church is the Church in history, the gathered throng of all professing households, assembled in covenant around the Word and Christ's sacraments. At the end of all history, *this same Church* will be revealed to an astonished universe as a bride of extraordinary beauty—a beauty that is *visible*. Many times throughout her history, she did not seem a suitable bride for our Lord. But then, on that last day, she will be presented and given away, without spot or wrinkle, or any other blemish.

Chapter Nine

New Life and Apostasy:

Hebrews 6:4–8 as Test Case[1]

Rich Lusk

Hebrews 6:4–8 is a highly controversial passage in Calvinistic circles. This essay will not attempt an exhaustive interpretation,[2] but rather debunk some flawed readings of the passage that have become quite commonplace. After a brief examination of the passage, we will look at broader theological questions raised by our reading of the text and seek to understand how it fits into pastoral practice and systematic theology.

Basically, the problem is in reconciling the notion of "falling away" with the five points of Calvinism, sometimes summarized by the acronym TULIP: total depravity, unconditional election, limited atonement, irresistible grace, and perseverance of the saints.[3] If God is sovereign in salvation, His elect cannot fail to persevere to the end. So what is going on in this troubling passage? What kinds of people are being described and what happens to them? Is apostasy real or illusory? What bearing does this passage have on Christian assurance?

Some Reformed commentators claim the warnings found here and elsewhere are hypothetical. This reading is hardly worthy of refutation. Why would an inspired writer use such terrifying language to scare his readers into avoiding something that could never come to pass anyway? Doug Wilson has humorously compared this approach to placing "Watch out for the cliffs" signs in Kansas. Moreover, there are enough recorded cases of actual apostasy in the pages of Scripture that we can put the hypothetical theory to bed (e.g., 1 Tim. 1:19, 20; Judas).

Other Reformed commentators claim the package of blessings in Hebrews 6:4–5 is less than full regeneration. After all, if these persons were regenerate, they would not fall away. The fact that they do (or may) fall away proves whatever grace they experienced was something less than full saving grace. This is true enough, perhaps. But there are still several problems with this way of reading the text.

Let us imagine, for the sake of the argument, that there is some qualitative difference between what the truly regenerate experience and what future apostates experience, *and* that this distinction is in view in Hebrews 6:4–6. The question every believer has to ask himself, then, is, "How do I know I won't apostatize? How do I know I won't fall away?" To take one example, Puritan John Owen, in his work *Nature and Causes of Apostasy from the Gospel*, says we must distinguish between merely "tasting" (6:5) the heavenly gift (which future apostates may do) and really "feeding" upon it (which the genuinely regenerate do).[4] But subtle psychological distinctions of this sort are bound to make one hopelessly introspective, always digging deeper into the inner recesses of one's heart to find some irrefutably genuine mark of grace. We are always left asking, "How do I know I am feeding on the heavenly gift, and not merely tasting of it? How do I know I've experienced *real* regeneration, and not its evil apostate twin? How do I know I have the real thing and not merely a counterfeit?" One's assurance is swallowed up in the black hole of self-examination.

As Scripture continually testifies, no man can know the depths of his own heart. Introspection has its limits. Frankly, our tools of self-analysis are not nearly as refined as the subtle linguistic analysis Owen and others apply to Hebrews 6. Therefore, on this model, assurance becomes virtually impossible.

But there is a more serious problem with this way of reading Hebrews 6. *Nothing in the text calls those warned to engage in a process of self-examination.* Rather, *Hebrews as a whole functions as an extended exhortation to perseverance.* In fact, the writer never calls into question whether or not he and his readers have experienced the grace of God. That is taken for granted. What is called into question, again and again, is whether or not they will *continue* in that grace. In terms of the theology of the book of Hebrews, the difference between the truly regenerate person and the person who will fail to persevere is not clear on the front end; rather, it only becomes clear as the one continues on in the faith and the other apostatizes.[5] Hebrews does not call us to construct two differing psychologies of conversion (or regeneration), one for those who will persevere and one for those who will not. Instead, it calls us to look away from ourselves to Jesus, the Author and Finisher of our faith. We are assured not by figuring out if we've received "real" regeneration, but by keeping our eyes fixed on Christ, the One who persevered to the end (cf. Heb. 12:1ff.).[6]

Hebrews 6:7–8 is often ignored in the interpretation of 6:4–6, but in reality these verses are critical for getting at the meaning of the passage. The writer turns to a familiar Scriptural metaphor: His readers are like the earth (cf. Gen 2:7) that has been watered (an obvious allusion to baptism or perhaps the means of grace more generally). New life has sprung up from the ground. We might call this new life "regeneration" in a generic, unspecified sense. There is no question the person has been made *alive*.[7] The question is, What will this new life produce? Will it bring forth a useful crop and receive God's blessing? Or will it produce thorns and thistles that are only fit to be burned in the fires of God's wrath? The writer clearly does not know which category each of his readers will fall into. He expects them to produce "better things . . . things that accompany salvation" (6:9). But the conclusion of the story has yet to be seen.

One further argument for this reading is discovered if we turn the warning of apostasy inside out. Remember, the threat of Hebrews 6:4–6 does not ensure that those who have received these blessings will fall short of salvation. It only says such falling away is a *possibility*. But if the author intended the blessings in verses 4–5 to be understood as less than full regeneration, then shouldn't he have said "*when* they fall away" rather than "*if* they fall away"? How could a partially regenerate person *avoid* falling away? We simply *must* assume the writer did not intend for us to distinguish the blessings described in these verses from "real" regeneration. It is an open question for the writer, and we must beware of making finer theological distinctions than he has intended to give us. What is at stake is not what these potential apostates have experienced in the past, but whether or not they will persevere into the future in the grace that is already theirs (cf. 2 Cor. 6:1).

This also refutes those who would take the blessings attributed to apostates in an ironic or sarcastic sense.[8] We certainly must acknowledge the presence of irony in the Scriptures.[9] But here it is simply impossible to suggest the text has an ironic counter-meaning. Again, the blessings are undifferentiated. Presumably, some of those persons described in Hebrews 6:4–6 will apostatize while others will not. But the passage cannot speak ironically to some and genuinely to others at the same time! There is a "rhetoric of reproach" in the Bible, to be sure, and there is a great deal of mocking laughter at the expense of the wicked. But irony simply does not explain the way this text actually works. Invoking irony to save a theological system (e.g., the TULIP) simply isn't sound exegesis. Apostates are ridiculed in Scripture, but not in this manner (e.g., Deut. 32:37; Ezek. 16:15ff.; Mark 2:17). An ironic reading of Hebrews 6 does not fit the writer's overall pastoral strategy, which is one of exhortation and encouragement. Such sarcasm would only be appropriate after the fact of their apostasy had become evident.

A Real Apostasy

Clearly, then, Hebrews 6:4–8 teaches the possibility of a real apostasy. Some people do indeed fall away, and it is a *real* fall *from* grace. Apostates actually lose blessings they once possessed. Apostasy is so terribly heinous precisely because it is sin against grace.

So how can this be reconciled with the TULIP? We satisfy the doctrinal requirements of Calvinism by insisting that all those God elected to eternal salvation will receive the gift of perseverance and will not fall away. Their perseverance is assured not by their own power or by some inner, irreversible metaphysical change that has taken place. Rather, their final glorification is guaranteed because God continues to work in them until he has brought their salvation to completion (e.g., John 10:28–29; Phil. 1:6).

Meanwhile, non-elect covenant members sooner or later will turn away from Christ and will perish because God withholds from them the gift of perseverance. The TULIP remains important because it reminds us that *all* of our salvation, including our perseverance, is a gift of God's grace. Those who fall away have no one to blame but themselves; those who persevere have no one to thank but God. He is the Sovereign Lord of salvation as well as apostasy.

Five significant lessons follow from this reading of Hebrews 6:4–8 (and similar passages).

First, the biblical warnings never call into question whether or not the church members they address have received God's grace. Nor do they typically call church members to examine themselves to determine if they've received real saving grace, or just partial, non-saving grace. They simply do not make the fine distinctions that Owen and others attempt to read into them. They take for granted the covenant community's objective standing in grace.

It is critical for our spiritual health that we recognize this because it reminds us that the antidote to the danger of apostasy is *not* ever-deepening self-examination, but looking away from ourselves to Christ. Even the very troubled Corinthians are addressed as the recipients of God's grace. But they are called to make sure they do not receive this grace *in vain* (2 Cor. 6:1). They are called to examine their works, not their hearts; in other words, the self-examination called for is ethical, not ontological (2 Cor. 13:5–7). The objectivity of the covenant of grace provides sure footing for faith's grasp of the divine promises. The question is not, "Am I elect? Am I truly regenerate?" The question is "Am I believing the promises and embracing the benefits God has given me as a covenant member? Am I pressing onward in the grace I have already received?"

Second, this is not to say that there is no actual difference between the grace that the "truly regenerate" (e.g., elected to persevere) receive and the grace that future apostates receive. No doubt, there *is* a difference, since God has decreed and made provision for the perseverance of the one and not for the other (Eph. 1:11).[10] Systematic theologians certainly have a stake in making such distinctions a part of their theology, so the TULIP must stand unchallenged. Whatever grace reprobate covenant members receive is qualified by their lack of perseverance. Augustine rightly distinguished "predestination unto grace," which was only temporary, and did not lead to final salvation, from "predestination unto perseverance," which did issue forth in eternal life. Perseverance is not merely the caboose on the end of the salvation train (to quote Doug Wilson once again); rather, its presence or absence qualifies one's whole participation in the *ordo salutis*.[11]

The point here, however, is that this qualitative difference is not in view in warning passages such as Hebrews 6, and it is an illegitimate move to make it a part of one's exegesis. These passages simply speak of the *undifferentiated* grace of God.[12] Moreover, such a distinction is of no pastoral significance since it is one of the Lord's secrets (cf. Deut. 29:29). It is simply impossible to determine who has persevering grace apart from the unfolding of time.[13]

Third, none of this exegesis undermines a properly grounded assurance. In fact, the writer of Hebrews makes assurance internal to the act of faith itself (Heb. 11:1, 6). The necessity of perseverance is a promise, not a threat, so long as we keep our eyes focused on Christ. It is only when we mix in some degree of self-reliance that we begin to doubt if we will persevere. Those who look to Christ have every reason to believe that the promises of John 10:28–29 and Romans 8:31ff. are for them. As Calvin said, Christ is the "mirror of our election," and as we look to Him through the means of grace, we have utter confidence in our standing before God. Just as we trust Christ to save us from past sins, so we trust Him for the future grace of perseverance. Every blessing, past, present, and future, is found in Him alone.

Assurance is thus a function of faith in Christ, not our own ability to gut it out to the end. But this full assurance does not make us immune to the warnings of Scripture. Assurance has a paradoxical quality: we can only be assured of our salvation against the backdrop of our possible damnation. It is the ever-present danger of apostasy that drives us to continually cling to Christ as the One in whom saving grace and full assurance are found. When God warns His people against apostasy, He is not playing games with them. If we think we're standing firm, we're in danger of falling.[14]

Fourth, the warnings force us to come to grips with the strong covenantal language of the Scriptures. Calvinists are used to speaking in terms of God's decree. When we speak of the elect, the regenerate, the sanctified, and so forth, we usually have reference only to those who enter into final salvation. This decretal perspective is biblical and is important to maintain. But it is not the Bible's primary way of speaking. More often than not, the Bible speaks covenantally and does not draw immediate distinctions between those in the covenant who are eternally saved and those who will someday apostatize. The Bible is a pastoral book and uses direct, personalized language to remind covenant members of their privileges and responsibilities.

A simple glance at Romans will show this. Paul can assuringly call his readers elect (8:31ff.) and then warn them about being cut off a few chapters later (11:20ff.). This explodes ordinary Calvinistic logic. In modern Calvinistic parlance, if someone is elect, they cannot fall away. But Paul is viewing election through the lens of the covenant, so he can give, in very direct language, both promises and threats. Biblically, there is no problem addressing the entire covenant community as elect, regenerate, sanctified, etc., even though (sadly) some of these covenant members will apostatize.[15] In other passages, election serves as a motivation to obedience and perseverance rather than their guarantee (e.g., Col. 3:12ff, 2 Pet. 1:5–11).

Fifth, the Bible consistently presents apostates as moving through three phases, with their final end worse than their beginning. In the first phase, they are spiritually dead, without hope and without God in the world. Then they are "made alive" after a fashion (e.g., Matt. 13:20, Heb. 6:7–8), and experience blessings within the context of the ecclesial community (e.g., Heb. 6:4–5). Finally, they forsake the Lord of the covenant and lose those blessings. This three-chapter story of spiritual death, temporary spiritual life, and final spiritual death is confirmed by Jude's description of apostates as "twice dead" (12).

Apostates are judged more severely than other unbelievers precisely because they entered into God's gracious covenant and then broke that covenant. In the same way that Israel's civil law punished adultery with harsher penalties than fornication, so those who were once members of the bride of Christ and have deserted Him can expect to end up in the hottest places in hell. They are condemned not merely as unbelievers, but as unfaithful spouses, disinherited sons, and traitorous citizens. Their latter end is worse than their beginning (2 Pet. 2:20; cf. Heb. 10:26ff.).

A Brief Excursus on Bible Reading and Systematic Theology

We now have our interpretation of this passage before us. Hebrews 6:4–8 describes the real blessings that every covenant member receives. Some persevere in those blessings by grace through faith and enter into final salvation. Others do not and perish. The blessings listed in 6:4–5 can be applied to both those who will persevere and those who will fall away. We have shown that this reading is compatible with

the TULIP because the sovereign plan of God undergirds both perseverance and apostasy. Those who are saved will revel in the grace and
mercy of God for all eternity. No merit or self-contribution is involved
in their salvation. Those who are lost will only have themselves to blame
for their failure to persevere.

But some will wonder if this reading can be integrated into the
wider framework of Reformed systematics. I will deal with that question straight on at the end of this paper, but for now I want to make a
few auxiliary comments about how we approach texts like this, and
indeed the Scriptures as a whole.

Some have objected to the exegesis offered here. They have insisted that not every member of the covenant community is really a
recipient of grace. They argue that the elect are a subset within the
covenant community. When Scripture speaks of the covenant community as a whole as "elect" (e.g., Eph. 1) or "united to Christ," (e.g.,
Rom. 6) it is making a judgment of charity, not describing what is in
fact the actual case of every baptized person, head for head.

Those who reason this way have logic on their side, at least in
some sense. After all, if one is united to Christ, and all blessings are
found in him, surely that includes perseverance, precluding the possibility of apostasy. Those who do apostatize were never united to Christ,
blessed with the Spirit's presence, loved by the Father, etc. In other
words, those who reason this way treat "union with Christ" or "election" as theological axioms from which deductions about perseverance
are drawn. If Bob Smith is united with Christ, he will persevere because, after all, perseverance is found in Christ alone. If Bob Smith is
regenerate, he will persevere because, after all, regeneration is a link in
the "golden chain of salvation." There is no such thing as a genuine
falling away from grace. There is no exit ramp from the *ordo salutis*
super highway.

Those who argue this way will also usually make a case against the
efficacy of the sacraments from logic. Baptism, so they say, cannot be
an effectual means of salvation because so many of the baptized fail to
bear lasting fruit. Passages about baptismal efficacy must be speaking
of the "thing signified" rather than what God does in and through the
sign itself. Of course, only a segment of those baptized actually receive
the "thing signified" so the rite itself is merely a symbol. If baptism was

indeed an effectual means of uniting us to Christ, we'd have to infer that no baptized person is ever lost—clearly a counter-factual conclusion.

But there is a problem here. The problem is not so much with the application of logic or the theological formulations. The problem is with the way Scripture is being read and applied. The Bible is not a revealed "system" of truth from which conclusions are to be deduced.[16] Rather, it is a pastoral/liturgical/covenantal book. It is a literary work, full of poetry and stories. It is the narrative record (and prophecy) of God's great acts from creation to consummation. The Bible was not given as grist for the systematic mill. It was intended to function first and foremost in the community of faith, not in academic or philosophical settings. It was given to provide the covenant people with encouragement, comfort, and direction. We must beware of drawing illegitimate deductions from Scriptural premises. We must learn to bend our logic to the Bible, rather than the reverse. We must learn to reign in our logical extensions at times.[17]

Thus, promises about perseverance (e.g., John 10:28–29; Rom. 8:31–39; Phil. 1:6) are not mainly theological axioms from which conclusions are to be deduced; rather, they are promises to be believed and claimed by faith. Scripture is not given first and foremost to provide logical exercises. It is given to feed and nourish our faith. We don't deduce perseverance from a set of premises; we trust God in Christ to provide it. If we cannot figure out precisely how the pieces of the theological puzzle fit together (in this case, promises of perseverance addressed to the community as a whole vis-à-vis the threats of apostasy), so be it.[18]

In the same way, if we cannot find a way to cleanly reconcile the Bible's robust teaching on sacramental efficacy[19] with the indisputable reality of apostasy, we dare not deny one or the other of these facts. Instead of trying to create laser-sharp theological categories, we must learn to live with fuzzy-edged mystery. The Scriptural warnings concerning apostasy are not there primarily to be theologically analyzed and worked into a dogmatic system; they are there to be heeded and observed, lest we perish.

In one sense, a good deal (though by no means all!) of the controversy taking place right now over covenant, salvation, the sacraments, and apostasy, is between those who are content to let loose ends dangle mysteriously and those who insist on tying up every last one. Are we willing to think "outside the box" of methodological scholasticism? Do we live by faith or by logic? Do we treat the promises of God as premises to be fed into syllogisms or as nourishment to feed our faith? I'm not necessarily saying we must choose between these two in every given case. The Bible can and should be the basis of a systematic theology. But I am saying there are significantly different approaches to the texts of Scripture. If we rush to systematize too hastily, we may fail to use the passages in the way God actually intended. The Bible was given primarily for purposes of pastoral care and nurture and must be used accordingly.

Where one side in the controversy sees a theological problem that must be solved in order to save the coherency of the system, the other side sees inscrutable mystery and lives with it by faith. Where one side sees axioms to be fitted into a logical system and from which deductions are to be drawn, the other side sees promises to be claimed and trusted. Our first task in approaching a passage such as Hebrews 6:4–8 is not to try to reconcile it with a system of truth we already possess (though we must do that in the end). Instead, we must see what the Spirit is saying to the Church in and through this living and active word of God. How does this passage comfort? challenge? convict? console? The passage's native habitat is the worshipping community; we must allow it to do its work there, rather than polishing off its rough edges in order to fit it into a dogmatic edifice we are busily constructing.

There are certainly hermeneutical and terminological issues to wrestle through in the current debate—most especially, the major divide between those Reformed theologians and pastors who read the Bible in a biblical-theological/redemptive-historical fashion and those who read it in a systematic/dogmatic fashion.[20] But more to the point, the basic divide is between those who read the Bible as a "promise book" versus those who read it as a "theology textbook." We must ask ourselves: Is Scripture a Father's love letter (warnings included: "Do not run away from home!") to his children? Or is it a professor's lecture notes to his students? Those are really the questions at the heart of this whole controversy.

Answering Objections

This view of apostasy obviously raises numerous questions. We would be remiss if we did not take up some of them here, replying to comments and criticisms.

First, it seems those who have argued against this position have canceled one another out. Some accuse this view of presumption, others of legalism. On the one hand, we are guilty of *presumption* because we insist that baptismal grace is universal. All those in the Church are recipients of God's favor and have "tasted the good word of God and the powers of the age to come" (Heb. 6:5). To be in the covenant is to be in Christ. It is to be enlightened and indwelt by the Holy Spirit (Heb. 6:4). On the other hand, we're *legalists* because we insist on the necessity of perseverance in faithfulness. There is no salvation apart from repentance and obedience (Heb. 5:9). Only those who stand firm to the end inherit the promises. Only those who persevere enter the final Sabbath rest of God (Heb. 3–4).

But the way to cut through these criticisms is simply to keep in mind the two-sided nature of the covenant. The covenant is structured in such a way that it includes *both* gracious promises *and* gracious responsibilities. We've been given grace in the form of union with Christ through the Holy Spirit. What is now objectively true of us obligates us to live a certain way. It is precisely because we have *already* received so great a salvation that we are to persevere to the end that we might enter into that salvation in its eschatological fullness. There is no presumption or legalism; just covenant grace and covenant faithfulness. Covenant keeping is not a matter of works righteousness; it is by grace through faith.

Also, some have wondered how those who possess all things "in Christ" can be vulnerable to falling away. If, after all, every Spiritual blessing is found in Him, including perseverance, how can we who are in Christ be in any danger of apostasy? How can those who have received the packet of blessings described in Hebrews 6:4–5 fail to persevere? Frankly, this is a great mystery. In fact, it is a double mystery. At one level, this is simply the age old "problem" of God's sovereignty in relation to human freedom. Calvinists have always confessed that predestination's inclusion of human responsibility is a mystery insoluble by human reason.[21] Those who have left Egypt behind for the sake of Christ are "free" to return to their old slavery, just as a dog may return to its vomit. Neither sin nor salvation strip man of his ability to choose.

But there is a darker enigma here as well. Questions about apostasy are really questions about the origin of evil. Apostasy is the ultimate mystery within God's creation and providence, going all the way back to the fall of Adam. How could a man who was created good, in knowledge, righteousness, and holiness, turn away from God to follow the lies of Satan?[22] How could Satan himself, originally an angel of light, apostatize? How could Israel, the elect and firstborn son of God, lose her kingdom inheritance (cf. Matt. 21:41, 43)? These questions are simply unanswerable by us. In fact, if apostasy were explainable, it would not be so utterly evil. We could rationalize it away.

It is clear that apostasy is part of God's eternal plan, however enigmatic that might be. The fall of "new men" in Christ is of a piece with the mysterious fall of the first man Adam. If we cannot explain the fall of Adam in the garden, neither will we be able to explain the fall of those who were once united to the new Adam.[23]

Additionally, we should note that tension between the assurances and threats of the new covenant, however mysterious, is an *inner-biblical* tension. In other words, the tension here is not simply the product of a theological system drawing unwarranted deductions; it is plainly on the pages of Scripture itself. For example, Peter reminds those who have been given "all things that pertain to life and godliness" (2 Pet. 1:3) that they must not succumb to false teaching and destructive heresies (2 Pet. 2:1ff.). Jesus spoke a parable in which a man received forgiveness and then had that blessing revoked (Matt. 18:21–35). Paul tells the Ephesians in one place they have received every Spiritual blessing in Christ (Eph. 1:3). The entire community, head for head, is regarded as chosen and redeemed. But elsewhere, he warns these same Christians that apostasy will arise from within their own community (Acts 20:28ff.). In Paul's view, assurance of election and the possibility of apostasy are twin features of the Church's life as a pilgrim community on the way from initial salvation to final glorification.[24]

If we decide to ignore the Bible's teaching on apostasy for fear that it might upset people's assurance or wreck their systematic theologies, we are pretending to be wiser than God. Pastors and teachers simply *must* be faithful to the Scriptures at this point. And they must not only deliver teaching *about* apostasy; they must actually warn their people in the way that Scripture warns them. Certainly, anyone issuing the covenant community warnings about apostasy should do so with humility and compassion. At the same time, these *are* warnings, so they should also be delivered with appropriate rhetorical forcefulness. But let's not outwit ourselves. These warnings are commonplace in Scripture. If there is a staggering disproportion between the frequency of warnings in Scripture, and the infrequency of their being sounded forth in our churches, we must reform our teaching practices. On page after page after page, one finds the inspired authors threatening the covenant community. It seems, then, that warnings of this sort, terrifying as they may be, should be a matter of course, a regular part of church life. We should find ourselves continually encouraged with the promises we have received, but almost as often, find ourselves warned about what will happen if we spurn these promises.

This is the answer to the charge of nominalism as well. Our attitude should be like that of Paul, who knew infallibly he belonged to the Lord (e.g., 2 Tim. 1, 4:6ff.), and yet lived in healthy fear of the danger of falling away (1 Cor. 9:24–27). Assurance must never lead to presumption, complacency, or carelessness. Part of the reason for provocative formulations is not simply to be faithful to Scripture (which uses deliberately provocative, envelope-stretching formulations), but to shock us out of our spiritual doldrums. Our preoccupation with the decrees tends to make us rather complacent (the "frozen chosen!"). There is a fine line between biblically-based assurance and presumption.

When I've talked to people who have had their assurance shaken by this kind of teaching and warning, in virtually every case, after conversation with the person, it came out that the basis of their assurance was flawed. They had grounded their assurance on a past experience, perhaps, with the result that they became overly introspective: "Did I *really* mean that prayer I prayed?" Or, they were trying to make their assurance a matter of iron-clad logic: "Systematic theology requires that God deal with me in such-and-such a way." Knocking down these props for people is often painful, but has a good result in the end. It throws us back onto the loving arms of Christ, not just for salvation, but for assurance as well. Again, as Calvin said, Christ is the "mirror of our election," and only by looking to Him within the community of His people can we know we are among God's chosen. In Christ, the hidden decree of predestination is manifested to us.[25]

Finally, some have wondered if this teaching entails the conclusion that salvation can be "lost." We've already dealt with this objection to some extent, but revisit it here. In many instances, the biblical writers view salvation as an eschatological concept—in this sense no one is saved till the last day. This is particularly evident in Hebrews. But salvation can also be understood as a past reality (we are saved in eternity past when God chose us in Christ, or when Christ died on the cross for us, or when the Spirit converted us) and a present and progressive reality (e.g., we are in the process of working out our salvation in fear and trembling: Phil. 2:11–12). To be sure, no elect person can lose his salvation, however much he may backslide. This is the point of Jesus' teaching in John 10:29—God the Father and God the Son will not lose their grip on those they have chosen for final salvation. The decree of God cannot be annulled or defeated. His promise to save His faithful people cannot be thwarted.

But the biblical language itself is more complicated. In one sense, all those in the covenant are "saved." They have been delivered out of the world and brought into the glorious new creation of Christ. They have escaped the pollution of the world through the knowledge of Christ, but not all will persevere. Jude 5 speaks of the Israelites as having been saved, and then destroyed, because they did not persevere. The preface to the Ten Commandments addresses Israel as God's redeemed people. But many of those redeemed did not continue trusting their Deliverer and perished (1 Cor. 10:1ff.; Heb. 3–4). 2 Peter 2 speaks of a similar class of people—fallen teachers who have been redeemed by Christ, who then deny him, and are destroyed.[26] To take yet another example, 1 Peter 3 says eight people in all were "saved" from God's wrath in Noah's ark. But if we read the Genesis narrative, we find one of those saved, Ham, apostatized and came under a curse. Even today, there are "Hams" in the ark of the Church. They were "saved" by God in baptism, but fail to persevere in that salvation and fall away.

What are we to do with these examples? Some might say, "Those are cases drawn from Old Testament types. Those were *pictures* of salvation—not the real thing. Salvation in the New Covenant cannot be lost." But the problem with this is that it draws a contrast precisely where the New Testament writers themselves draw a parallel. Paul, Peter, and Jude all use these Old Testament stories to warn New Covenant believers, lest they too fall from grace. Imagine a reader of 1 Corinthians 10 saying, "Well, those Israelites who were redeemed out of Egypt perished, but that was the old covenant. In the New Covenant, it's 'once saved, always saved.'" But Paul specifically says the record of the Israelites who failed to persevere and were destroyed *was "written for our admonition" in the New Covenant era.* It is a narrative warning written for us. The basic structure of the covenant, with attendant blessings and curses conditioned on grace-enabled perseverance in faithfulness, remains in tact through every age of biblical history.

Besides, as we have seen, the New Testament itself has many warnings which parallel the Old Testament warnings. Thus, Jesus spoke of those in the New Covenant who would be united to Him, but then cut off because they did not persevere in fruit bearing (John 15:1ff). The vine and the branches imagery is rooted in the Old Covenant Scriptures and is used by Jesus in the same way as in Isaiah 5. If Jesus himself is salvation personified, then, in some sense, being cut off from Him entails being cut off from the source of salvation. Likewise Paul says the Galatians have been adopted by God as old Israel was, but they are also in danger of falling from grace (Gal. 3:26–4:6, 5:4).[27]

Again, there is no question that God's elect, predestined for final salvation, will persevere to the end. They cannot fall away because God is determined to keep them in the path of life. But reprobate covenant members may temporarily experience a quasi-salvation. They were, in some sense, bought by Christ (1 Pet. 2:1), forgiven (Matt. 18:21ff.), renewed (Matt. 13:1ff.), written into the Book of Life (Rev. 22:19), etc., and lost these things.

Perhaps all this can be made more palatable and plausible if we learn to think of salvation in more relational, narrative, and covenantal categories, rather than metaphysical categories.[28] "Salvation," in this sense, is not a thing we possess that can be lost and found, like car keys. Rather, it is a matter of relationship, of being rightly related to God. But relationships are not static, timeless entities. Rather, they are fluid and dynamic. Some marriages start well; the couple is really in love. But then things go sour. Our salvation covenant with the Lord is like a marriage. If we persevere in loyalty to Christ, we will live with Him happily ever after. If we break the marriage covenant, He will divorce us. It may not be wise to call this "losing one's salvation," but it would be unbiblical to say nothing at all was really lost or rejected. That would simply be a denial of the reality of the covenant.

Final Thoughts: Integrating This Reading of Hebrews 6:4–8 into Historic and Systematic Reformed Theology

The teaching offered here is not un-Reformed in any sense. Calvin is known for his doctrine of predestination, but he was also the covenant theologian par excellence. Calvin had a robust doctrine of apostasy. In various places, he speaks of apostates as those who had been formerly "reconciled to God" and "adopted" by Him, joined in "sacred marriage" to Him, recipients of "illumination" and "grace," having "faith," and so on. He says the eternally reprobate can, for a season, share in the special, effectual call of the Holy Spirit. Those who fall away have forsaken their salvation and forgotten that they were cleansed. He clearly says the warnings are for those elected by the Father and redeemed by the Son—in other words, they're for us![29]

In more recent Reformed theology, John Murray has had quite a bit to say about the relationship of the work of Christ to common grace and the non-elect within the covenant. For Murray, many benefits from Christ's work accrue to people who ultimately do not reach final salvation. And yet, the "L" in TULIP (limited atonement) remains in tact because the atonement does in history precisely what God designed for it to do.[30] Following on the heels of Murray, Norman Shepherd sought to reformulate some Reformed doctrines, not to alter their substance, but to take into account more fully the Bible's covenantal perspective. In particular, Shepherd points out that biblical writers frequently look at election through the lens of the covenant.[31]

Going back behind the Reformation, everything set forth here can be found in Augustine. This great Church father was certainly the most significant influence on Luther and Calvin. Augustine taught that believers, called by God, and regenerated (in some sense) by Him, might still fall away. This is obviously identical to our exegesis of Hebrews 6, terminological differences aside. Of course, Augustine also taught unconditional election: All those chosen in Christ from the foundation of the world to receive eternal salvation will indeed do so. God's purposes cannot fail. Perseverance is a gift given to the elect alone, and it ensures their entrance into final salvation. Augustine felt no contradiction between these two poles of election and apostasy; in fact, he felt it was necessary to keep them together in order to be faithful to Scripture.[32]

In terms of systematic theology, I do not think it is all that difficult to incorporate a stout view of apostasy into our decretal, covenantal dogmatics. Briefly sketched out, it looks something like this (with the admission that it is not the final word, only a word on the way to a longed-for better understanding and articulation of these issues):

God, in eternity past, elected in Christ a great multitude to salvation. This election was wholly gracious and unconditional, having its source only in the free mercy and good pleasure of God. Those the Father elected to eternal salvation, he sent his Son to die for. His atoning work is fully sufficient for their salvation and completely accomplished their redemption. The Holy Spirit works in these same chosen ones to apply Christ's saving work to them and keep them faithful to Christ their whole lives. Because of the hardness of their hearts in sin, this work of grace must be, ultimately, irresistible. No elect person can be lost and no non-elect person can attain salvation. In Christ, the Last Adam, the fall of the first Adam is reversed and overcome for God's chosen family.

God's eternal decree to gather His elect into a people for His name is worked out in history. We do not emphasize God's action in eternity at the expense of His work in history, or vice versa. Nor do we pit individual election versus corporate election. Chosen individuals only come to realize their election in the context of the history of the elect community. One's election becomes manifest in the administration of Word and sacrament, as one responds to the gospel and enters the Church in baptism. Christ is present in His Church by His Spirit, to see to it that all His elect ones are brought to faith in Him. The church is the kingdom, family, and house of God. In and through the church, God nurtures, equips, and perfects those He has chosen, called, and gathered. The church is the means of grace through which perseverance into final salvation is granted.

However, God mysteriously has chosen to draw many into the covenant community who are not elect in the ultimate sense and who are not destined to receive final salvation. These non-elect covenant members are actually brought to Christ, united to Him and the Church in baptism, receive various gracious operations of the Holy Spirit, and may even be said to be loved by God for a time. They become members of Christ's kingdom, stones in God's living house, and children in God's family.[33] Corporately, they are part of the chosen, redeemed, Spirit-indwelt people, just as Israel was God's elect and adopted people until 70 A.D. They experience blessings in the sphere of grace which are common, at least for a time, to both those elected to persevere, and those not so elected. But, sooner or later, in the wise counsel of God, these individuals fail to bear fruit and fall away. They do not persevere in the various graces they have received; their faith withers and dies. In some sense, they were really joined to the elect people, really sanctified by Christ's blood, and really recipients of new life given by the Holy Spirit. The sacraments they received had objective force and efficacy. But God withholds from them the gift of perseverance and all is lost. They break the gracious new covenant they entered into at baptism. They fail to inherit the promises and are excommunicated from the family of God.

Of course, there are different varieties of apostasy. Even as those who are ultimately saved will have a variety of "salvation stories" to tell and rejoice in for all eternity, so the finally damned will end up in hell by a wide array of routes. Some never directly encounter the saving revelation of Christ in preaching and the sacraments, but still reject the revelation of God through the things He has made (Rom. 1:18ff.). Their condemnation is just because they have refused to thank and glorify their Creator who has showered them with good things (Acts 14:14ff.). They apostatized in Adam. Others enter into the covenant community for a season. They experience real grace and perhaps even real fruitfulness. But in due time, they are drawn away from Christ and His people by the lures of Satan. Because they received much, they will answer for much. Still others are hypocrites from the beginning. They only enter into the Church on a pretense. They may fool the officers and members of the Church for a time, but they cannot fool God. Their objective membership in the church is a blessing, considered in itself, but because of their unbelief, it only brings instant and intensified curse. Their sin is willful and deliberate. Their covenant status and heart condition do not match and they know it. Covenant blessing is poured out upon them in the means of grace, but they reject it again and again. Even if their apostasy escapes the detection of the church discipline process, their condemnation does not sleep.

The covenant, then, is a true revelation of God's salvation, for in the covenant community, all God's people, elect and non-elect, find gracious blessings. The covenant really is gospel—good news—through and through. The administration of the covenant really is salvific. Yet only those who continue to persevere by grace in loyalty to the covenant and the Lord of the covenant inherit final salvation. Those who fall away lose the temporary covenantal blessings they had enjoyed. Ultimately, this is because God decreed that these covenant breakers would not share in the eschatological salvation of Christ. Everything happens according to His eternal counsel and will. Of course, these apostates cannot blame God for their falling away—it's their own fault, since God's overtures of love towards them in the context of the covenant were sincere. And those who do persevere to the end cannot claim any credit or make any boast—all they have done has been because of God's grace at work in them to keep them faithful.[34]

All covenant members are invited to attain to a full and robust confidence that they are God's eternally elect ones. Starting with their baptisms, they have every reason to believe God loves them and desires their eternal salvation. Baptism marks them out as God's elect people, a status they maintain so long as they persevere in faithfulness. By looking to Christ alone, the preeminently Elect One, the One who kept covenant to the end and is the Author and Finisher of the faith of God's people, they may find assurance. But those who take their eyes off Christ, who desert the Church where His presence is found, who forsake the external means of salvation, will make shipwreck of their faith and prove to have received the grace of God in vain. The requirement of perseverance is non-negotiable. But it is not a threat to us; rather, it is a promise to be claimed in Christ. A passage like John 10:28–29 is not given to make us wonder, "Am I one of those the Father and Son are holding?" Rather, this is a promise to be claimed by faith: "God, you've promised to keep me in Your grasp! For the sake of Your name, do so!"

This, then, is the biblical picture. The TULIP is still in place, but has been enriched by a nuanced covenant theology. By framing the issues as we have, we are able to preserve God's sovereignty in salvation and hold covenant breakers accountable for their own apostasy. Plus, we can do justice to the Scripture's teaching on the nature of the Church and efficacy of the sacraments, as well as the genuineness of the covenantal promises and threats. Nothing has been lost by our reformulation of the popular Reformed picture, and a great deal has been gained.

Notes - Chapter 9

[1] Thanks to Kris Lundgaard, whose thoughtful, probing questions provoked me to dig deeper into this passage and Joel Garver, whose writing on apostasy (unfortunately unpublished) sets a new benchmark in Reformed theology.

[2] For example, I will not attempt to explicate the meaning of each of the blessings listed in verses 4–5. I will also ignore the once-and-for-allness of the apostasy in view since I think it very likely pertained to the unique circumstances of the first century audience. Ordinarily, apostates are not barred from repenting and returning to the Church. In the situation facing the original readers of Hebrews, apostasy would be irreversible most likely because the apostates would die in the Jewish War of 66–70 A.D., defending their now-obsolete temple against the Romans. For all practical purposes, if someone apostatizes and is cut off from the covenant community in excommunication, that person is always free to repent and return to the Church and to the Lord. Indeed, we must recognize that one purpose of excommunication is the ultimate reclamation and restoration the wayward brother (1 Cor. 5, 1 Tim. 1:19–20). We see at least one such apostate repenting and returning to the church in Paul's Corinthian correspondence. Traditionally, texts such as Matthew 12:31ff. and 1 John 5:16 have sometimes been used to deny the freedom of apostates to return. But this is a misreading of these passages. The unpardonable sin seems to be related to Jews who first had the ministry of Jesus and rejected Him, and then also rejected His Spirit after the resurrection and Pentecost. It was a unique danger for Jews living at that peculiar, transitional time in redemptive history as they received the witness of the Son and the Spirit in succession. They rejected God's double witness to the Messiah. True, there may still be a form of aggravated apostasy from which one may not repent, but we shouldn't try too hard to gauge if someone has committed this kind of sin. We should always seek the repentance and restoration of apostates.

[3] Numerous expositions of Calvinism are available. See, for example, Edwin H. Palmer *The Five Points of Calvinism* (Grand Rapids, MI: Baker, 1972). The Five Points derive not from Calvin himself (though he certainly affirmed them) but from the Synod of Dordt, which convened from 1618–1619, and formulated a five-part response to the Arminian movement.

[4] John Owen, *Nature and Causes of Apostasy From the Gospel* in the *Works of John Owen*, Vol. 7 (Edinburgh, Banner of Truth, 1965) p. 24. In light of Hebrews 2:9, the "tasting" vs. "feeding" distinction looks very artificial.

[5] Several biblical narratives bear this out. For example, the same terminology that describes the Spirit coming (literally, "rushing") upon Saul in 1 Samuel 10:6 is used when the Spirit comes upon David (1 Sam. 16:13), Gideon (Judg. 6:34), Jephthah (Judg. 11:29), and Samson (Judg. 14:6, 9; 15:14). But in four of these five cases (David, Gideon, Jephthah, and Samson), the man in question was clearly regenerated and saved by the Spirit's work (cf. Heb. 11:32). This means that at the outset of Saul's career, the biblical narrative itself draws no distinction between his initial experience

of the Spirit and the experience of those who would enter into final salvation. Saul's apostasy was not due to any lack in God's grace given to him, but was his own fault. While God no doubt predestined Saul's apostasy (since He foreordains all that comes to pass), God was not the Author of Saul's apostasy (cf. WCF 3.1). From one perspective, at least, Saul received the same initial covenantal grace that David, Gideon, and other saved men received. His failure to persevere was due to his own rebellion.

[6] Note further that Hebrews 10:32 uses the same word ("enlightened") to describe true conversion as found in Hebrews 6:4 of those who might apostatize in the future. Again, the difference is not between two kinds of enlightenment, but those who *abide* in the light they've received and those who do not.

[7] Cf. Matt. 13:20ff.

[8] For example, this is Fowler White's approach in his unpublished essay, "When Words of Praise Implied Reproach: A New Strategy for Interpreting Hebrews 6 and 10" (a paper presented at the 1984 national meeting of the Evangelical Theological Society).

[9] See, for example, my unpublished paper, "The Ironic Gospel."

[10] Thus, I fully affirm WCF 10.1 and 10.4: only those actually predestinated unto life are effectually called and the reprobate never "truly" come to Christ. There are numerous passages which differentiate the grace of the elect and the reprobate within the covenant (e.g., John 8:35, Rom. 8:29–30, etc.). But this differentiation between elect and reprobate covenant members only becomes evident over time. Insofar as history is real to us (and to God!), we must take undifferentiated covenant grace seriously.

[11] Following Anthony Hoekema, I would rather speak of a "way of salvation" than an "order of salvation," but the point is the same either way. See his *Saved by Grace* (Grand Rapids, MI: Eerdmans, 1989), ch. 2. Richard Gaffin also critiques the *ordo salutis* model. See his *Resurrection and Redemption* (Phillipsburg, NJ: Presbyterian and Reformed, 1987).

[12] In some warnings, this is inescapably obvious. There is no way the writer of Hebrews intends for his readers to distinguish between the kind of objective sanctification received by the genuinely regenerate and those who will apostatize (10:29). See also Galatians 5:4, 2 Peter 2:1, 20–21, Revelation 22:19, etc. The WCF speaks of blessings that are "common operations of the Spirit," shared by both the elect-unto-salvation and the reprobate covenant member (10.4).

[13] The systematic decretal perspective is fine so long as we are dealing with a timeless, abstract system. But when we start to deal with actual persons and lived history, it becomes inadequate.

[14] Note that WCF 14.2 teaches that one function of saving faith is to "[tremble] at the threatenings" of Scripture. Many modern Calvinists assume glibly the warnings do not apply to them, but this is an unconfessional attitude. It is the response of faith, not doubt, that takes the covenant warnings seriously.

[15] This point is obviously of immense significance for pastoral ministry. We should not hesitate to speak to our fellow covenant members the way Paul addressed his churches. We can say to our fellow churchmen, "You're elect! God loves you and Christ died for you! You're forgiven and regenerated!" Covenantally, these things are true of them. Until and unless they apostatize, their covenant membership must be taken as a sign of their eternal election. Pastorally we identify covenant and election in order to nourish and assure, even as we distinguish covenant and election in order to give warnings and threats. This point is also critical for liturgics, for in the liturgy we speak the direct, personal language of the covenant, not the abstract language of the decree. The Bible is a liturgical book and we should imitate its language. When we say in the liturgy, "*We* are gathered in the name of God the Father, God the Son, and God the Holy Spirit" we are speaking covenantally. Without this covenantal perspective, a consistent Calvinist would have to say "Those of us here who are elect are gathered . . ." Not exactly the stuff of beautiful worship! Another example is the pastor's declaration of absolution. A pronouncement to the congregation, "*Your* sins are forgiven!" is very powerful, much more so than, "Whoever here is elect and regenerated and penitent is forgiven!" The conditions and qualifications are true enough, but they all too easily point us in the wrong direction. Given the Puritan obsession with predestinarian theology, at the expense of the covenant, it is not surprising most Puritans rejected liturgical worship forms. A decretal theology, abstracted from the covenant, cannot support liturgical language. The liturgy speaks the language of the covenant, not the language of the decree. In Calvinistic churches, a good many pastoral problems related to assurance are due to a failure to properly relate covenant and election. We need to learn to use terms such as "elect," "regenerate," etc., not just in a narrow decretal sense, but also in a broader covenantal sense, as they so often function in Scripture.

[16] This is not to say the Bible's teaching cannot be translated into systematic theology. Behind Scripture stands the mind of God, which is perfectly consistent. God is Absolute Rationality (among other things). But that's still quite a bit removed from claiming that we can actually reproduce the system of Scripture in our theology textbooks. In fact, while nothing in Scripture is irrational, to be sure, there is no doctrine that does not terminate in mystery for finite (and now fallen) minds. Systematic theology is useful in organizing our understanding of the Bible and erecting barriers to keep out heresy. However, it is also dangerous, unless we are willing to live with an "open-ended" system. For an excellent introduction to "open-ended" systematics, see Cornelius Van Til, *An Introduction to Systematic Theology* (Philipsburg, NJ: Presbyterian and Reformed, 1974). In dealing with the NT epistles (usually regarded as the most "systematic" writings within Scripture), we must always keep in mind the ad hoc nature of these documents. They were written to deal with various pastoral issues, not to provide a philosophical system or an ideology. They are pastoral letters addressed to communities of faith, not abstract treatises delivered to classrooms

full of seminary students. The epistles can be transformed *into* systematic theology, of course, but should not be read *as* systematic theology.

[17] WCF 1.6 acknowledges the use of logic as a hermeneutical tool. But even then, Scripture itself, not autonomous reason, is the "supreme judge by which all controversies of religion are to be determined" (WCF 1.10). In other words, Scripture itself controls our application of logic to Scripture.

[18] There is a great deal of mystery here. For example, why would the Spirit inspire Paul to address the Ephesian community, "[God] blessed us with every spiritual blessing in the heavenly places in Christ, just as He chose us in Him before the foundation of the world, that we should be holy and without blame before Him in love," when some of those referred to as elect and blessed and beloved would not persevere? Paul's declaration was not to be read as a head-for-head guarantee that every member of the visible covenant community in Ephesus would be eternally glorified. Rather, Paul tells them (head-for-head) who they are objectively as a way of encouraging and nurturing faith. It's as though Paul said, "Don't you see who you are? You're elect in Christ and blessed with every Spiritual blessing in him. Live accordingly!" Colossians 3:12 reflects the same logic. Paul moves from their objective status as "the elect of God, holy and beloved" to their duties within the covenant community to "put on tender mercies, kindness, etc." The election Paul is attributing to these churches is not one of God's hidden things any longer (Deut. 29:29); in Christ and his covenant administration, the decree of election has now been revealed. And yet not all who are united to the Elect One, Jesus Christ, remain in Him and fulfill the high vocation that election brings with it. It is still to be seen who will persevere and who will fall away from within the elect people. We have much to learn from Paul's pastoral practice in these letters.

[19] On baptismal efficacy, see my essay on baptism in this book, as well as "Baptismal Efficacy and the Reformed Tradition: Past, Present, and Future," available online at http://www.hornes.org/theologia/content/cat_sacraments.htm.

[20] That's not to say these two approaches are incompatible. But in our day, cross-communication between those who favor one approach towards those who favor the other is quite difficult, given different theological lexicons, different motivating questions, different methodologies, and so forth.

[21] See WCF 3.8 and 9.1–5. It misses the mark to suggest that emphasizing apostasy leads us to *over-emphasize* human responsibility. It's actually impossible to over-emphasize human responsibility because we are infinitely accountable to God. Only if we deny the Creator/creature relationship, and put human responsibility on a continuum with divine sovereignty, is it possible to think of one being emphasized at the expense of the other. It's not a matter of either/or but both/and. Of course, God's sovereignty is always the ground and presupposition of human responsibility. But we have maintained all along that salvation is a work of God's sovereign grace.

[22] The analogy between Adam's apostasy and new covenant apostasy is entirely warranted, exegetically, theologically, and confessionally. The description of Adam's virtues (knowledge, righteousness, and holiness) given in WSC 10 is actually derived from passages which describe our re-creation in Christ (Eph. 4:24, Col. 3:10)!

[23] Adam and Israel, of course, are the standard paradigms from which we must develop a biblical theology of apostasy. Interestingly, the whole biblical narrative turns on critical acts of apostasy. The apostasy of the first Adam and the crucifixion of the last Adam by apostate Israel are the key junctures in the biblical story. But it might be helpful to briefly survey another paradigmatic example of apostasy. The case of Saul is very instructive here (and has relevance even in the new covenant, unless we take a dispensational approach to soteriology). When Saul was anointed, the Holy Spirit came upon him in a mighty way. (This does not mean the Spirit had not been active in his heart prior to his anointing. No doubt the Spirit was active in the life of Saul prior to his full reception of the Spirit at his anointing/baptism. Nor can the Spirit's work be reduced to merely equipping Saul for office.) Saul has already shown signs of piety, but now he is adopted by God in a special way and receives new creation life from the Spirit (1 Sam. 10:6–9). We see the fruit of this new heart in the following chapters as he displays faithfulness, humility, fights against the Lord's enemies, etc. However, in 1 Samuel 13, he begins to backslide, resulting in a threefold fall and his ultimate rejection by the Lord. His heart grows harder and harder towards the Lord, till finally he grieves the Spirit so deeply that the Spirit departs from him in 1 Samuel 16. Note that his fall (like Adam's) involved a food test, as he sets himself in the place of God (14:24ff.). Saul is thus the classic case of apostasy, of falling away from the Lord. David acknowledges this in his famous prayer of repentance when he prays, essentially, "Do not let me be a Saul!" (cf. Ps. 51:11, alluding to 1 Sam. 16:14).

Of course, Saul may not be used as a counter-point to the teaching of Scripture elsewhere (and the confessions of the Reformed churches) that God is sovereign in salvation. Saul did not fall *in spite of* God's decretal attempt to save him; rather Saul's renewal as well as his apostasy were *both* part of God's sovereign orchestration of history (WCF 3.1,8). Theologically, we can even say God chose to withhold the gift of perseverance from Saul for His own wise and holy purposes. In an *ultimate sense*, then, Saul was not elect, not purchased by Christ, not fully regenerate, etc. In retrospect, his failure to persevere qualifies his entire experience of God's grace. In the book of Samuel, he is like the first Adam. His fall makes way for a Second Adam, David, who will be a man after God's own heart. The narrative of Samuel hangs on this familiar two-Adam biblical-theological motif.

But Saul's case shows how far apostates can enter into God's grace before falling away. A snapshot of Saul's life prior to 1 Samuel 13 would give a picture seemingly identical to that of an elect person. Saul really did taste of God's mercy and love; he really did possess the Holy Spirit and the new creation life the Spirit brings; he really was adopted into God's family and really lived a godly, exemplary life for a time. But he failed to persevere. No doubt, there is a great deal of mystery in this, just as there is a great deal of mystery in the fall of the first man, Adam. Saul, as a new Adam figure, had been restored to God's image, but fell back into the corruption of the world. He experienced the powers of the age to come, but slipped back into bondage to the world, the flesh, and the devil.

We cannot deal adequately with Saul's case if our only theological categories are elect and non-elect. We must understand the place of the covenant as well. It is not enough to say that Saul's fall proved he was non-elect. In some sense, he was, for a time, part of God's elect people in and through the covenant. When he fell he lost all the blessings of his covenant relationship with the Lord. He did not go to hell simply as a non-elect person, but as a disinherited son, as an unfruitful branch, as a covenant breaker, as an unfaithful spouse of the Lord, etc. So long as Saul remained in covenant with the Lord, he had every right to think of himself as "elect" and "regenerate." Those around him would have also considered him to be elect, since he had all the marks of one called by God to eternal salvation. But he sinned grievously, failed to manifest any genuine repentance, and was formally cut off from the elect/covenant community by Samuel. Saul became a defiled house for the Spirit, and so the Spirit departed from him.

The application to Christians should be clear: In terms of the "already" and the "not yet," we are like Saul in 1 Samuel 10. We have received the Spirit and been adopted by God in our baptism/anointing, but now we must persevere. If we sin, we must not make excuses, blame shift, pridefully try to save face, etc., but must, like David, cry out in humble repentance and brokenness and move on knowing God has forgiven us. Like David, we beseech the Lord, "Do not take your Holy Spirit from me" (Ps. 51:11; cf. 1 Sam. 16:14) because we do not want our stories to end as Saul's did. Lest we fall into "soteriological dispensationalism," we must acknowledge the reality of both Sauls and Davids in the new covenant. Lest we fall away from the Lord, we must take narrative warnings like the case of Saul with utter seriousness.

[24] In the Bible, election is always presented as good news—as pure gospel—for the covenant people of God. Yet, in many modern Calvinistic presentations, the doctrine takes on an ominous, threatening character. It raises the question, "Am I elect?," a question anxious souls want to have answered. But we cannot peer into the eternal decrees of God to see his roll of chosen ones. Nor do we have spiritual x-ray vision ("cardio-analytic abilities," as one theologian puts it) that allows us to gaze into the depths of our hearts to see if we are *really* "regenerate." But here is a place where the Bible must be allowed to trump the deductions we might otherwise draw from premises provided by systematic theology. The inspired writers, after all, often speak of the covenant people of God as elect. The elect are not viewed as a "secret society" within the visible Church. The biblical authors speak of the entire covenantal community as chosen by God; surely this knowledge of who is elect cannot be due simply to the fact that the Spirit is working in them as they write. Continually, the apostles

address real words of comfort and assurance to visible churches—often very troubled visible churches!—and this is to serve as a model for pastors today. As has already been suggested, our theology must allow us to speak the gospel in the first and second person, in a very personal and direct way. If Paul had been writing Ephesians 1 as a modern scholastic Calvinist, he would had to have said to the community, "He chose *some* of us in Him before the foundation of the world, that we should be holy and without blame . . . " and then remain agnostic about the identity of the "some." But Paul's theology of election permits him to speak of the *whole* covenant community as elect in Christ, even when he knows some members of that congregation will apostatize. Various attempts to solve this dilemma (e.g., distinguishing special or individual election from general or corporate election) may be helpful, but do not fully resolve the complex mysteries involved.

[25] It is important to remember that the TULIP is not an exhaustive biblical theology. The TULIP was formulated in response to a particular doctrinal controversy at a particular time and place in history (seventeenth-century Holland). It was never intended to serve as a systematic grid for interpreting the Scriptures. Systematic theological paradigms like the TULIP can serve as helpful checks on our reading of Scripture and can erect boundaries for orthodoxy. But they are like *Cliff's Notes*—they really only serve their purpose if we actually interact carefully with the primary text itself. In this case, moreover, there is great potential for confusion since the terminology of our systematic theology and our theological slogans do not always match the Bible's own terminology. Indeed, the Bible has no systematic theological vocabulary; it speaks more in metaphor and imagery than technical terminology.

While allowing creeds, confessions, and the history of dogmatics to serve as hermeneutical tools, we should always be careful to not allow the demands of a theological system to override the exegesis of particular texts. Whatever problems apostasy might create for what philosophers have called the "theoretical intellect," there is no problem at all for the "practical intellect:" I stand in fear of falling away, all the while trusting Christ to preserve me completely. I am spurred on by both the promises made directly to me as a covenant member, and the threats about the possibility of apostasy. Logically, we may have to fight to hold these things together, but practically there is no difficulty. Consider an analogy: Married persons usually feel no practical tension between a commitment to marital fidelity and guarding themselves against the possibility of adultery. Promise and threat, assurance and vigilance, can go together quite easily in the real world!

For better *and* for worse, we have numerous popularizers of Reformed theology around today. The result is that what most of us think of as "Reformed" is greatly truncated. American Reformed theology is like a bad cassette recording of the real thing. In this essay (and in this book as a whole), we are simply trying to recover nuances that were originally in the tradition, but have been lost.

[26] In 2 Peter 2:1, the pattern of being "redeemed" by the Lord, then denying him, is simply an intensified, eschatologized replication of Israel's exodus ("redemption" is an exodus term after all), followed by her rejection of the Lord in the wilderness. Jesus exodused Israel (Luke 9:31) in His cross; many who were "redeemed" by Him later rejected Him. This typological model fits with the recurrent NT theme that Christians from 30–70 A. D. (and beyond, in several senses) were like that generation of Israelites after the Red Sea crossing: in danger of perishing in the wilderness as they trek on their way to the promised land of the new covenant in its fullness (cf. 2 Pet. 3).

[27] The biblical illustrations can help us understand the relational dynamics at work here. An adopted child has *all* the privileges that come with being part of the family. Some of those privileges are still future (e.g., inheriting the family fortune), but in principle they belong to the child (cf. Gal. 4:1). But what if the child runs away from home? What if he forsakes all he has been given and returns to the orphanage? He loses the future inheritance that was his, along with everything else. In the same way, a married person has all the privileges of marriage, including the promise of a future life together, companionship, children, etc. But if the spouse deserts or commits adultery, he loses everything, including the future. That, I would suggest, is analogous to what happens in cases of apostasy. It's not just that blessings received in the past are lost; the promised future is forfeited as well. (Certainly the case of Adam's apostasy reveals that as well.)

[28] See Peter Leithart, *The Priesthood of the Plebs: A Theology of Baptism* (Eugene, OR: Wipf and Stock, 2003), for some forays into recasting theology along these lines. Of course, I'm not suggesting a relational, narratival approach is devoid of ontology. However, the older, more rationalistic, Cartesian models of Reformed scholasticism generally factored relational change over time out of their soteriological formulations. We must resist the temptation to flatten out history.

[29] I am drawing from Calvin's discussion of apostasy and temporary faith in *Institutes of the Christian Religion*, ed. John T. McNeil (Philadelphia: Westminster Press, 1960), 3.2. See also his commentaries on various "apostasy" passages such as Hebrews 6 and 10, John 15, Romans 11, 1 Peter 2, etc. Of course, in terms of God's decree, Calvin also differentiates between what the reprobate experience and what the elect experience.

[30] See John Murray, "The Atonement and the Free Offer of the Gospel," pp. 59–85 in *Collected Writings of John Murray*, vol. 1 (Edinburgh and Carlisle, PA: Banner of Truth Trust, 1976). The theology of apostasy laid out in this paper can be thought of as simply an unpacking of Murray's provocative statement on page 63: "Many benefits accrue to the non-elect from the redemptive work of Christ." We are not abandoning effectual atonement; we are making nuances within its parameters.

[31] See Norman Shepherd, *Call of Grace: How the Covenant Illuminates Covenant and Evangelism* (Phillipsburg, NJ: Presbyterian and Reformed, 2000).

[32] Specifically, see Augustine's *A Treatise on the Predestination of the Saints, A Treatise on the Gift of Perseverance, A Treatise on Rebuke and Grace,* and *A Treatise on Grace and Free Will,* all available in Philip Schaff, ed., *A Select Library of Nicene and Post Nicene Fathers* (first series; 14 vols.; Grand Rapids, MI: Eerdmans, 1974). Of course, Augustine also integrates a robust doctrine of sacramental efficacy into his soteriology. He knew that God's salvation was applied through outward means. Unfortunately, Augustine failed to fit a fully biblical doctrine of assurance into his understanding of predestination, salvation, perseverance, and apostasy. On that score, this paper may be regarded as a corrective to traditional Augustinianism.

[33] Confessionally, I find all of these things embedded in the WCF's description of the visible Church in 25.2. "The visible Church . . . is the kingdom of the Lord Jesus Christ, the house and family of God, out of which there is no ordinary possibility of salvation." Such an understanding of the visible church obviously has its corollaries in a high doctrine of baptismal efficacy (WCF 27.3, 28.1–2, 6; WLC 153, 154, 161, 167; WSC 85, 88, 91, 92) and the possibility of a real apostasy (WCF 10.4). Sadly, these sections of the confession, and their rich implications for systematic theology and pastoral practice, have been neglected. Much of our present controversy is due to a failure to take seriously the teaching of WCF 25.2 on the church. Lord willing, this book will help correct that flaw in current Reformed theology and praxis.

[34] Calvin's discussion of election in the *Institutes* begins with the empirical observation that not all who hear the gospel respond in faith. The differentiated responses are traced back up into the sovereign decree of God. The view offered here simply extends Calvin's logic past conversion to perseverance. God's decree is the ultimate explanation of why some in the covenant persevere and others don't. But an appeal to the decree cannot be used to cancel out other equally valid truths concerning human responsibility, the graciousness of church and covenant membership, and the efficacy of the sacraments. The covenant remains gracious, even if some break it, causing covenant blessings to devolve into covenant curses.